STEPPING
STONES
SUCCESS

to

EXPERTS SHARE STRATEGIES
FOR MASTERING BUSINESS,
LIFE, & RELATIONSHIPS

Stepping Stones to Success
Copyright © 2010

Published in the United States by
INSIGHT PUBLISHING
Sevierville, Tennessee • www.insightpublishing.com
ISBN 978-1-60013-502-6

Cover Design: Emmy Shubert
Interior Format & Design: Chris Ott

Disclaimer: This book is a compilation of ideas from numerous experts who have each contributed a chapter. As such, the views expressed in each chapter are of those who were interviewed and not necessarily of the interviewer, Insight Publishing or the other contributing authors.

A Message from the Publisher

There are many things I've come to understand throughout the many years I have been in this business. I've learned that it's never too late to grow and learn, to change course, to expand perspectives, and to admit I don't know everything.

Because I know it's important to learn from the experience of others, I reached out to many experts when putting this book project together and I gained some valuable information from them. The people I talked with have presented some insights that will expand your horizons and make you realize that you can be the key to your own success.

This book, *Stepping Stones to Success,* is your golden opportunity to profit from the knowledge of others. It will give you the facts you need to make important decisions about your future.

Interviewing these fascinating people was a unique learning experience for me. And I assure you that reading this book will be an exceptional learning experience for you.

—David Wright

The interviews presented in
Stepping Stones to Success
are conducted by David Wright,
President and Founder of
International Speakers Network
and Insight Publishing.

Table of Contents

Introduction

SUCCESS DEFINED
By Dr. Steve Cady

Don't confuse success with fame.
Success is much more than fame or power or money or possessions.

In every civilization, there are people who have committed their lives in service of success for others. What can we learn from them? What can we learn from the best life and career coaches out in the world working with people from all corners of the planet? What can we learn from integrative medical professionals who have healed thousands; have helped thousands heal themselves? What can we learn from those who have counseled thousands of people in finding and living their calling in life? What can we learn from professionals who bring people together to experience each other in new and inspiring ways? What can we learn from innovators who have developed techniques and methods to help people overcome challenges, find meaning, and accomplish great things? In this book, we set out to find answers to these questions and bring that collective wisdom to you.

A common bond shared by the experts interviewed as part of The *Stepping Stones to Success* project is that they view success as a quest to be whole. Wholeness is literally a "healing" experience. The entomology of "whole" and of "healing" is found in an old English word:

Weal \Weal\, n. A sound, healthy, or prosperous state
of a person or thing; prosperity; happiness; welfare.

In essence, "whole" means more than "all of something," it is a healthy balance, unity, and completeness. It refers to the interdependent parts of a human being unified under the influence of related forces.

The *Stepping Stones* project began with a search for such experts in order to interview them about their work. The criteria for inclusion was simple—each person has an established practice, a track record of success, a widely used framework or model, a solid educational background, and is a recognized leader in her or his area of expertise.

In this book, you will find compelling stories and insights that will shift you—nudge you—and even jolt you in positive ways. In addition, these interviews have been analyzed to uncover the patterns in their stories, approaches, and advice. A simple, yet powerful, qualitative research technique was used to uncover their collective secrets to success. There were simple research questions applied to the interviews:

1. What is success?
2. What are the key actions that lead to success?

If you are looking at success, then it is necessary to begin by addressing the first question—how does one define success? What does success look like? What I found is that true success is multidimensional and can be represented by a star. Stars through the years have served as targets, guides, windows, and signposts. The six points of the star represent individual outcomes and together define that wholeness we yearn to have.

What makes these points unique is they are results oriented. You don't do them directly—you realize them as outcomes or goals in your life. For example, your personal wellness is a result. This includes having healthy blood pressure, weight, energy, and more. These are results that people aim for in their life. The concluding chapter in this book answers the second question above. It describes the actions you can take to realize the six results in the Star of Success—these actions are called Stepping Stones.

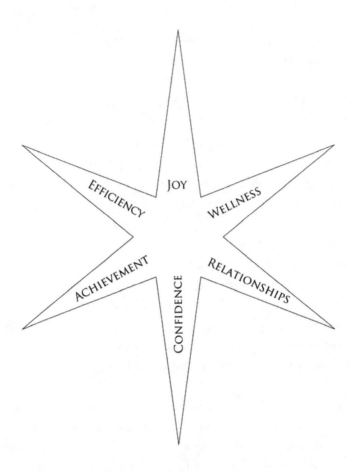

The Star of Success

Don't confuse success with fame. Success is much more than fame or money or power or possessions. When you arrive at your last days and look back over your life, fame and possessions will seem trivial. What we found in the interviews is that true success transcends the surface definition to become multi-dimensional:

- Success is achievement. Successful people get things done in the service of their purpose or calling in life. They finish projects. They keep their commitments. They follow through on what they set out to do. Some successful people are rapid-fire accomplishers—getting lots of things done in bursts. Other successful people get things done over time. In both cases, truly successful people build a solid track record of concrete purpose-driven accomplishments.

- Success is efficiency. Successful people do things with ease, sometimes described as effortless. Yes, successful people fail, make mistakes, and more. The key is they make fewer mistakes because they don't repeat them as much. They waste less time and energy. They figure things out, while others watching are mystified. Truly successful people adjust quickly, innovate solutions when faced with obstacles, and execute fluidly.

- Success is wellness. Successful people are healthy in mind, body, and spirit. They experience high levels of energy. They have strong immune systems. They sleep better at night. They recover from surgery quicker. They have less unfinished personal issues and unattended emotional trauma to deal with, and carry less psychological "baggage." They are spiritually grounded. Truly successful people openly discuss their wellness practices and their healthy connection with a higher power or God.

- Success is relationships. Successful people connect on a deep level with friends, family, co-workers, and the community at large. They get along well with others. They have a genuine love and regard for each other. They read people well and are aware of their own impact on those around them. People seek them out. People feel safe with them. Sometimes, successful people are quiet and other times they are charismatic. In all cases, people like themselves when they are with truly successful people.

- Success is confidence. Successful people are "comfortable in their own skin." They are grounded and centered. They know themselves and can describe who they are with a sense of purpose in life. They are able to make decisions and can explain their reasoning. When others are hurtful or judgmental of them, they have a calm demeanor that lets the judgments pass on by them. And, when observed by others, truly successful people are seen as a blend of power and compassion.

- Success is joy. Successful people experience an overall feeling of happiness and gratitude. They feel blessed and freely express how they feel—how happy they truly are. And, this feeling is genuine. They also enjoy moments of exhilaration often described as peak experiences. Their senses are heightened as they savor smells, tastes, sights, sounds, touch, and more. These experiences of joy are complemented by peacefulness. Truly successful people notice and appreciate the smallest of things and express a wonder for all things.

How successful do you believe you are? Are you experiencing all or some of these qualities of success above? What I have found is that success is a journey and not a destination. Nobody fully experiences all six dimensions all the time. They experience moments of success. It might be an extreme experience of joy in the midst of a health crisis. And, there are moments where they click on "all cylinders"—where each and every one of the above success dimensions are fully realized. The experts interviewed consistently mention one thing. You can have more and more success in your life. The question is this:

What are the steps you can take to experience true success?

The experts interviewed prescribe a set of actions for success called steppingstones. These are practical ways for living the life you yearn to live. Next, you will be presented with these interviews of leading experts. In the last chapter, you will find the results from qualitative analysis of the interviews to uncover common themes that they share. These themes are presented as "10 Steppingstones to Success" that you can take in your life.

As you read the interviews, notice the patterns. What do the interviews have in common? What is unique to one or two interviews? Notice the shared advice, techniques, tools, stories, examples, and evidence that they provide. Take note of what you think will work for you. Pay special attention to those things that push your buttons—these are clues for you as well. The one interview that you have the hardest time accepting may just be the one interview you need the most. Make up your own mind as to what you see as the keys to success. Do your own analysis. Then, compare your conclusions with the "10 Stepping Stones to Success" provided in the final chapter.

CHAPTER ONE

Self-Rescue: Your First Step to Success

An interview with...

ABBY LEORA ROHRER

DAVID WRIGHT (WRIGHT)

Today we are talking with Abby Leora Rohrer, visionary, transformational healing journey mentor, author, and educator. She is the creator of Self-Rescue 101™ and the Pull-Free, At Last! Transformational Healing System.

Abby guides others to identify painful life-long patterns and to fully transform them into healing and personal freedom. In other words, she helps people escape and expand the boxes within which they hold themselves hostage.

While many teach about personal transformation, Abby Rohrer has lived all sides of it—from the wounding of a traumatic childhood, through to freedom and redemption. In the process, she uncovered the connection between people's early relationship wounds and their painful repeating patterns. These unhealed patterns block the path to achievement.

Abby, you believe that some of our daily habits and ways of coping with life create barriers that interfere with our ability to achieve success, isn't this so?

ABBY ROHRER (ROHRER)

Yes, David, that's true. The seemingly innocent ways in which we handle life offer hidden clues about why we feel unfulfilled or unable to achieve the success we desire.

We all want to be free and to soar. We want to pursue our goals and dreams without obstacles, but so many find that as they head toward their goals, those dreams slip further and further away.

We're told by all of the experts that maintaining a positive attitude is crucial to the ultimate fulfillment of your dreams. But it can be incredibly difficult to hold onto a positive attitude and envision a better life when how your life looks *today* supports the fear of lack more than the belief of success. In other words, the "evidence" in front of you seems to confirm that you have little real chance of getting what you want. So your attitude begins to spiral down and you lose your passion and momentum. You begin to believe that others can achieve great things but, for some reason, you just aren't capable of it. You can't see what's holding you back or standing in your way. So you blame it on something beyond your control, shove your dreams to the back of your closet and go on with daily life, but you're not building toward your best future!

One of the main things that stops you from achieving your dreams is how you cope with the emotionally challenging moments that crop up in your life. Many people use ways of coping with life that severely limit and keep them stuck again and again. But these are hard to spot so you usually don't question them or realize that your daily "habits," even those that aren't official addictions or compulsions, often restrict and hold you back.

The way you use any habit, even one that is commonly considered to be healthy, can turn it into a coping mechanism that interferes with forward motion in life. This happens when you use it to push away or shove down your emotions.

Exercise is a good example. For most it's a productive experience, but there are some people who use it as a way to suppress their feelings. Unfortunately, we are often unaware that, by doing this, we create and perpetuate our own difficulties.

Then we go off and blame our lack of achievement on something outside of us that seems beyond our control.

I remember a woman who desperately wanted a child but was unable to conceive. She exercised so much that she stopped menstruating regularly but still was unwilling to change her routine. Rather than cutting back on the frequency or duration of her runs, she was considering expensive and invasive fertility treatments. She was unwilling to look inside herself to identify the true source of the problem because it would have meant changing the way that she coped with her emotions.

In our culture we tend to define addiction as "the use of a substance" that is unhealthy or creates an insatiable hunger. It's true that some substances *are* highly addictive. We may see ourselves as being at the mercy of these evil substances, for example, cigarettes, but it's important to remember that not everyone who smokes a cigarette will ultimately become addicted.

When you focus on the *what*, you end up seeing yourself as a victim who is subordinated by a substance, rather than seeing the deeper reasons of *how* you're using it and *why* you're using it. It's really not having that drink every night after work that's the problem, but rather, whether you're using it to *dampen your feelings and why you're doing that*, instead of directly feeling and resolving any uncomfortable feelings, which would be a healthy approach that keeps you moving forward in life.

WRIGHT

Why do we do this to ourselves? Why do we adopt these habitual ways of coping?

ROHRER

In a nutshell, it's easy and we're on auto-pilot. To a great extent, we're programmed to operate in this way. We live in a culture that is based on external solutions—there's a quick-fix or a pill for every purpose. Most of us know a handful of people who are on emotion-dampening medications, and those who are not have other ways of self-medicating.

We forget that our uncomfortable feelings belong to us and that they serve an important purpose in our lives. They can provide us with crucial information *if* we will allow it. Since they come *from* us, we cannot simply send them off to someone else to deal with. We must personally handle them! But, we fail to remember that our feelings are our responsibility to live with or to resolve. We don't realize what a gift they are to us and that emotions can help us to achieve our dreams *if* we will simply befriend and learn to work with them.

Instead, many of us have bought into the belief that we shouldn't have to think about them or do anything to face our demons and fears without a "rescue team" of therapists or doctors standing close by.

We've become much too comfortable with numbing away our emotions. We believe that self-medicating through a coping method can, on some level, keep us safe from our feelings and issues. Most of us have been trained since childhood to shove our emotions under the rug and get on with life, rather than face our problems directly.

We don't recognize that these coping styles stem from old mistaken beliefs that can be corrected fairly easily. You may have adopted a certain belief because of a relationship hurt that happened when you were two years old. You continue to carry this old belief and rarely, if ever, question or update it to the kind of present-day, adult standard that you would demand in any other area of your life.

These "wounds" are the result of painful interactions in early relationships that remain unhealed, usually with those whom you loved dearly or who were most important to you, for example, your parents or siblings.

WRIGHT

So early relationship wounds often interfere with our ability to achieve success in one or more areas of life?

ROHRER

Yes, David. Our early relationship wounds set the stage for many of our present day perceptions. Many of our beliefs are based on these unhealed wounds and our choice of actions and habits are largely based on them as well. If we have never resolved or updated these, we unconsciously carry forward and act from beliefs that originated from a young child's mistaken perceptions. We don't recognize we are doing this and then we wonder why we can't accomplish our goals. Now you can see how our old unhealed relationship wounds create our present-day barriers to success in all areas of our lives.

Here's a real-life example: I was recently working with one of my students who is a very successful businessman. But he struggles with feeling unfulfilled in his personal life. In his last mentoring session, we identified how his blocks to achieving the intimacy he desires go back to when he was just four years old. We found this out by using a method I'll share with you later in this chapter.

He and I talked about how this issue is most likely responsible for some of his wife's feelings of mistrust and when he resolves *his* issue she will finally trust that he will support a precious dream of hers. My student knows how to fully resolve it because he has now successfully practiced the path to resolution many times before. Through this, he now has the knowledge that he is capable of full completion of old feelings and perceptions that interfere with his happiness and success in relationships.

I'd like to tell you about another student, Patty, who resolved a longstanding rift with her mother. Because Patty had made a life-choice that conflicted with her family's spiritual path, she was shunned by the family and religious community. Patty and her mother didn't have a relationship *for more than twenty years.* Her mom had missed out on Patty's wedding and many precious years with her grandchildren. My student missed her mother terribly, and believed that her mother, now elderly, might die before she saw her again.

Because of Patty's pain and lack of knowing another way to proceed, she was open to looking for an unhealed pattern through my method. Patty followed the process and quickly found clarity and resolved the block *within herself.* Before long, she had reconnected with her mom and things "magically" resolved themselves. They now have a closer relationship than ever before. Patty continues to use the same technique to move forward in many other areas of her life.

WRIGHT

Thank you for those powerful examples. Might these same early unhealed wounds also be the basis of a full-blown addictive or compulsive behavior?

ROHRER

Absolutely! Many students come to me about a significant problem in our culture—compulsive hair-pulling. In fact, the male student I mentioned earlier came to me for that reason. There are twelve to fourteen million compulsive hair pullers in the United States alone. The large majority of them are in hiding and you would never know they have the problem at all. But it interferes with their relationships and some cannot get a job because they aren't able to hide it well enough. Others spend hours every day camouflaging their lack of eyelashes or bald spots so that you will never guess the secret shame they carry.

Now at the age of thirty-eight, the student I mentioned earlier has his first beard ever. Through our work, he quickly realized that his hair-pulling was just the tip of the iceberg. Now, he has chosen to get to the bottom of the painful issues in his personal relationships. Because of his commitment and progress, his wife became motivated to work on things that she was hiding from that interfered with mutual satisfaction in their marriage. Their communication has improved and they are individually resolving underlying issues that have plagued their relationship from the beginning.

WRIGHT

But what about the average person who doesn't struggle with an addiction but who simply can't achieve his or her business dream or get a venture off the ground? Or the woman whose internal clock is ticking and, more than anything, wants to build a family but can't seem to find the right guy? All the guys who ask her out are duds—what can she do?

ROHRER

There are people who don't identify with having a recognizable addictive or compulsive behavior, that's true. But, many of them would be willing to acknowledge that there is one or more area in life in which they constantly *yearn* for greater satisfaction. They may recognize that their vision can only be achieved by playing a bigger game or playing in a bigger arena. They may even be able to see that no matter how hard they try, they simply have not been able to break through whatever is blocking their success.

There was a man like this at a business meeting that I regularly attend. I watched him struggle for a year and a half unable to make any inroads toward his self-identified dream. No matter how much the group attempted to help him, all we heard were what I call the "yeah, buts." I'm sure you know what I mean, it's when someone complains that they feel victimized in a certain situation or stuck and you offer a number of suggestions and each time you do, the response you are met with begins with "yeah, but—." In other words, "Yeah, but that won't work because I don't have a computer." "Yeah, but I can't do that because my father won't like it." "Yeah, but that will cost too much." You see?

I suggest that you begin to see that you are stuck in repeating patterns—in a revolving door—and you can find your way out of it. Begin to consciously use your wounds as a signal that you need a personal "pattern-busting" strategy. Commit to rescuing yourself and make it a priority so that you can begin to *resolve* this stuff for good and find the success that you deserve.

WRIGHT

How can we do this?

ROHRER

When you get your "buttons pushed," instead of running away from the pain, run *toward* it. So often, when people hurt your feelings, you lash out at them, ignore it or wait for the pain to dissolve and go away. More often than not, however, you're using an unhealthy coping strategy to numb that pain away. This doesn't solve anything. It only suppresses your discomfort, and after enough years of suppression you may find that your dreams have passed you by. This is a terrible tragedy. There are dreams that you are being called to achieve and gifts that only you are capable of offering the world *if* you can just move through your blocks to achievement.

You keep looking *outside* yourself for the next magical quick-fix, when the answers that you need are really right *inside* of you. In other words, every single time you get your feelings hurt, instead of suppression, I recommend that you go inside yourself to discover if the hurt is connected to a repeating pattern.

So the next time you are passed over for a promotion or get a poor performance review, instead of blaming that idiot boss of yours, go inside yourself and find the core wound that causes you to be a magnet for receiving that poor review and resolve it at its origin. When you do this, you will begin to see how these challenges and difficult life-moments are really gifts calling you to free yourself from your chains.

You can use each and every bit of the emotional pain *that you're already dealing with* to identify and fully resolve and heal these difficult lifelong patterns. You can get free!

WRIGHT

Will you tie this back to how it relates to mastering life and achieving success for us?

ROHRER

Sure. This strategy will finally free you to achieve success in areas you have never before been able or courageous enough to tackle because you've been resisting facing the pain. Once the issue is resolved, you will be completely free to walk in a direction that was never before available to you.

Let's say that you're a gifted artist and all of your friends and family know it. You make absolutely striking sterling silver jewelry that you give to friends and family members on their birthdays and at Christmas. When you go out in public wearing your own creations, women stop you on the street to ask where you found such a great necklace. They're astounded when you tell them that you made it yourself. In those rare moments when you gather up your courage to present your wares to your local fine arts and crafts gallery, they instantly take them on consignment or order a dozen pieces without batting an eye. But you are still reluctant to really go for it in your business. Something always gets in the way. Your family needs you for the next six months. A friend is going through a rough time and you couldn't possibly tell her you're too busy making earrings, right? But, this work is your passion and you will never feel truly fulfilled until you make your big statement out in the world.

I once met this sweet, but excruciatingly shy young man who was a gifted songwriter and singer. I mean *gifted!* He was every bit as talented as any well-known artist today. He reminded me of Bruce Cockburn—he was that good! But he was so terrified and blocked that he simply couldn't pursue his passion so we have lost out on experiencing the magnitude of his ability. Can you just imagine if Susan Boyle had never stepped up to sing on *Britain's Got Talent?* How much worse off would we all be? The world learned so much the day she sang on that show! We learned never to judge the talent of a singer by her appearance. We also learned that every single person has a chance at greatness if we can just move through our blocks enough to show our gifts publicly.

WRIGHT

Will you give us a few examples from your own life? How did you go from struggling with twenty-seven years of compulsive hair-pulling to healing it, and come to understand the relationship connections involved?

ROHRER

Well, it was through the process of finally becoming willing to face my pain. When I first became aware of my own repeating patterns, I was shocked. I realized that I was using hair-pulling to hide from my emotional pain in relationships. I saw how I was making my world smaller and smaller in my attempts to keep myself safe. It was actually the pain of my emotionally abusive marriage that finally caused me to begin to heal myself. I had gone to counseling for years to fix my marital pain, childhood pain and hair-pulling but I hadn't found resolution there. It was a gift when my marriage finally deteriorated enough to push me over the edge into facing myself because that led to my healing.

You see, I had always blamed my husband for my pain and problems but what I couldn't see all of those years, even in counseling, was that I was helping to perpetuate my own pain. I was magnetized by an unhealed verbally-abusive childhood to repeatedly attract and even encourage the same type of treatment from my spouse. I had to come face-to-face with that. I had to begin to see that there were repeating patterns at work in my life and that there was a quick way for me to get to the core and resolve them. It was a true miracle for me when I finally began to see the freedom that resulted from doing this.

I used to be so very afraid of everything. My life was riddled with anxiety. Unconsciously I thought that I could find my way to safety by continuing to squeeze myself into smaller and smaller "boxes." But the reality is, that eventually I would have squeezed myself into such a small box that my oxygen supply would have run out. I would have suffocated. I think this is what happens when someone who previously had vitality suddenly becomes physically ill and succumbs completely to that illness. It's as if he or she could see no other way out of an *inner* box.

Life is continually asking us to expand. You don't see nature attempting to make a tall tree smaller and smaller, right? Trees keep growing and expanding throughout their lifetime. Life asks us to become as big as we can possibly be, but instead, so many of us try to play smaller and smaller. And even though we want to play a bigger game, to do more, give more, and go for our dreams, we seem to hit one wall after another. We let these walls stop us, but we really need a new model that can help to culturally move us toward expansion for all! We need to learn how to support one another in expanding as far as each of us is capable of going.

WRIGHT

What's the biggest challenge keeping most people from resolving these things?

ROHRER

There are cultural and family norms that bind us. While competition is useful for cultures to progress, at this point, we have created an extreme amount of social competition that the media fuels with a barrage of negative judgments.

Underneath some of our family norms, we may not want to dishonor or "show up" our mother or father. There are power and loyalty issues that must be internally resolved. This is a familiar but hidden box that many people have put themselves in.

And, again, people are not aware that there are these big painful *patterns* operating in their lives. They don't seem to realize that this year it's with *this* person rather than *that* person or this time it's come along in pink instead of last year's blue, but *the underlying pattern is still the same.*

Once they begin to see the *underlying pattern,* they can start to clearly understand that the manifestations of that pattern are not simply going to go away. They stalk you and you must face and resolve them. If you don't, chances are that they will only get worse. And eventually, they might turn into a big life crisis that you would much rather not have to deal with, like illness, financial loss, divorce, or midlife woes.

WRIGHT

How can anyone begin right now to identify their issues and painful patterns?

ROHRER

Actually, doing this can be quite fun. It's like becoming the Sherlock Holmes or Indiana Jones of your own inner life. You become a detective who explores the mystery of your bigger life themes, the matter of your soul. Honestly, doing this is very satisfying! After all, when you really think about it, what could possibly be more interesting to you than learning about *you?*

And this process even has a bit of international intrigue! It's a lot like one of those Chinese finger traps. You know, the one where you insert your index fingers into that woven straw contraption and the more you try to pull your fingers out the tighter it gets and the more trapped you are? Then you figure out that the way out of the puzzle is by moving in the opposite direction. *You must go further in, all the way in, to get free.* It is the very same with your emotional pain. When you start running *toward* your pain rather than away from it and allow yourself to drop to the bottom and release your old, trapped energy, that's where you'll heal the pattern for good!

WRIGHT

What are the concrete steps people can take to fully resolve these quickly and easily?

ROHRER

I'm glad you asked because I really want to offer readers a practical method they can use to achieve fast results. Here's a process that I personally use and teach my students. In using these steps you will come to a deep understanding that allows your painful pattern to make complete sense to you.

In other words, the whole structure of the pattern should become clear to you in very practical terms. If this doesn't happen, go through the steps again and *release any resistance* you have to discovering your authentic truth about the pattern. After doing this, if you still are unable to come to a clear understanding, you will need to consciously work on decreasing your level of resistance. It is always our resistance to seeing our deeper truth that interferes with resolution. This may show up as fear, anxiety, denial, an attitude that this is a waste of time, and other thoughts like this, so we need to keep an eye out for these emotions and attitudes.

Here's the method. It's called "Six Simple Steps to Emotional Freedom" and it's an integral part of my Self-Rescue 101™ System:

    a. First, take some time to build a foundation for yourself. You want to ensure that you are *in a solid relationship with yourself to get the best results with this process.*

11

A lot of people have become disconnected from themselves or have never had an authentic conversation with themselves. So you want to be sure that you are listening to your own inner truth on a regular basis and are solidly focused on what you think and feel, rather than other people's pronouncements about your circumstances and desires.

I suggest that you start now with this preliminary step and begin to journal in a way that allows you to really listen to yourself and your desires. This helps you to form or deepen the *relationship* with yourself. I recommend Julia Cameron's wonderful technique "The Morning Pages" from the book, *The Artist's Way*. If you don't have access to that book, it's basically about hand-writing three full-sized notebook pages, completely unplanned, using stream of consciousness, each and every day. *But I would add one more important rule: do not reread what you have written and do not allow anyone else to read it.* In fact, go ahead and shred your pages immediately after writing each day. I don't have space to fully explain why here, but this is very important so that you will not criticize or negatively judge yourself, which would quickly stop you from receiving the big benefits of journaling in this way.

> b. Next, set aside 5 to 10 percent of your awareness on alert for an emotionally uncomfortable moment when one of your buttons gets pushed.

At this point, you may begin to wonder what this has to do with your present-day desire to push toward your dream of success in some area. Let's say that your dream is to open a dance studio. Yesterday, your sister said something that hurt you but you were unwilling to look at it. Instead you're at your computer beating your brains out trying to write a plan for your business but you can't seem to find enough clarity to accomplish it. If you were willing to look deeper at the hurt, you might see that what's really standing in the way of your business plan is an unhealed wound stemming from a very old belief. This wound began over an early incident within your family in which you had a painful perception that "you'll never amount to anything in the world." Now that might be worth facing and sorting out, don't you think?

c. Life magically brings up these painful moments to help us move forward. You simply need to *trust* that if a painful moment has appeared, it's trying to help you transform something that's in the way of your forward movement. All you need to do is to begin by recognizing that your sister's comment hurt you. Think back to the way she made you feel yesterday. Use the sensations in your body, but don't get stuck in the *emotions* or try to analyze what you're feeling. Feel your body's *sensations*—are your shoulders tense, is your jaw tight? Stay with those sensations.

Now ask yourself, "Have I ever felt this way before?" Are the sensations familiar?

d. See if you can trace them back. Watch that you don't jump into analyzing your feelings or telling yourself a story that justifies the way you feel emotionally—simply stay with your body. Keep tracing your sensations back to the beginning where they originated. Keep going back and further back. Make sure that you're following the thread of the very same body sensations all the way back to their *origin*. You may encounter incidents that happened in the intervening years, but keep going back to find the original source.

e. Once you find the original source, take a look. Can you see the connection to your present-day hurt? If you've done this right, there should be a crystal-clear path from the early wound to the present-day issue and you will see your pattern fully.

f. Now return to your original wound and finish the leftover feelings from that time long ago. This will release the emotional energy that's been keeping the pattern in place. I provide my students with lots of tools for finishing up this old energy and there are many books that offer good tools, as well. I also recommend that people get creative and develop their own solution in the moment. Mostly, finishing your feelings is a natural process but sometimes a tool can be useful to help you along.

WRIGHT

What would you say to someone who is reluctant or thinks this process is a waste of time? What are the top benefits of resolving our painful patterns?

ROHRER

I think that people are sometimes reluctant because they simply don't realize the toll that this is taking on their life and, as I mentioned earlier, it goes against our cultural norms. But here's the truth: The world is waiting for you to share your gifts with us. And time is wasting. We need you to get moving so we can all benefit!

Face the fact that if you don't or won't, both you and the world will miss out. If you don't break through your blocks, then you can expect that life will give you more of the same thing that you're experiencing right now. So if that's dissatisfaction or frustration, then that's what you have to look forward to in the future. I know it's not always easy to face this old stuff, but we need to remember that we're capable adults now and we have so many more resources at our disposal than the wounded three-year-old of long ago. He or she didn't have *you* to stand by his or her side back then. You can be his or her champion now!

The situation that we have in terms of current global economic problems is a great analogy for what happens when we continue to operate with our old, programmed ways of coping and dealing with life. We eventually get to the point where growth and expansion simply cannot occur without addressing the underlying core issues. Things begin to break down on a bigger scale and to spiral down rather than up (remember those smaller and smaller boxes?). And just like those economic problems may have begun in one area (mortgages) and one location (the United States), they are now impacting the entire economic outlook of the world.

We all need to begin to address the deeper systemic issues rather than just attempting to move forward on the surface of life or trying one quick, but useless fix after another.

Here's another important point. You've probably heard that you are the creator of your life. It's difficult to accept this until you see exactly how you are creating. Many people are hooked on repeating patterns that produce a great deal of negative drama in their lives. This is another coping style that takes up so much time and energy that you have little ability to create positive life experiences. But, once you begin to recognize your patterns and take care of them, you will quickly lose interest in creating or participating in pointless drama. You'll finally have the energy to create the life that you really wanted all along!

I want to encourage you to do this because you will be so much freer, not just to pursue your dreams but to *achieve* them. In a culture where we're programmed to push through rather than resolve the past, every year of carrying the old load can take a toll on you and contributes to aging faster and a decline in feeling robust. In other words, lack of resolution ages us, causes us more stress, and keeps us in a perpetual cycle of unhappiness and not achieving our dreams. Eventually, it can cause physical illnesses and the general decline of your health and of the ability to even pursue the deeper yearnings of your soul. When this happens, many people feel that life has been wasted.

Your time is now! Don't put off going for it and achieving the greatest satisfaction that you can within your lifetime. Deal with your patterns now so you can achieve the biggest, most outrageous and expansive dreams that you are capable of dreaming in all areas of your life!

ABOUT THE AUTHOR

Abby Leora Rohrer, founder and CEO of Facilitated Recovery, LLC, is a pioneer in teaching people how to identify and break through the barriers to success in all areas of life.

Abby has studied, taught and lived self-healing for more than fifteen years. Her workshops and guiding principles offer powerful blueprints for people to turn self-judgment into self-compassion and connect with themselves on the deepest level. Once they've truly connected within—and discovered the source of their emotional turmoil—they are transformed and free of their negative coping behaviors, free of the past, free of their emotional pain and free to fully resolve relationship problems. Rohrer was first known for her groundbreaking work in helping compulsive hair pullers to achieve freedom and is the founder of Colorado-based TrichotillomaniaFree™ Women's University, an online curriculum and healing system for women hair pullers. Since 1995, she has cracked the hair-pulling code by offering sufferers the critical information and innovative support needed to permanently release themselves from the debilitating grasp of this disorder and many other painful emotional issues.

ABBY LEORA ROHRER

Facilitated Recovery, LLC
P.O. Box 664
Lafayette, CO 80026
303.546.0788
www.PullFreeAtLast.com
Coming soon: www.SelfRescue101.com

CHAPTER TWO

Find a Mentor and Believe in Your Dreams

An Interview with...

JACK CANFIELD

DAVID WRIGHT (WRIGHT)

Today we are talking with Jack Canfield. You probably know him as the founder and co-creator of the *New York Times* number one bestselling *Chicken Soup for the Soul* book series. As of 2006 there are sixty-five titles and eighty million copies in print in over thirty-seven languages.

Jack's background includes a BA from Harvard, a master's from the University of Massachusetts, and an Honorary Doctorate from the University of Santa Monica. He has been a high school and university teacher, a workshop facilitator, a psychotherapist, and a leading authority in the area of self-esteem and personal development.

Jack Canfield, welcome to *Stepping Stones to Success*.

JACK CANFIELD (CANFIELD)

Thank you, David. It's great to be with you.

WRIGHT

When I talked with Mark Victor Hansen, he gave you full credit for coming up with the idea of the *Chicken Soup* series. Obviously it's made you an internationally known personality. Other than recognition, has the series changed you personally and if so, how?

CANFIELD

I would say that it has and I think in a couple of ways. Number one, I read stories all day long of people who've overcome what would feel like insurmountable obstacles. For example, we just did a book *Chicken Soup for the Unsinkable Soul.* There's a story in there about a single mother with three daughters. She contracted a disease and she had to have both of her hands and both of her feet amputated. She got prosthetic devices and was able to learn how to use them. She could cook, drive the car, brush her daughters' hair, get a job, etc. I read that and I thought, "God, what would I ever have to complain and whine and moan about?"

At one level it's just given me a great sense of gratitude and appreciation for everything I have and it has made me less irritable about the little things.

I think the other thing that's happened for me personally is my sphere of influence has changed. By that I mean I was asked, for example, some years ago to be the keynote speaker to the Women's Congressional Caucus. The Caucus is a group that includes all women in America who are members of Congress and who are state senators, governors, and lieutenant governors. I asked what they wanted me to talk about—what topic.

"Whatever you think we need to know to be better legislators," was the reply.

I thought, "Wow, they want me to tell them about what laws they should be making and what would make a better culture." Well, that wouldn't have happened if our books hadn't come out and I hadn't become famous. I think I get to play with people at a higher level and have more influence in the world. That's important to me because my life purpose is inspiring and empowering people to live their highest vision so the world works for everybody. I get to do that on a much bigger level than when I was just a high school teacher back in Chicago.

WRIGHT

I think one of the powerful components of that book series is that you can read a positive story in just a few minutes and come back and revisit it. I know my daughter has three of the books and she just reads them interchangeably. Sometimes I go in her bedroom and she'll be crying and reading one of them. Other times she'll be laughing, so they really are "chicken soup for the soul," aren't they?

CANFIELD

They really are. In fact we have four books in the *Teenage Soul* series now and a new one coming out at the end of this year. I have a son who's eleven and he has a twelve-year-old friend who's a girl. We have a new book called *Chicken Soup for the Teenage Soul and the Tough Stuff*. It's all about dealing with parents' divorces, teachers who don't understand you, boyfriends who drink and drive, and other issues pertinent to that age group.

I asked my son's friend, "Why do you like this book?" (It's our most popular book among teens right now.) She said, "You know, whenever I'm feeling down I read it and it makes me cry and I feel better. Some of the stories make me laugh and some of the stories make me feel more responsible for my life. But basically I just feel like I'm not alone."

One of the people I work with recently said that the books are like a support group between the covers of a book—you can read about other peoples' experiences and realize you're not the only one going through something.

WRIGHT

Jack, we're trying to encourage people in our audience to be better, to live better, and be more fulfilled by reading about the experiences of our writers. Is there anyone or anything in your life that has made a difference for you and helped you to become a better person?

CANFIELD

Yes, and we could do ten books just on that. I'm influenced by people all the time. If I were to go way back I'd have to say one of the key influences in my life was Jesse Jackson when he was still a minister in Chicago. I was teaching in an all black high school there and I went to Jesse Jackson's church with a friend one time. What happened for me was that I saw somebody with a vision. (This was before Martin Luther King was killed and Jesse was of the lieutenants in his organization.) I just saw people trying to make the world work better for a certain segment of the population. I was inspired by that kind of visionary belief that it's possible to make change.

Later on, John F. Kennedy was a hero of mine. I was very much inspired by him.

Another is a therapist by the name of Robert Resnick. He was my therapist for two years. He taught me a little formula: E + R = O. It stands for Events + Response = Outcome. He said, "If you don't like your outcomes quit blaming the events and start changing your responses." One of his favorite phrases was, "If the grass on the other side of the fence looks greener, start watering your own lawn more."

I think he helped me get off any kind of self-pity I might have had because I had parents who were alcoholics. It would have been very easy to blame them for problems I might have had. They weren't very successful or rich; I was surrounded by people who were and I felt like, "God, what if I'd had parents like they had? I could have been a lot better." He just got me off that whole notion and made me realize that the hand you were dealt is the hand you've got to play. Take responsibility for who you are and quit complaining and blaming others and get on with your life. That was a turning point for me.

I'd say the last person who really affected me big-time was a guy named W. Clement Stone who was a self-made multi-millionaire in Chicago. He taught me that success is not a four-letter word—it's nothing to be ashamed of—and you ought to go for it. He said, "The best thing you can do for the poor is not be one of them." Be a model for what it is to live a successful life. So I learned from him the principles of success and that's what I've been teaching now for more than thirty years.

WRIGHT

He was an entrepreneur in the insurance industry, wasn't he?

CANFIELD

He was. He had combined insurance. When I worked for him he was worth 600 million dollars and that was before the dot.com millionaires came along in Silicon Valley. He just knew more about success. He was a good friend of Napoleon Hill (author of *Think and Grow Rich*) and he was a fabulous mentor. I really learned a lot from him.

WRIGHT

I miss some of the men I listened to when I was a young salesman coming up and he was one of them. Napoleon Hill was another one as was Dr. Peale. All of their writings made me who I am today. I'm glad I had that opportunity.

CANFIELD

One speaker whose name you probably will remember, Charlie "Tremendous" Jones, says, "Who we are is a result of the books we read and the people we hang out with." I think that's so true and that's why I tell people, "If you want to have high self-esteem, hang out with people who have high self-esteem. If you want to be more spiritual, hang out with spiritual people." We're always telling our children, "Don't hang out with those kids." The reason we don't want them to is because we know how influential people are with each other. I think we need to give ourselves the same advice. Who are we hanging out with? We can hang out with them in books, cassette tapes, CDs, radio shows, and in person.

WRIGHT

One of my favorites was a fellow named Bill Gove from Florida. I talked with him about three or four years ago. He's retired now. His mind is still as quick as it ever was. I thought he was one of the greatest speakers I had ever heard.

What do you think makes up a great mentor? In other words, are there characteristics that mentors seem to have in common?

CANFIELD

I think there are two obvious ones. I think mentors have to have the time to do it and the willingness to do it. I also think they need to be people who are doing something you want to do. W. Clement Stone used to tell me, "If you want to be rich, hang out with rich people. Watch what they do, eat what they eat, dress the way they dress—try it on." He wasn't suggesting that you give up your authentic self, but he was pointing out that rich people probably have habits that you don't have and you should study them.

I always ask salespeople in an organization, "Who are the top two or three in your organization?" I tell them to start taking them out to lunch and dinner and for a drink and finding out what they do. Ask them, "What's your secret?" Nine times out of ten they'll be willing to tell you.

This goes back to what we said earlier about asking. I'll go into corporations and I'll say, "Who are the top ten people?" They'll all tell me and I'll say, "Did you ever ask them what they do different than you?"

"No," they'll reply.

"Why not?"

"Well, they might not want to tell me."

"How do you know? Did you ever ask them? All they can do is say no. You'll be no worse off than you are now."

So I think with mentors you just look at people who seem to be living the life you want to live and achieving the results you want to achieve.

What we say in our book is when that you approach a mentor they're probably busy and successful and so they haven't got a lot of time. Just ask, "Can I talk to you for ten minutes every month?" If I know it's only going to be ten minutes I'll probably say yes. The neat thing is if I like you I'll always give you more than ten minutes, but that ten minutes gets you in the door.

WRIGHT

In the future are there any more Jack Canfield books authored singularly?

CANFIELD

One of my books includes the formula I mentioned earlier: E + R = O. I just felt I wanted to get that out there because every time I give a speech and I talk about that the whole room gets so quiet you could hear a pin drop—I can tell people are really getting value.

Then I'm going to do a series of books on the principles of success. I've got about 150 of them that I've identified over the years. I have a book down the road I want to do that's called *No More Put-Downs,* which is a book probably aimed mostly at parents, teachers, and managers. There's a culture we have now of put-down humor. Whether it's *Married . . . with Children* or *All in the Family,* there's that characteristic of macho put-down humor. There's research now showing how bad it is for kids' self-esteem when the coaches do it, so I want to get that message out there as well.

WRIGHT

It's really not that funny, is it?

CANFIELD

No, we'll laugh it off because we don't want to look like we're a wimp but underneath we're hurt. The research now shows that you're better off breaking a child's bones than you are breaking his or her spirit. A bone will heal much more quickly than their emotional spirit will.

WRIGHT

I remember recently reading a survey where people listed the top five people who had influenced them. I've tried it on a couple of groups at church and in other places. In my case, and in the survey, approximately three out of the top five are always teachers. I wonder if that's going to be the same in the next decade.

CANFIELD

I think that's probably because as children we're at our most formative years. We actually spend more time with our teachers than we do with our parents. Research shows that the average parent only interacts verbally with each of their children only about eight and a half minutes a day. Yet at school they're interacting with their teachers for anywhere from six to eight hours depending on how long the school day is, including coaches, chorus directors, etc.

I think that in almost everybody's life there's been that one teacher who loved him or her as a human being—an individual—not just one of the many students the teacher was supposed to fill full of History and English. That teacher believed in you and inspired you.

Les Brown is one of the great motivational speakers in the world. If it hadn't been for one teacher who said, "I think you can do more than be in a special education class. I think you're the one," he'd probably still be cutting grass in the median strip of the highways in Florida instead of being a $35,000-a-talk speaker.

WRIGHT

I had a conversation one time with Les. He told me about this wonderful teacher who discovered Les was dyslexic. Everybody else called him dumb and this one lady just took him under her wing and had him tested. His entire life changed because of her interest in him.

CANFIELD

I'm on the board of advisors of the Dyslexic Awareness Resource Center here in Santa Barbara. The reason is because I taught high school and had a lot of kids who were called "at-risk"—kids who would end up in gangs and so forth.

What we found over and over was that about 78 percent of all the kids in the juvenile detention centers in Chicago were kids who had learning disabilities— primarily dyslexia—but there were others as well. They were never diagnosed and they weren't doing well in school so they'd drop out. As soon as a student drops out of school he or she becomes subject to the influence of gangs and other kinds of criminal and drug linked activities. If these kids had been diagnosed earlier we'd have been able to get rid of a large amount of the juvenile crime in America because there are a lot of really good programs that can teach dyslexics to read and excel in school.

WRIGHT

My wife is a teacher and she brings home stories that are heartbreaking about parents not being as concerned with their children as they used to be, or at least not as helpful as they used to be. Did you find that to be a problem when you were teaching?

CANFIELD

It depends on what kind of district you're in. If it's a poor district the parents could be on drugs, alcoholics, and basically just not available. If you're in a really high rent district the parents are not available because they're both working, coming home tired, they're jet-setters, or they're working late at the office because they're workaholics. Sometimes it just legitimately takes two paychecks to pay the rent anymore.

I find that the majority of parents care but often they don't know what to do. They don't know how to discipline their children. They don't know how to help them with their homework. They can't pass on skills that they never acquired themselves.

Unfortunately, the trend tends to be like a chain letter. The people with the least amount of skills tend to have the most number of children. The other thing is that you get crack babies (infants born addicted to crack cocaine because of the mother's addiction). As of this writing, in Los Angeles one out of every ten babies born is a crack baby.

WRIGHT

That's unbelievable.

CANFIELD

Yes, and another statistic is that by the time 50 percent of the kids are twelve years old they have started experimenting with alcohol. I see a lot of that in the Bible belt. The problem is not the big city, urban designer drugs, but alcoholism.

Another thing you get, unfortunately, is a lot of let's call it "familial violence" — kids getting beat up, parents who drink and then explode, child abuse, and sexual abuse. You see a lot of that.

WRIGHT

Most people are fascinated by these television shows about being a survivor. What has been the greatest comeback that you have made from adversity in your career or in your life?

CANFIELD

You know, it's funny, I don't think I've had a lot of major failures and setbacks where I had to start over. My life's been on an intentional curve. But I do have a lot of challenges. Mark and I are always setting goals that challenge us. We always say, "The purpose of setting a really big goal is not so that you can achieve it so much, but it's who you become in the process of achieving it." A friend of mine, Jim Rohn, says, "You want to set goals big enough so that in the process of achieving them you become someone worth being."

I think that to be a millionaire is nice but so what? People make the money and then they lose it. People get the big houses and then they burn down or Silicon Valley goes belly up and all of a sudden they don't have a big house anymore. But who you became in the process of learning how to be successful can never be taken away from you. So what we do is constantly put big challenges in front of us.

We have a book called *Chicken Soup for the Teacher's Soul.* (You'll have to make sure to get a copy for your wife.) I was a teacher and a teacher trainer for years. But because of the success of the *Chicken Soup* books I haven't been in the education world that much. I've got to go out and relearn how I market to that world. I met with a Superintendent of Schools. I met with a guy named Jason Dorsey who's one of the number one consultants in the world in that area. I found out who has the bestselling book in that area. I sat down with his wife for a day and talked about her marketing approaches.

I believe that if you face any kind of adversity, whether it's losing your job, your spouse dies, you get divorced, you're in an accident like Christopher Reeve and become paralyzed, or whatever, you simply do what you have to do. You find out who's already handled the problem and how did they've handled it. Then you get the support you need to get through it by their example. Whether it's a counselor in your church or you go on a retreat or you read the Bible, you do something that gives you the support you need to get to the other end.

You also have to know what the end is that you want to have. Do you want to be remarried? Do you just want to have a job and be a single mom? What is it? If you reach out and ask for support I think you'll get help. People really like to help other people. They're not always available because sometimes they're going through problems also; but there's always someone with a helping hand.

Often I think we let our pride get in the way. We let our stubbornness get in the way. We let our belief in how the world should be interfere and get in our way instead of dealing with how the world is. When we get that out of that way then we can start doing that which we need to do to get where we need to go.

WRIGHT

If you could have a platform and tell our audience something you feel that would help or encourage them, what would you say?

CANFIELD

I'd say number one is to believe in yourself, believe in your dreams, and trust your feelings. I think too many people are trained wrong when they're little kids. For example, when kids are mad at their daddy they're told, "You're not mad at your Daddy."

They say, "Gee, I thought I was."

Or the kid says, "That's going to hurt," and the doctor says, "No it's not." Then they give you the shot and it hurts. They say, "See that didn't hurt, did it?" When that happened to you as a kid, you started to not trust yourself.

You may have asked your mom, "Are you upset?" and she says, "No," but she really was. So you stop learning to trust your perception.

I tell this story over and over. There are hundreds of people I've met who've come from upper class families where they make big incomes and the dad's a doctor. The kid wants to be a mechanic and work in an auto shop because that's what he loves. The family says, "That's beneath us. You can't do that." So the kid ends up being an anesthesiologist killing three people because he's not paying attention. What he really wants to do is tinker with cars.

I tell people you've got to trust your own feelings, your own motivations, what turns you on, what you want to do, what makes you feel good, and quit worrying about what other people say, think, and want for you. Decide what you want for yourself and then do what you need to do to go about getting it. It takes work.

I read a book a week minimum and at the end of the year I've read fifty-two books. We're talking about professional books—books on self-help, finances, psychology, parenting, and so forth. At the end of ten years I've read 520 books. That puts me in the top 1 percent of people knowing important information in this country. But most people are spending their time watching television.

When I went to work for W. Clement Stone, he told me, "I want you to cut out one hour a day of television."

"Okay," I said, "what do I do with it?"

"Read," he said.

He told me what kind of books to read. He said, "At the end of a year you'll have spent 365 hours reading. Divide that by a forty-hour work week and that's nine and a half weeks of education every year."

I thought, "Wow, that's two months." It was like going back to summer school.

As a result of his advice I have close to 8,000 books in my library. The reason I'm involved in this book project instead of someone else is that people like me, Jim Rohn, Les Brown, and you read a lot. We listen to tapes and we go to seminars. That's why we're the people with the information.

I always say that your raise becomes effective when you do. You'll become more effective as you gain more skills, more insight, and more knowledge.

WRIGHT

Jack, I have watched your career for a long time and your accomplishments are just outstanding. But your humanitarian efforts are really what impress me. I think that you're doing great things not only in California, but all over the country.

CANFIELD

It's true. In addition to all of the work we do, we pick one to three charities and we've given away over six million dollars in the last eight years, along with our publisher who matches every penny we give away. We've planted over a million trees in Yosemite National Park. We've bought hundreds of thousands of cataract operations in third world countries. We've contributed to the Red Cross, the Humane Society, and on it goes. It feels like a real blessing to be able to make that kind of a contribution to the world.

WRIGHT

Today we have been talking with Jack Canfield, founder and co-creator of the *Chicken Soup for the Soul* book series. Chicken Soup for the Soul reaches people well beyond the bookstore, with CD and DVD collections, company-sponsored samplers, greeting cards, children's entertainment products, pet food, flowers, and many other products in line with Chicken Soup for the Soul's purpose. Chicken Soup for the Soul is currently implementing a plan to expand into all media by working with television networks on several shows and developing a major Internet presence dedicated to life improvement, emotional support, and inspiration.

CANFIELD

Another book I've written is *The Success Principles*. In it I share sixty-four principles that other people and I have utilized to achieve great levels of success.

WRIGHT

I will stand in line to get one of those. Thank you so much being with us.

ABOUT THE AUTHOR

Jack Canfield is one of America's leading experts on developing self-esteem and peak performance. A dynamic and entertaining speaker, as well as a highly sought-after trainer, he has a wonderful ability to inform and inspire audiences toward developing their own human potential and personal effectiveness.

Jack Canfield is most well-known for the *Chicken Soup for the Soul* series, which he co-authored with Mark Victor Hansen, and for his audio programs about building high self-esteem. Jack is the founder of Self-Esteem Seminars, located in Santa Barbara, California, which trains entrepreneurs, educators, corporate leaders, and employees how to accelerate the achievement of their personal and professional goals. Jack is also founder of The Foundation for Self Esteem, located in Culver City, California, which provides self-esteem resources and training to social workers, welfare recipients, and human resource professionals.

Jack graduated from Harvard in 1966, received his ME degree at the University of Massachusetts in 1973, and earned an Honorary Doctorate from the University of Santa Monica. He has been a high school and university teacher, a workshop facilitator, a psychotherapist, and a leading authority in the area of self-esteem and personal development.

As a result of his work with prisoners, welfare recipients, and inner-city youth, Jack was appointed by the State Legislature to the California Task Force to Promote Self-Esteem and Personal and Social Responsibility. He also served on the Board of Trustees of the National Council for Self-Esteem.

JACK CANFIELD
The Jack Canfield Companies
P.O. Box 30880
Santa Barbara, CA 93130
Phone: 805.563.2935
Fax: 805.563.2945
www.jackcanfield.com

CHAPTER THREE

Life Inspired: Six Ways to a Passionate Soul

An interview with...

STEVE CADY

DAVID WRIGHT (WRIGHT)

Today we are talking with Dr. Steve Cady. Steve is a tenured graduate faculty member in the College of Business at Bowling Green State University and author of *The Change Handbook.* His published article and WBGU-PBS video on *Following Your First Best Alternative in Life* articulates his mission to "inspire the world to passionately pursue its dreams."

Steve, welcome to *Stepping Stones to Success.* Why don't you start by telling us little about your background and what influenced you to conduct research on passion?

STEVE CADY (CADY)

Thanks David. The best place to start is with my dad, Robert Cady. When I was a kid I would crawl into bed with him on Saturday mornings. We would watch cartoons on television and he would run his hands through my hair. I love a good head massage. My dad would do it until his arm hurt and he'd stop. When he did, I'd pick his arm back up and put it on my head.

Years later, when I was heading to graduate school, I got to spend a few last moments with my father before he died. I stopped by our house and walked into the living room where my dad was on the couch. He was sick and frail. I sat down on the floor and curled up next to him and we watched a TV show about dolphins by Jacques Cousteau. Dad just reached down and started rubbing his hands through my hair. I began reflecting back on the time when I was a little kid. He said something to me in that moment that I will never ever forget. He said, "Steven, if I could do it again, I would have been a marine biologist."

You see, my dad was a credit manager for a finance company. He had lived his second best alternative in life. He was a good dad. He loved my brother and sister and me a lot. He kissed a lot. He hugged a lot. He drank a lot. He yelled a lot. He encouraged a lot, and in his own groping, wounded, beautiful way was a good dad. He died two weeks later.

Dad gave me a gift in that moment that I want to share with you and that I hope you'll take with you. I want to inspire you, and those who are reading this, to live your *first best* alternative in life—your *first best* alternative.

WRIGHT

Steve, share with us what living an inspired life of passion means. How is this related to living one's first best alternative?

CADY

Let me give you a *Reader's Digest* version of my life's work. Many years ago I became fascinated by people who live their first best alternative, and I called them Passionate Souls. I've spent the last fifteen years researching this concept – studying thousands of people. Interestingly, my first research study on the concept back in 1991 looked at how people define success in life. Since then, I have been exploring concepts of inspiration and passion with my students and other scholars. I have interviewed dozens of people. I have reviewed years of literature, analyzed surveys and conducted research studies to learn how Passionate Souls live their life.

WRIGHT

What did you discover?

CADY

Well, first of all I learned that about 7 percent of the population is living their calling—living their first best alternative. That means 93 percent of people are not— 93 percent!

WRIGHT

Wow! Why is this? What's preventing people from living their calling?

CADY

Let me answer this by getting you to do something.

You know I'm a teacher, so bear with me. I would like this interview to be an experience for you and the readers.

Take out a blank sheet of paper. O.K. now write down those things that limit you from being your best self. What are those things that hold you back? Who's the person who holds you back? What are the past events or set of circumstances in your life that hold you back? What are those thoughts in your head that keep you from believing in yourself? Write them down; just like a random stream of thoughts or consciousness. Who's that person? What's that event? What's that thought? What are those things?

[Few minutes pass]

CADY

OK, now let me tell you a story about Socrates.

Socrates is a great philosopher. And he's sitting under a tree talking with his students. He tells them about this guy who's a jerk—a real jerk. This guy goes on a two-year journey to find himself. He comes back two years later, and guess what? He's still a jerk.

One of the students raises his hand and says, "Socrates, I don't get it. He goes on this two-year journey. He's supposed to find himself. How in the heck did he come back, still a jerk?"

"Well," Socrates replies, "because he took himself along."

Here's the point of the story for us ...we too are on a journey, whether we like it or not. The question is this – are you being intentional on your quest to live the rest of your life? I want you to be ready for this journey and move beyond those things that hold you back. And, it begins with a choice. So I want you and the readers to do something symbolic right now. I want you to turn the page on what holds you back from a new page of possibilities in your life. I want you to set aside the things that limit you; you can have them back later. Before we go through the rest of the interview, I want you to turn the page to a new page of possibilities, and say 'yes' if you're ready.

WRIGHT

Yes, I'm ready. What's next?

CADY

In my work, I've discovered that there are *six ways to a passionate soul*. These are the ways Passionate Souls *live their life*.

One or more of these ways is going to speak to you. It's going to knock you in the forehead. It's going to surprise you. Let it guide you into exploring and finding your passion and living more of your life.

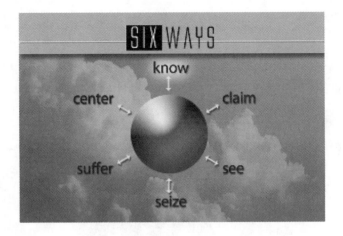

To guide you through the six ways, I have created a Passion Wheel. It's a checklist of sorts. Here it is. When I present this, I start at Way One and rotate all the way around to Way Six.

WRIGHT

O.K., so Way One is Knowing. Does that mean that passionate people have a clear vision of what their calling is or what they're meant to do?

CADY

Yes, Passionate Souls *know* their calling. Take, for example, the tallest towers in the world in Kuala Lumpur. Imagine if I take an I-beam and I bolt it down on the first floor window reaching over to the other building. I go to the other building and bolt it down to the first floor there.

Would you, just for fun and with no safety equipment, cross that I-beam?

WRIGHT

I'd probably do it. It's not too high.

CADY

Now go up forty-four floors, bolt it down between the two buildings. Would you cross it, with no safety equipment, just for fun?

WRIGHT

No, way.

CADY

All right. Now, how about if I give you some money to go across. How about a thousand dollars…or ten thousand dollars—would you cross it for ten thousand or a hundred thousand dollars? How about a million dollars?

WRIGHT

Okay, maybe a million dollars would get me to try.

CADY

Now, let's just take that I-beam and go up all the way to the top. It's cold out. It's windy. It's rainy. And those buildings sway. If you know anything about construction, high-rise buildings sway about fifteen feet in the wind. Imagine this…they're swaying. The I-beam is bolted down. You are on one end of the I-beam. Down at the other end is someone you love, for instance, a child. Okay? Would you know cross the I-beam to save that child's life?

WRIGHT

Without a doubt, I would cross the I-Beam. What does this have to do with knowing my calling?

CADY

You see, Passionate Souls take great risks in the service of something greater than themselves. Without any ambiguity, they know what they'd cross that I-beam for. This is their calling.

A calling is simply defined as a person's talent used to make a difference in the world. There are two key parts to this definition, talent and difference. First, let me first talk about talent. A talent is something you do well. It's hard to imitate and it's unique to you.

Passionate Souls have a talent that they really *know*—they know it and own it. It's unique to the passionate soul. They put their own signature on it.

WRIGHT

Many people have great talents and they know they are talented whether or not others are aware of their gifts. Does that make them passionate?

CADY

Here's the second part of the definition that brings it to life. It's life itself. It's what gives meaning or purpose for getting up in the morning. Passionate Souls take their talent out into the world beyond their family and make a difference that affirms life. A talent without a purpose is like a ship with a big high-performance engine and no rudder. When a talent affirms life, it turns living into *acts of service*.

Have you ever heard of the helper's high? What researchers have found is that service creates high bursts of energy and exhilaration followed by calm and serenity that lasts for a long period of time. What's also interesting is that when you reflect back on your act of service later—months later—you still get the same helper's high experience.

Take it a step further. When you serve another, your immune system is improved, you get rid of insomnia, and you have greater satisfaction in life. Now let's take it even further. The people watching someone perform an act of service— someone living his or her calling—get the same effect themselves.

So if you're looking to get high, my suggestion is to get the all-natural high of living your calling.

[A bit of laughter]

WRIGHT

Is knowing your calling something you are born with or find early in life? In other words, is it too late for, say, someone in their sixties?

CADY

I had one lady run up to me after I gave a talk and say, "My life's over. I agree with what you are saying. But I have wasted a ton of time. I don't even think it's worth starting now. It's too late for me."

"Look," I replied, "you're just a junior [in college], what are you talking about?"

It's refreshing, and when I share this story with an audience, they laugh because they are so surprised that this 19 year old student would think that she already lived her whole life.

And then there's T. Boone Pickens the billionaire venture capitalist. He's living his calling to change the world around energy use. I saw him being interviewed by Charlie Rose who said to him", You're eighty years old."

"Yes," Pickens replies, "And I'm going to use every minute I've got!"

So the answer is clear – it's never too late. Heck today is all you've got; live it like it's your last and plan on living a long time making a difference.

WRIGHT

T Boone is changing things on a big scale. Does that mean I have to change the whole world? It's a pretty big place.

CADY

When you look at the people that have changed the world, the one thing you see is that they started in their neighborhoods. They didn't intend to change the whole world, they just got started, usually close to home. And, many stay close to home making a lifelong difference in their community; heck, on their street or in their workplace.

WRIGHT

Okay, how does one find one's calling?

CADY

This is the most frequent question I get—how do I find my purpose in life? And there are two distinct paths that I've seen in Passionate Souls' stories when they share them.

One is, it's emergent—it sneaks up on them. They're living their calling. They're living their gifts. They're making a difference in their world. And then one day, they look around and they think, "Hey, I am <u>really</u> making a difference! Wow! Look, I love this!"

And in other situations, it's *Bam!*—a punctuated event. It's sometimes during a tragedy and sometimes it's during an inspiring moment that just jolts people. In that moment, they know what they are supposed to do with their life.

Whether it is emergent or punctuated, there is one common ingredient in finding one's calling. It's self-reflection. You have to look inward to better understand your potential in the world. Passionate Souls take a good and hard look in the mirror.

Let me ask you a question. Would you date you? Would you marry you? Would you hire you? Would you pick you? Would you be your best friend? As Gandhi said, "Be the change you want to see in the world."

Try this. Make a list of all the things you want your family, friends, and co-workers to change about themselves. Now, re-write it as your personal growth and development list. Change it from "Joe needs to..." to "I need to..." Those items you push back the hardest on are the ones to take into serious consideration.

WRIGHT

Those are good questions. I want to get very specific here. How can someone use this to identify what difference they want to make in the world?

CADY

What Passionate Souls do is notice the moments that matter. And if you're seeking to find your calling, it's sometimes in small little moments, but as I said, it's can also be in lightning-bolt moments.

Here is one way. Reflect on a moment when you felt you mattered. I want you to jot down what that moment was. What was happening in that moment? Who were you influencing or what were you affecting? How did you make it different? What did you do? What talent or gift did you bring to that moment? How did you feel in that moment?

Let me tell you about Kwazi, a guy I met in Uganda. I call him the reluctant king. A woman by the name of Cory who was my host when I visited Uganda said, "Steve would you talk to Kwazi? The life has just drained out of his eyes." She went on to say, "This is a beautiful talented man."

Kwazi is the eldest, and he's in line to be the next chief. He left his village to go to the capital to make money because he's good at fixing things. So he went into the capital, and he began working for the U.N., driving people to and from the airport. He also had an auto mechanics store.

We sat down and sipped black African tea on this beautiful green lawn. I asked Kwazi, "Tell me about a moment when you felt you mattered."

"It was this morning at three a.m.," he replied.

"Really? What happened?"

"I was driving somebody to the airport from the U.N. and this dog ran out in front of me." (Small clue: "this dog ran out in front of me.")

"What happened?" I asked.

"I didn't hit it."

"Okay, well, what was different?"

He said, "I saved its life."

"Kwazi," I said, "you save lives!"

"Yeah, I save lives."

"Tell me, how do you save lives?"

"I'm in the capital," he replied. "There are lots of homeless kids. I help them find homes. I help them find health care. I help them find food and shelter. My village still sees me as the eldest, so they come and talk to me about cattle and water and those kinds of things."

"What are you doing, Kwazi?" I asked.

"I'm sharing my life."

"Ah, so you save lives through sharing your life."

And this strong, kingly African man got small.

"Kwazi," I said, "can you say that? Just try saying it."

"I can't."

"Are these your words or did I make them up?"

"No, no. I said those things."

"Let's try here—just try here. Right now, for just one moment, try."

He sighed, took a breath, and said, "I save lives through sharing my life."

"Kwazi, say it a little bit louder."

He sighed again, "I save lives through sharing my life."

And he began to cry, and I started crying and Cory started crying. I actually have this recorded on tape. You can hear us all sitting there crying.

And at some point he calmed down, and he said, "Steve, I've taught my children to not deny who they are. I know what I need to do now."

WRIGHT

Wow! That's a powerful story. Do people find it difficult to accept their calling or profess their passion?

CADY

Well, that is one thing Passionate Souls do differently than those who don't. Passionate Souls *claim* their purpose. Way One is in your head and in your heart.

Claiming your calling is Way Two of the Six Ways and it is out in the open—it's public. Passionate Souls love to talk about what they do—about their calling. They share with people on planes, or trains, in grocery stores—anywhere. It's public. And they're enthusiastic about it. There's a childlike awe they have with living their calling. And it's authentic. Think about what authentic means. Authenticate. Who authenticates a passionate soul's calling? Nobody but the passionate soul can decide if they are living their calling.

One of our best thinkers in leadership and community is Peter Block, and he says, "When I meet you, I meet your commitment." And, this brings attention to someone living their calling.

When Passionate Souls make a commitment, they become a target for better or for worse. Have you ever seen a Rorschach inkblot test? Psychologists have been using these for years. You throw ink up on a page, and you ask somebody, what do you see? One person says, "I see two people in love." Another person says, "I see two people that hate each other." Both are the same inkblot test. When Passionate Souls claim their calling, they are like an inkblot test for those around them. They're a mirror for other people. Those that are inspired are seeing the inspiring part of themselves. Those that are hypercritical are seeing the negative side of themselves.

Regardless, they face this mirror by themselves; they really take the time alone necessary to be totally aware of who they are.

WRIGHT

So Passionate Souls have to 'go it alone' as it were?

CADY

No, it's not quite like that. On one hand, Passionate Souls have supporters—people who love them. They accept support from people. They welcome it.

And they stand on the shoulders of those who have come before them. They honor their elders.

On the other hand, Passionate Souls have to deal with what I call "ankle-biters." These are people who love to nibble around on the ankles saying, "Can't do it—no way, not here, not in these times. I can't see that person doing this. No way."

What Passionate Souls do is they focus on the supporters and not on the ankle-biters. They allow the resistance to be informative as they move forward. It is, however, not a focus. They are very good at focusing on the vision of what they yearn for in the world and don't allow the distractions to take over.

I want you to try this. Say this with me, "I am not who I think I am. I am not who *you* think I am. I am who I think *you* think I am."

WRIGHT

[laughing] Brain twister, right?

CADY

The point is that Passionate Souls know who they are, in spite of what they may think others think of them.

Pat McClagan is an author friend of mine. When she was in the fourth grade she was out on the playground. She had braces on her legs. She ran up to some kids who were in a big circle holding hands playing a game. One of the kids turned around and said to her, "Get out of here. We don't want cripples." Pat ran off the field crying, and sat down.

She told me, "Steve, in that moment, I felt so alone. And in that moment, I chose to no longer to be a victim. I was going to choose my path in life and I wasn't going to let what other people said or thought about me dictate who I was going to become. I chose in that moment to do something great with my life." And she has gone on to do great things.

Here's what Passionate Souls tell me: They say that they see the ankle-biters and the resistance as an indication they're on the right path. They expect people to doubt. They expect to choose something that is going to be hard.

WRIGHT

How can someone work on being brave like that?

CADY

They are committed to getting out their message as an invitation to others to be part of something that matters. The importance of what they yearn to do is greater than the fear. It's less about them and more about the difference. And, they are willing to be publically accountable.

I like to take people through a Way 2 activity. Begin with reviewing your thoughts around a moment you felt you mattered. There's a clue in there. There was a difference you made. There was something you did really well.

One thing you can do is write down that one thing you did really well and claim it for yourself or for the world. It's something you commit yourself to—something about yourself, your talent, your gift. Write down one simple little phrase, couple words, or a sentence. Now, here is the clincher. Sit with a friend or even at dinner with a group of people. Ask for their attention and share with them what you are claiming.

WRIGHT

That sure can be scary. Knowing it is one thing. Claiming it is another. What keeps people from standing up and claiming it?

CADY

I call it the syndrome of the *second best alternative*. People choose second best to avoid fear and stay comfortable. On one hand, you've got fear. And on the other hand, you've got comfort. On one hand, there's the fear of success. On the other, there's the comfort of mediocrity. On one hand, there's the fear of failure. And on the other hand, there's the comfort of dreaming what could be. On one hand, there's the fear of being noticed. On the other hand, there's the comfort of hiding in the crowd. On the one hand, there is the fear of living. On the other hand, there's the comfort of dying.

Passionate Souls do not like to be comfortable. The pressure is a welcomed. They step into their fear like a samurai looking at the edge of his sword.

WRIGHT

You seem like an outgoing person or extrovert. Did you naturally fall into living like this?

CADY

Actually, when I graduated from high school, I was afraid to go to into public places. Malls scared me. Check-out lines petrified me. When I went to college, I was exposed to leadership and personal growth programs, and my world opened up. One night I dreamed there was a sea of people, and in that moment I was touching their hearts. It was simple and powerful. And, it was counter to my anxiety for being in public. This positive image of what I yearned for gave me the motivation to go for it.

I woke up the next morning, grabbed one of my friends, and said, "I know what I'm supposed to do with my life! I know!" The next week I started a program called LEAD—Leadership Education And Development. The focus was on students who wanted to find their path and succeed in college.

I chose an opening night, put flyers up all over campus, got my agenda, and I told myself that no matter how much my voice quivered or my knees buckled or how much I shook, I was going to do it! I expected about twenty people. I walked into the room and there were two hundred people sitting in there, including the college's vice president of student affairs! I was literally, honest to God, shaking uncontrollably. I stood in front of the audience and said, "Welcome," holding my agenda behind my back because my hands were shaking so much. But I did it. I was shaking and nervous, but I stepped out and did it. And, after a few minutes I felt better and it became easier at the next event.

What I learned in that moment was that you have to step into your calling and into your fear. Stay in it long enough to calm yourself down and know you'll be okay. But only *you* can do that. Nobody else can do it for you—nobody else.

WRIGHT

So you have to begin somewhere, right?

CADY

Yes! When you know your calling, which is Way One, when you claim your purpose, which is Way Two, you open the door for possibilities and this leads to Way Three.

WRIGHT

So tell me about Way Three.

CADY

Way Three is about *seeing* the possibilities. Passionate Souls see the possibilities. And when I talk about "seeing," I'm talking about all the senses—anything the mind can see and believe can be achieved. And there are two kinds of seeing— *synchronicity* and *equifinality*.

WRIGHT

I think I've heard of synchronicity but I don't know what you mean by equifinality.

CADY

Equifinality is studied by psychologists and by quantum physicists who examine the smallest particles of matter in order to understand the vastness of our universe. Scientists took a random number generator and in a three-dimensional space they put out a dot in the space randomly. They were looking to see what happens when random dots are placed into this three dimensional space many times. And they did it more than a billion times.

What do you think they saw?

WRIGHT

Maybe a full, completely filled in box?

CADY

No. They saw a picture that looks like butterfly wings.

This is referred to as chaos theory or the butterfly effect. And what it tells us is that synchronicity is all around you at any one point. Swimming around you, are the opportunities and possibilities to follow your passion—to live your calling. They are there already, just waiting for you to see them.

WRIGHT

Give me an example of how this plays out

CADY

You know how it is when you buy a new car, you're driving down the street, and suddenly you say, "Hey, there's my car. Hey, there's my car. Oh, there's one in my color." Those cars didn't just show up that day. They were there the day before when you were driving down the street. They were always there. But you are just now noticing them. You are just now *seeing*. Now that you see, the question is what path do you choose? And, this is known as equifinality.

WRIGHT

What is equifinality?

CADY

Equifinality means there are multiple paths to the same goal. So I can cross the I-beam we discussed earlier from one end to the other directly. Or, I can go down the stairs, across the street, and up the elevator. There are all kinds of ways that I can get from point A to point B. I don't have to cross the I-beam directly to save that child's life. There are other ways to get there.

Have you ever noticed how some people have all the luck? Things just seem to fall their way. People seem to think it just comes easy for those who are passionate.

But here's what Passionate Souls say. They see all the possibilities. They see the path. They expect it to unfold in unexpected ways, and what they do is unleash the power of synchronicity. So when a door shuts, they see other possibilities open up. And they notice all the various choices. While other people are scared and paralyzed, Passionate Souls have a calm, peaceful demeanor because they see lots of different ways. It's just a matter of deciding which way to go"

WRIGHT

So when things don't go as planned, Passionate Souls find another angle and keep going? Sounds like they are less likely to be pessimistic?

CADY

Well, some people want their path to unfold exactly as planned. Passionate Souls relish the unexpected. They realize that linear and fixed plans are unrealistic and set one up for failure.

Try this one on. Seeing is believing or believing is seeing. And, some people simply don't see the possibilities at all.

I'd like to tell you about the parable of the house flood. This is one of my favorites. There is this guy is in his house. He walks over, turns on the radio, "Evacuate immediately! There is a flood coming."

"No thanks!" he says, "God will protect me!"

The rains come. He crawls out onto his roof and sits down. A boat comes by and the people offer to take him to safety.

"No thanks," he replies, "God will protect me."

The waters come up higher, and now he's up on the chimney. A helicopter flies over and drops down a ladder.

"No thanks!" he calls out. "God will protect me!" He drowns. He dies. He goes to heaven. He walks up to God and says, "Hey, I thought you were going to protect me!"

God says, "Well, let's see. I sent you a radio announcement, a boat, and a helicopter."

[Laughter]

WRIGHT

It appears people get locked in to how they view their world. How do you get unstuck?

CADY

Well first, to get unstuck, you have to know what stuck means and then recognize that you are indeed stuck yourself. What keeps us from seeing the possibilities is this notion of *learned helplessness*. It's been demonstrated in lots of different ways.

One way is with fish. If you take a fish tank with a glass divider in the middle, and you put a barracuda (and this has actually been done) on one side and its prey on the other side, it bangs into the glass. It bangs into the glass over and over again going after its food. Over time, the barracuda stops. Scientists take the glass out. The barracuda never tries again to go to the other side to eat the fish it likes to eat, and it starves to death.

Learned helplessness is defined like this—when you are presented with an opportunity to change or leave a challenging, difficult, punishing, noxious situation, you don't even see it as an opportunity. You don't even recognize it as an possibility.

To get unstuck is to break the cycle of learned helplessness. So, Way One is to know your calling. Way Two is to claim your purpose. Way Three is to notice or see the possibilities. This takes unlearning our limiting beliefs.

WRIGHT

If we are not naturally inclined to notice or see our possibilities, can we train ourselves to do this?

CADY

Yes, we can change our thoughts. Chaos theorists have taught us that our thoughts are powerful and the things we look at actually change based on the way we look at them and what we notice.

Dr. Masaru Emoto from Japan has done some controversial research. Some people are debating it, but I will tell you that chaos theory and quantum physics supports what he is finding.

He takes a Petri dish and puts in a drop of water. He then puts a label with a word on it, on the dish. He directs specific thoughts at the Petri dish. He speaks words to the water and then they photograph the water as it freezes to see how the water crystallizes.

For example, he labels a Petri dish "You fool" and takes a picture. And what appears is misshapen, diseased-looking water.

He then takes another dish of water and labels it "Thank you" and takes a picture. And what shows up is an elegant structure.

He then took another Petri dish, and he had some children sit with it and ignore it. What showed up was water that was misshaped.

The children then said "You're beautiful," just a few times to the water, and it just started to take shape. They said, "You are beautiful" a lot of times, and a beautiful elegant structure formed.

Now consider the following facts: Your body is 85 percent water. The kinds of thoughts you have, and the things you pay attention to have a major effect on you for good or for bad. Look around you and notice what kind of environment you have created or allowed yourself to be in. What kind of people do you gravitate toward?

Gene Poor, a professor friend of mine, tells his students, "You are the product of the five closest people to you in your life."

WRIGHT

So are you saying that if I think and speak out positive thoughts I can change not only the way I view the world but my outcomes as well?

CADY

Yes, that's exactly what I'm saying. A couple days after learning about Dr. Emoto's work, I was really ragging on myself and being quite self-critical. A good friend cut me off and said, "Hey! Would you just be nice to your water?"

I think that would make a great bumper sticker. You know? Be nice to your water.

WRIGHT

So, this is where we begin to change our realities? Is it possible for us to change just by how we think and what we surround ourselves with?

CADY

Yes, we absolutely can. And what chaos theory shows us is there are two realities at any one time in our life. In that moment when you see both realities, I have to tell you, in every single case, it is the loneliest moment because it is only you who can make the choice. You have to choose from the two realities that co-exist. And the question is which one will you choose—success or failure? Self-confidence or self-doubt? Supporters or ankle-biters? Which will you choose?

WRIGHT

Is that it? I know my calling, I claim my calling, and now I see the possibilities? Synchronicity happens and equifinality shows me the paths...and, I am on my way?

CADY

Yes, but there's more. Passionate Souls *seize* the moment. Try this, put your finger on your nose. Try to take it off. Noooooo. Put your finger back on. Try to take it off...Yoda says, "There is no try, only do."

Seizing the moment is about action. It's two things—*choice* plus *focus* equals *action*. And what Passionate Souls do is make tough choices between two mutually desirable options, oftentimes, in the short-term and in the long-term.

WRIGHT

Say more about choices.

CADY

For example, in the short-term, do you go out at night, have fun with your friends, stay up late? What do you have going on tomorrow? A big project? A major event? You want both of them. They are mutually desirable. Which do you choose?

A good friend of mine will often go to parties and then say, "Hey, everybody, I've got to leave early because I have to be brilliant tomorrow!"

Passionate Souls also make tough choices in the long-term. Sometimes they stay home, close to friends, but then they have to make a tough choice, whether to be close to family and friends or to go off to a faraway place to get an education or to pursue a project or something that is really in service of their calling. Again, these are two mutually desirable choices.

Passionate Souls make the tough choice. It's about priorities.

WRIGHT

Prioritizing also takes discipline, especially when one wants to do it all—have my cake and eat it too.

CADY

There is a fun experiment I learned and now share with my audiences. I hold up a large glass bowl containing one grapefruit and ask, "Is the bowl full?"

Most people say no. All right, so let's try filling this thing up some more.

I add more fruit to the bowl—grapefruit, apples, grapes, and more.

I ask, "Is it full now?" Ah, maybe, some people say yes, some people say maybe.

I add a pitcher of rice to the bowl. "Is it full now?" "Yes," some people say, "it looks pretty darn full to me."

Lastly I add a pitcher of water to the bowl. A lot of people say, "The bowl is now full."

What is the point of the story? People often say they can always put more into their lives; they can always do more. No, that's not it.

I then pull the big grapefruit out of the bowl. And, then try to stuff it back in and it will not fit into the bowl. The grapefruit is your *calling*. If you don't put the grapefruit in first—if you don't make your calling first priority—you will not get it in later after the bowl or your life is filled with everything else.

I pull out the other pieces of fruit from the bowl and hold them up. These are your *goals*. Again, the point is, if you don't get those big things in first, they are not getting back in at all.

The rice represents your daily activities. If you don't have the goals in support of your calling in place, then you are running around doing a lot of stuff that doesn't make any sense. You end up wondering what you are spending your life doing—hopelessly running on that wheel you see mice running on.

WRIGHT

That's a great metaphor. So it's a choice to set priorities?

CADY

Yes, the choice is about priority. Passionate Souls make tough choices, and then they focus. Once you make your choice, train yourself to stay focused.

Think about golfing. All right. I tee up. Whew. There's a lot of water up there! Man, look at that tree. Oh, those sand traps, my goodness! Look at that water. Oh, look at that water. I am not—I am *not* hitting it into that water! I am not going to hit it into that water. No way, Jose! I am not going to hit it in that water!

Where do I hit it?

WRIGHT

In the water!

CADY

Right, in the water it will go. I've found there are three kinds of people who approach something like this: die-ers, survivors, and thrivers.

Die-ers use the event and the conditions in their life to give up. They accept the water. The water becomes their outcome or result they guarantee themselves.

Survivors use the events and the conditions in their life as reasons to get by. "I think I'll just hit it on the green, just the green. I'm happy with the green. Just let me get on the green. A bogey isn't that bad. It's better than the water."

Passionate Souls are often told that their goals and their dreams are too grandiose. They're too big. They're going for too much. "Pull back a little bit and go for the green, man." Passionate Souls are *thrivers*. They go for the hole-in-one every time, and every time they focus on making that hole-in-one.

When Tiger Woods played, his dad would walk around him jangling change and keys. He would be the epitome of an ankle-biter for Tiger. And Tiger made the choice to win, and he focused.

WRIGHT

Can you give another example of seizing the moment that is not associated with just one instant or action?

CADY

Absolutely. I want to read a story to you from Charles Garfield.

Have you ever gone through a tollbooth? You know that your relationship to that person in the booth is not the most intimate you'll ever have. It's one of your life's frequent non-encounters.

Late one morning, when Charles Garfield was heading to lunch, he drove to one of the booths. He heard loud music and wondered what was going on. He came up and the guy in the booth was dancing.

"What are you doing?" he asked the guy.

"I'm having a party," came the reply.

"What about the rest of us?"

"You're not invited."

"I had dozens of questions for him," Garfield wrote. And he found the guy months later. Again he asked, "Look, what are you doing?"

"Yeah, I know you," the guy said. "I'm still in the booth dancing. I'm still having the same party."

"Well, what about the rest of the people in the booths?"

"Stop. What do they look like they're doing?" he said as he pointed down the row of tollbooths.

Garfield said, "I don't know."

"No imagination man. They look like vertical coffins. People get in these booths in the morning at 8:30, and then get out at the end of the day after checking their brain. They do this over and over and over again."

Garfield went on to write that sixteen people were dead on the job, and the seventeenth, in precisely the same situation, had figured out a way to live! The man was having a party in a boring situation in which you and I would probably not last three days.

"He and I did have lunch later," Garfield wrote.

"I don't understand why anyone would think my job is boring," the guy with the tollbooth job said. "I have a corner office, glass on all sides. I can see the Golden Gate Bridge, San Francisco, and Berkeley Hills. Half the Western civilization vacations here and I just stroll in every day and practice dancing."

You sometimes have to act like a winner before you become a winner.

WRIGHT

What about those who carry great burdens or extreme unhappiness? It must be hard for them to act like a winner. Do they need to fix what is causing their unhappiness before seizing their calling?

CADY

We all carry burdens. Passionate Souls embrace the tough road of life. This leads us to Way Five—*Suffer.* The root meaning of "passion" is to suffer. Passionate Souls embrace their suffering, and there are three embraces.

Their first embrace is to *reframe* it. When I ask Passionate Souls, "Do you suffer?" What they'll say is, "Nah, I don't suffer. What are you talking about?"

"Well, do you have trials, and tribulations?"

"Yes. Okay. Yes I do, but I don't suffer."

What Passionate Souls do is embrace their suffering, they *reframe* it, and they see it as important to the person they are today and who they are becoming.

WRIGHT

They see suffering as necessary?

CADY

Yes, take the butterfly for example.

On the left is a cocoon. Alfred Wallace, a botanist, decided to snip the butterfly out. It came out, and its wings were shriveled, and it died. What he learned is that if you cut the butterfly out early, it doesn't experience the struggle it needs to redistribute the fluid in its body so its wings can open up and it can fly. Like the butterfly, the struggle is important to who you are and who you are becoming.

WRIGHT

Of course, suffering shapes us. But how do you move beyond it? I mean, how do you let go of the hurt and heal the wounds? I too hear about people speaking of the "battle wounds" from doing what they believe is right or good.

CADY

This is the second embrace. They see life as a grand experiment and the key to healing from those battle wounds is forgiveness. They forgive themselves and they forgive others.

Corrie Ten Boom spent many years in Ravensbruck, a Nazi concentration camp. Many years later she was telling her story of Ravensbruck, and after her talk, she came down to the front and started greeting people in the audience.

A man walked toward her and immediately she had a flashback to an incident in the camp. It turned out that this man had been a guard in Ravensbruck.

She had just given a talk on forgiveness. He walked up to her and said, "It's so good to know that I can be forgiven. Will you forgive me?" She went on to share that she who had been talking on forgiveness was now faced for the first time with one of the most challenging moments in her life.

She reached up her hand and she put it in his hand, and she said, "I forgive you." And she said in that moment, the weight of her burden of anger and hate fell off her shoulders.

WRIGHT

Taking a step like that takes a lot of strength. Do Passionate Souls naturally have this strength?

CADY

Actually, they believe that there is a good reason for everything. The third embrace of suffering for Passionate Souls is that they are *persistent learners*—they never ever give up.

You can see from Nick's picture that he is a happy-looking guy. He looks like he is full of energy and life.

He has a program called, "No Limbs, No Limits."

Nick was born with no arms and no legs.

What Nick will tell you in his message is, "never, ever give up." He swims, surfs, rides around, he shaves, and cooks. He says his message is that wherever you are, never, ever give up. You can figure it out because he figured it out. You can find him on YouTube.

WRIGHT

It sounds like burdens and sufferings can be turned into positive experiences.

CADY

Yes. Let's do this. You came to this interview today with a burden that you carry. Those of you who are reading this are carrying a burden, a weight on your shoulders. Imagine that burden as a rock. Go find a rock. Hold that rock, that burden out and see it in the palm of your hand. Imagine it as a gift. How has that burden helped to shape you? How has it helped you to become the person you are? What is the gift of the burdens you carry?

I advise people to write down their suffering. Then write down the gifts they have received from their burdens. I encourage them to keep the gift of that burden. Get rid of the weight and use the gift. And this leads us to Way Six.

WRIGHT

The Passion Wheel says Way Six is Center. What does that mean?

CADY

It means that Passionate Souls *center* themselves. When you look around the world there are dualities—there's black and white, there's heaven and hell, right and wrong, yin and yang.

Passionate Souls are challenged by obsession and depression. They go back and forth. They experience obsession, checking and rechecking, over and over again.

Then, things flip and they experience depression. This is the opposite of obsession. This can range from feeling the blues all the way to complete inactivity and checking-out.

All people, including Passionate Souls, experience degrees of obsession and depression. For some it is a minor experience of feeling down or feeling anxious. For others, it can be extreme obsession, depression, checking out, loneliness, and they go back and forth.

Here is the irony. Whether they like it or not, Passionate Souls are a gift to those around them. Sometimes, they are serving others in need, while they themselves are feeling very down and out. The ironic thing is that the Passionate Soul is not experiencing the JOY of living their calling. Yet, people around them are benefiting from their gifts and talents.

When Passionate Souls find the exact center, they experience the joy of living their calling.

WRIGHT

This is surprising because people living their calling appear to be centered and balanced most of the time. I didn't know they tend to waver between extremes. What advice do you have to help someone stay centered?

CADY

Focus on two things - the implementation and inspiration in your life. For inspiration, create an "inspiration station." Find a place in your house where you can put the things that remind you of all the great things about you. Put cards, awards, successes, the things you aspire to have, all the things you love, put them there, and stop by your inspiration station each day and focus on it for three minutes.

Second, develop a personalized project and time management system. Write down your plans and put commitments into a calendar. Hold yourself accountable. You can also unleash the power of the present, because the present is a flash of light. And what Passionate Souls do is imagine their future and they write it down. When you write it down, your future is brought into the present with you.

WRIGHT

Steve, this has been a fascinating conversation. Do you have any closing thoughts to add for our readers?

CADY

Yes. I'd like people to reflect on the dash of their life. You have your birthday and you have your death day, but on your tombstone, in the middle, is the dash. That's the magic of your life. That's where it all happens.

That's where you *know* your calling.

That's where you *claim* your purpose.

That's where you *see* all the possibilities there to support you and love you.

That's where you *seize* the moment, when you embrace the *suffering* and let it inspire you to live more mighty.

That's where you find the *center*—the joy in your life.

Here is a poem I love to end with.

"And he said, 'Come to the edge.'
And I said, 'I can't, I'm afraid.'
And he said, 'Come, to the edge.'
And I said, 'I can't. I will fall.'
And he said, 'Come to edge.'
And I did,
And he pushed me,
And I flew. "

ABOUT THE AUTHOR

Dr. Steven H. Cady is strongly committed to using cutting-edge approaches that inspire innovative solutions and collaborative strategy creation. He is a Graduate Faculty member at Bowling Green State University where he serves as Director of the Institute for Organizational Effectiveness. He has also served as Director of the Master of Organization Development Program and the Chief Editor for the Organization Development Journal. Steve publishes, teaches, and consults on topics of organizational behavior & psychology, change management, and organization development. Some of his clients include DaimlerChrysler, The Tavistock Group, Dana Corporation, The Diocese of N.W. Ohio School System, Lake Nona, The Area Office on Aging, Anne Grady Corporation, Alcoa, BGSU, and British Petroleum. Prior to receiving his Ph.D. in Organizational Behavior with a support area in Research Methods and Psychology from Florida State University, Steve studied at the University of Central Florida where he obtained an MBA and a BSBA in Finance.

He is co-author of *The Change Handbook*. His published article and WBGU-PBS video on Following Your First Best Alternative in Life articulates his mission to "inspire the world to passionately pursue its dreams."

STEVE CADY

www.stevecady.com
580 Craig Drive
Perrysburg, OH 43551
419.255.6800
www.stevecady.com
office@stevecady.com

CHAPTER FOUR

Transition

An *Interview with....*

NANCY FAUST

DAVID WRIGHT (WRIGHT)

Today we are talking with Nancy Faust. Nancy has over twenty-eight years' experience in corporate positions including HR Director, strategic planner and entrepreneur. She has helped many people go through the difficult and challenging process of career transitioning to find their dream job using her proven methods and techniques.

Nancy, welcome to *Stepping Stones to Success.*

NANCY FAUST (FAUST)

Take a deep breath and release it slowly. Repeat twice. Make sure your room is quiet and cozy. Shut your eyes and picture the most beautiful scene you have ever seen. Stay there for a few minutes; time does not matter right now.

If you are in transition you must care for yourself first, then the rest of your world. When you are relaxed, bring your higher self to the present and read this chapter. My hope is that you will see all things are possible in transition and even the worst things are there to teach us lessons, which makes them good instead of bad.

WRIGHT

What is transition?

FAUST

That is the same as asking what ice cream is and tastes like. It can be defined by the dictionary, as well as by hundreds of types of flavors. Transition is *Change* from the simplest form right up to the most major change you have experienced in your life. Your marriage, your first child, death, moving, and changing jobs are some of the most important transitions in your life. How you deal with them is a whole other story. There is no magic ten-step manual to tell you how to deal with any of these transitions. You have to go through the process yourself to figure it out.

WRIGHT

What type of Transition are you speaking about in this chapter?

FAUST

I want to discuss the stressful transition and steps to job or career change. I said earlier there is no ten-step program, but what I didn't say is that there really is help for the person getting ready to do the work of career transition.

If you have a newborn you can hire a nurse or a sitter, or your friends and family can help you get used to and settle the newborn in your environment. They talk of the next steps to come in raising a child and what the future could bring. What a help! You will do the work to raise the child but you can fall back on their expertise or previous experience during confusing times.

In career transitions there is also support available for you called consultants and coaches. If you decide to go it alone, then you know that step one is updating your resume. Either you type it yourself or go to a resume service and get someone there to type it.

Step two, you will call your friends, search your newspaper and the Internet for any job you can perform and apply for it. If you are granted an interview you will take your latest "job description," your resume, and your last state of thinking into the interview to try and make a square peg fit into a round hole. I have even heard people say, "I will take this job until another comes along." Wow! That is stressful. It certainly does not sound as though this is a good way to find the perfect job or even a long-term fit going in this direction. Actually, this starts the cycle over and over again. Why not focus on finding the job you love?

WRIGHT

What should I do if my career changes or I am unhappy with my current position?

FAUST

First you should recognize your personal growth and welcome it as a part of your growing and changing. Be happy and realize this is not the job for you any longer. With new clients, my partner starts her conversation with, "Congratulations! If this is a time you have been terminated or laid off, then realize that things do happen for good reasons and this is the beginning of the new you."

This is a time to change your thinking. You are no longer someone doing another person's job description. You are yourself with your own likes and dislikes; you are good at some things and not so good at others. You now have an opportunity to fix those things you have wanted to be better at or to bypass them altogether in your next job. Now is the time to think outside the standard box. It is also time to remember that career changes take time. Do not picture landing your perfect job in a few days or even weeks.

Step One is to update your resume with a new focus! Pull your gifts and talents to the top and advertise. According to reports, the number of long-term unemployed grew to 4.4 million in June 2009, with the average job search lasting twenty-seven weeks or more. The first thing to do is stop thinking about how you can impress a new employer by listing your prior job description duties. Spend a great deal of time recalling the "above and beyond" accomplishments you made at each employer on your list.

Most important is to stop thinking of yourself as others at work saw you. You are a bright, intelligent being with wonderful characteristics and a lot of worthwhile work to give. Own the fact that you are the person the entire employment field has been looking for! When you own this fact it is reflected in how you carry yourself, the presence felt when you enter a room, how people respect you, and how you feel about yourself. Truly own this fact because if you just wear it, you will come off as arrogant and not a team player.

Employers want to hire people who can follow their job description but really want that person to show what an asset he or she was to the last employer and that the person feels confident about taking the job.

If you never had the opportunity to make an above and beyond accomplishment for an employer, then think of the ways you helped oil the wheels. Were you a team player? Did you volunteer for extra work or harder parts or mentor new hires? What positive things can you say about yourself and your time at a prior job? Were you recognized with awards, gifts, and/or a bonus? Now is the time to share all of your great qualities and accomplishments with the interviewer.

Once you have written down these items, you are ready for Step Two. Get a career coach/consultant. The coach will help guide you through the process of locking in your perfect job. Keep in mind that your coach is not getting the job for you and is not a counselor for you. You will do a lot of soul-searching and homework to get your perfect job; they say nothing worthwhile is ever free or easy. A consultant is a person you hire to talk about your last jobs and what you want in a new job. The consultant will work with you to build a standard resume, review with you basic interview steps, and maybe send you off on one or two suggested employment offers, then leaves you to your own job search.

WRIGHT

Is Step Three in your search getting ready for the job interview?

FAUST

This is not an easy step, especially when done alone. We call this shifting your mindset. If you are walking this path alone, buy a tape recorder or better yet, find a friend who listens well and is *totally* honest with you. We find ourselves saying the simplest or smallest of things like, "I have to" when we really don't mind doing it or really don't "have" to do it. Your friends should say, "Stop; did you hear that negative you just said?" You should change your sentence to "I get to," or "I want to"—anything other than the words "have to." Another thing about not making negative statements is you will slowly but really feel yourself start to feel better about your normal life duties and begin to see the positive surrounding you. Let go of negativity and let the true happy you show through.

Step Three is to prepare for the interview. You should spend time telling your friend about your professional self and your work history wrapped in a ball with major accomplishments, just as if your friend were performing the interview. Do these repeatedly; if you stumble in your answers, do it in practice so the real interview goes easier. Your interviewer will surely ask you to spend a few minutes talking about yourself.

Step Four is to be confident in the interview. At the actual interview, make sure you smile and make good eye contact with all the people who interview you and give a firm handshake. Presentation is really a one-shot deal. Use your first shot wisely. Dress appropriately, as though you were going to a business meeting. If you freeze during the interview, don't worry—we are all human. Simply be honest. Tell the interviewer that you are excited to get this job and that has put you slightly on edge. Stop and take a deep breath, then proceed again. You will be fine and your answers will be great.

Be patient with the process. If the interviewer is a few minutes late, it is not a slap to you—he or she is busy and has interruptions as well—stay focused on the exchange opportunity.

I have been in the Human Resource field for twenty-eight years. I remember interviews from the past and when I think of them, there are two groups that I immediately replay in my mind—the positive and the negative. The sleeper interviews I cannot even remember.

The positive:

I had a young man who was applying for an engineering position. He knew it would be ground level entry. He came straight out of college, nervous as could be. He was dressed in his suit and tie, and looked professional. I went into the conference room and started talking about the position we were hoping to fill.

This young man pulled out a notepad with writing on it and flipped to a new page. I noticed he did not write down everything I was saying but did put bullet points on his notes about key areas in the job or key requirements for filling the job. He had his "about me" question prepared and did a fine job of presenting who he was.

At this point I invited the other interviewers to join the interview because it had gone so well. This young man received business cards from all and placed them in front of him in a pattern that matched where each person was seated around the table. That way, when he addressed us, he knew the name of the person he was talking to. There is nothing wrong with "Well, ma'am," but a "Well, Ms. Faust" was so much more professional. It felt as though he was taking the same amount of time to get to know me as I was getting to know him.

After my questions I asked him if he had any for me before we went to the next step. He did in fact have several very pertinent questions about my company and the position. He had written down all of his questions before the interview. He had visited our Web site and knew a lot about the company culture and business. This was impressive and well noted on his interview form.

Interviews I conducted were of the panel protocol with a different mix of interviewees each time. This meant I had different peers I invited who wanted to know different things. I had peers who were very intense and some who were so freewilled that they never came out of an interview seeing anything other than the answers to their six questions, not even caring about the whole package of a person.

This particular interview started with me, then we were joined by three other engineers who were very considerate but wanted a good feeling of the candidate's knowledge. Having just come from college there isn't a lot to work with as far as job history. However, we can test methods and theory, equations, etc. to see if a candidate has retained the knowledge he or she has been given in college.

One of the engineers gave the job candidate a test. It had three problems on it. He told him he would be back in a few minutes. We all left the room to give him time to think. Upon returning the man had finished two problems but was stuck on the third. My engineer sat next to the candidate and reviewed the question with him. He asked different things about the equations used and why he chose them. Finally, the interviewer gave the correct answer and explained how he got it.

We had watched with great interest as this interaction happened. My candidate knew the correct formulas and that was a big plus. He stumbled on how to apply them in the correct order, a small minus. This young man had no actual experience but had the knowledge we needed. Nobody minds a small amount of on-the-job-training. It didn't matter to us if he came up with the correct answer or not, it was his thought process that told us what we needed to know. We hired this man as an entry level engineer. Within three weeks we changed his status to a level one group, which meant he was on the fast track to management of projects. He never let us down. That was a positive experience.

The Negative:

It was 3:00 PM and I was stuck on a telephone call. I sent my secretary to invite my candidate to sit in the lobby for a few minutes or to go ahead and enter the conference room. She assured him it would be just a few minutes. He decided to wait in the lobby. I could see the lobby from where I was and he had no idea who I was so it was interesting as I was ending my call to watch him pace the lobby and look at his watch in pure disgust every round he made. I was five minutes late.

I entered the lobby, shook his hand as I introduced myself and invited him to the conference room. I apologized for the delay, explaining that a call I had took longer than I planned. He said nothing, just stared at me and sat down. As usual, I started talking about the position we had and what type of person we were hoping to find to fill it. He assured me the job was a "piece of cake" and almost below what he was looking for. I offered to end the interview if that was the case but he asked to continue.

I invited my peers into the interview, once I established his skill set. He did have the qualifications we were looking for. We repeated the standard job history questions and asked him to tell us about himself. As I expected, he said everything I knew he would say and left the feeling that we should know he was a gift straight from heaven above.

We all took note of the fact that every statement was "I" and there was never a "we" in the speech. People who don't acknowledge that they are part of a team are people who are hard to work with; as for me, I don't hire them. The engineers who interviewed him all agreed that he may be a handful but if he turned out half as good as he stated he would be helping us fill an important gap. We decided to take a chance. I made an offer and he accepted.

During the first three weeks I expect new hires to ask lots of questions and make their share of mistakes. Mr. X fell right into that area. The problem with Mr. X, "sent straight from heaven," was he never learned from his mistakes and used information or help once and then forgot it.

He was great at showing his irritated and annoyed self to clients as well as peers. He was capable of the work given but after his introductory period when he was given a normal amount of work he fell apart. He was given three opportunities to clean up his act but never did. Needless to say, his stay with the company was not long lived. I followed his next three jobs by way of networking and found they were all identical to my experience with him.

The lesson learned here is that arrogant people need not apply and will not be hired. Also, those who don't prepare for and bring their best self to the interview will be rejected.

The Sleeper:

A "sleeper interview" is one where candidates are dressed appropriately, on time, had answers to standard questions but there was no depth to their answers, so it turned into a textbook interview. They probably read a book of interview questions, got the gist of what was supposed to be said, and did just that. I never left the room feeling that I'd found either a gold mine or a failure. I just found a warm body to fill a position. The shame is that people who are sleeper interviews may have had hidden potential that they had not presented or let me find

They normally were given a job and we planned on keeping them there until they showed us great improvement. Great improvement never happens with sleepers, so you find people doing the same job for fifteen years without very many raises and they are burned out. There is always a lack of communication on their part as far as their hopes and dreams. You cannot ask them what their five-year plan is because they can't see past Friday.

The lesson learned here, or moral of the story, is: don't be someone able to do the job at hand—be someone who communicates, takes the job at hand, and then make yourself shine so much that you cannot be ignored. You will move up the ladder quickly and be valued as a member of the team.

WRIGHT

What is next after the first interview?

FAUST

Step Five is the second interview. Most executive, managerial, or leadership roles will require more than one interview. Depending on the company, you will either be invited to the second interview while you are there or someone in the company will contact you within about one week to set the second interview date. If you are not the person the company is looking for, the interview should be followed with a few kind comments that point out qualities they needed that you do not show. Most companies are very quick to send out a "no thank you" letter.

Assuming you are one of the final candidates, you should be ready for tougher questions, tests, and a concept discussion for you to grasp and get into, possibly over a meal. The "jacket comes off" and we begin to really dig into your potential. You will be given some "what if" questions:

What if our client is very unhappy with the speed of the machine we built and decides to say this at delivery? How will you handle the problem at hand?

What about disagreements with other department managers regarding scheduling, technique, or other job issues? How will you handle the problem?

You will be given more tests to see how deep you are and how far out you reach. We gave you a direct test in the first interview; now it is time to drill deeper and wider into your talents. These tests are very important as far as drilling deeper but the wider is not that much of a problem if you don't pass it with flying colors.

Meal:

What can I say? You either practice good table manners or you don't. This was something that should have been taught and practiced at home during your youth. The reason a company takes you to lunch or dinner is because it is always your job to represent the company in and outside of work. If you take a client to dinner, it should be as pleasant an experience as working with you earlier in the day.

We took Dan to dinner at a local restaurant that had a casual atmosphere one night. We all ordered and asked that he order anything he wanted. This went well until drinks came around. Dan was a fish! He could drink faster than a thirsty teenager. This was noted. During dinner Dan chewed with his mouth open and spoke loudly with food in his mouth. At all times Dan's elbows were on the table unless he was lifting his glass—again. Needless to say, this part of the interview was a goose egg.

Concept discussions are lots of fun but nerve-wracking at the same time. This is your time to shine and it must be done on a dime. This process typically involves a hypothetical discussion around a new project and how it will be completed.

Everyone is given a sheet of paper and a pencil. We start to describe our individual ideas of what parameters we have to meet and what usable routines we have to do that. Then we develop a Bill of Material to include all the parts we need. After that we may start to draw a machine so we can place components and size the boxes we will need. Your input into this conversation is important, even if it is not the winning idea. We want to see you think and watch how you process information—did you take good notes, are you timid and did you sit back or were you outstanding and jump right in? We will learn about you at this point.

You should have in mind a salary range that you can work in. Be fair—not everyone will make six figures in the first year. Figure out what your market is worth. At some point near the end of the second interview, you will be told how much the job will pay. At this point you will either be thrilled or ready to scream. If the pay is so low that you cannot live in a lifestyle that satisfies you, then you will need to speak up and start negotiating. Most companies pay a certain amount during the first ninety days and then raise your rate as you become more valuable to them. If this is the case, you might accept a rate slightly lower than you had in mind. Please do not negotiate for salary using vacation, sick days, per diem, etc.

After the second interview, all involved will sit together and discuss strong and weak points during the interviews. Together they will make a decision. If you have owned and not worn the confidence I mentioned earlier, done your homework about the company you are applying to, presented yourself as having manners, a deep thinker, and a make-it-happen person, then you should be receiving an offer letter soon if not on the spot.

WRIGHT

Twice you have mentioned doing homework to check out the company the candidate will interview with. How is the best way to do so?

FAUST

I use the Internet for most of my discovery. Google is a great way to find stories and information about the company. The other thing is to go directly to the company's Web site. There you will find their mission, vision, and value statements. These statements are very hard to generate when done correctly. Just for information, a company should redo that work continually to see if it all still fits or if it needs updating.

For example, at my last job we spent a day to generate the ones we used. We all knew that elements such as integrity, customer care, and staying sharp in our field were important. We started with each word or thought and broke it out and wrote bullet points about each one. After we finished, it was clear what words were used over and over. Our point was made with these words. It was easy after that to create the sentence we wanted to use for our mission and our vision statements.

The value statement was processed the same way but took several writings to get it perfect. What was great about the whole process was when the entire company was brought in to view our new statements, everyone smiled and accepted proudly what our company was going to say to the world. It was a day I won't soon forget.

I also recommend that you look at the company's affiliations with other companies and check them out. If you know who your company represents and what exactly it is that they do, you will shine a little brighter at the interview.

Normally names of key executives are listed on the site as well. I Google every name I get to find articles about them also. Work they are proud of, or work that is typical to their company, may be listed to provide a look into what they can do for customers. This information is valuable to you during the interview and in deciding if you really want to interview with this company.

It is always an eye-opener when the candidate mentions that while the candidate was researching their company, he or she found X to be on the cutting edge, or that he or she found that the President was a great community service minded person, etc. Let them know you have invested time into finding out about them.

WRIGHT

Let's talk about general transition emotions, thoughts, fears, and feelings.

FAUST

I don't know many who welcome major changes like a breeze blowing in their hair. Most people experience some anxiety. After all, a change in job means a dip in money, your family may be uprooted to find your perfect job, or you may not find a job opening in your field right away. This is just plain scary the first few days.

I suggest that you take a week to sit back and think about the pros and cons of the field you have been working in. This is the perfect time to decide if you want to continue to be in a service world or if you would rather be in retail. It is time to decide if you want to lead or follow in a job. How close to retirement are you? Do you need a job with flexible hours or is the nine-to-five still feeling good to you? This is the time to decide if you even want to work for someone else.

My personal circumstances allowed me to take sufficient time to dream about my being back in the same type job, changing to a new job, or working for myself. I also considered if I did work for myself, should I make my work something that gives back to the world or something that is a product consumed by the world?

I knew I loved talking and have always taken on the role of teacher. I knew I needed more flexibility in my schedule and would feel bad taking advantage of a good employer asking for time off on a regular basis. I no longer sit behind a desk and follow a job description. I know I am capable of doing that should I need to, but it just isn't for the grown up me.

I decided to travel the path of the entrepreneur—one that gave back by teaching and helping people see their hidden potential. I am a job coach, an author, and a speaker.

Fears:

After deciding to own my own business, the fear set in again. I call them the one thousand "what if's" in life: What if nobody wants my service? What if clients don't pay on time—I am used to a regular paycheck! What if I find that I am really not cut out for this job I felt was my dream job? How do I start? Where do I start? When do I start? Do I need all my business equipment before I start? What about marketing? I should be able to market myself, but sometimes people are too close to the forest to see the trees.

This is the time to take a chill pill and calm down! You will be okay. If you did not have these questions or any others, you might be that arrogant person who will fail in the end. A caring, concerned person is one who will make sure all details are done and will succeed in most cases.

I wrote down each and every concern no matter how big or small. This was my "punch list." I put priorities on them, and then I started knocking them off my list one by one. As I did this I was building my business and getting closer to my kick-off date. It amazes me how much I can get done when under pressure if I have a "punch list." I bet it will work for you as well.

The same types of questions pop up when you decide to work for others. This is a time to speak with your Human Resource Officer who can take away most of those fears by explaining the process. You should also have a punch list for yourself so you can start knocking items off your list. You will be flying before you know it.

Emotions:

Most of us like to nestle into a nice warm corner of our own and feel secure. Losing your corner is a very emotional time. You may feel embarrassed, shocked, mad, sad, and just lost for a few days. It takes time to adjust. Don't beat yourself up. Spend time meditating, sleeping, thinking about the person you are and what your best qualities are. After this time you are ready to decide what to do and follow the advice given above.

WRIGHT

Before we end, will you give a few pointers on how to update a resume?

FAUST

Your resume is the door opener for you. It will determine if you are granted an interview or not. This is the place to showcase all of *your* talents. This is not the place to showcase what you did for your last employer on a daily basis.

It seems to me that the first resume ever written must have opened with "My Objective Is," and everyone has just accepted it as part of what must be in a resume. Think of how foolish it is to have this valuable space taken up with rubbish. *Everyone's* objective is to get a job and of course move up the line and be a part of a team. Standard sentence, sleeper candidate, boring interview probably.

I believe that the resume should open with a brief but concise description of your working background. Summarize in two to three sentences your strong points. Under that you should describe in more detail, using bullet points, the items that describe the key words written in your two to three sentences.

The next section is a statement section. If you feel that you have been a hands-on leader, then say that and describe what that means to you. Under that list three to four bullets describing how you have accomplished this.

If you feel you are an innovative thinker, a problem-solver, a team-builder, etc., then state those things as above with a description and several bullets.

The next section is for education. Use the standard format.

The experience section is last. You should list the company name, your title, a brief description of the company, its size, industry, and your position overview. There is no real reason to go into great detail of your standard job description's minor details. Everyone needs to know how to answer the phone, run a computer, use spreadsheets, etc. What the HR officer is looking for is "big bite" items that you performed and were successful at that saved the company money or made the company more efficient or if you got a contract that wasn't easy to get. Use your bullets for these items.

When I reviewed resumes, there were sometimes twenty years of previous experience listed. It is *not* necessary to go back to when you were just getting started. Most resumes I saw showed companies that were no longer in business and the candidate had lost touch with those who had supervised him or her. There was no one to talk to about work habits so this was a waste of space. You certainly should go back ten or fifteen years, depending on how many jobs you have had. Remember, we are trying to shoot for a one-page resume. If it runs over don't worry, just don't allow it to become three or more pages.

Entice prospective employers and make them have a desire to call you out of all the others.

WRIGHT

Is there anything else we should consider when faced with sudden change?

FAUST

Yes, if you find yourself in transition, be calm. I have found it interesting and almost comforting to review the Chinese symbol for crisis. Change can be fearful. Sometimes we fear and feel in danger (crisis). Yet this crisis is an offering to open a new window of opportunity that will allow you to grow and have wonderful new things in life. With all fear comes a great opportunity to change it to a positive.

Think positively about the new world in front of you. Take some evaluations to see if you are really thinking what you are feeling as far as what type of job you should be in. Select employment fields that make your heart sing. Working is a necessary evil for most of us, but working at a job you love makes the necessity easier to swallow.

Have fun, this is a great opportunity.

ABOUT THE AUTHOR

Have you lost the love, enthusiasm, and desire in your current job? Are you in transition? Do you know how to get from where you are to where you want to be? Nancy Faust can help you in your transition to achieve your dream job. Nancy's energetic, straightforward, punch list approach is easy to understand to build for yourself and to follow on your own schedule. With each major step that you add to your own punch list for success, there are many sub items that require thought and creativity to achieve. Nancy will cover the necessary thought processes to help you convert your desires into reality. You will also be given insight into the newest thinking about your resume, interview techniques, follow-up meetings, and business terms.

Nancy's most requested seminars focus on Transitioning and Executive Coaching. Nancy has over twenty-eight years' experience in corporate positions including HR Director. She has helped many people go through the difficult and challenging process and find their dream job using her proven methods and techniques.

NANCY FAUST

TransitionResourcesInc.com
NFaust@TransitionResourcesInc
800-IN1VIBE (800-461-8423)
304 E. Celestial Drive
Greer, SC 29651

CHAPTER FIVE

Presentation Power: The Lesson of the Bus

An Interview with...

JOEL WELDON

DAVID WRIGHT (WRIGHT)

Today we are talking with Joel Weldon. For over thirty-five years, Joel Weldon has been sought after as a professional speaker, seminar leader, sales trainer, and executive speech coach. He's one of the elite group of speakers to have earned all four of the highest honors in the speaking profession: the Golden Gavel *"for his profound impact on corporate America,"* the Communication and Leadership Award, induction into the Speakers Hall of Fame, and "Legend of the Speaking Profession."

His business card and corporate logo is actually a heavy eight-ounce can that says: *"Success Comes in Cans, Not in Cannots!"* Over half a million people have that Can of Success. Most of them keep it on their desks!

Joel, welcome to *Stepping Stones to Success.*

JOEL WELDON (WELDON)

Thank you, David.

WRIGHT

Since this chapter is about presentation skills, Joel, my first question to you is, in your opinion, why is the ability to speak in front of a group one of the most important steppingstones to success?

WELDON

When you develop the ability to speak in front of a group—confidently, authentically and with significant effect—that ability will set you apart from the majority. It's what gives you credibility and respect, and positions you to become a leader in your field. That's why it's such a vital steppingstone to success!

You can scream your lungs out, you can stamp your feet and pound your fists, but the chances that people will buy from you, follow you, or even listen to you, are slim to none! Yet no matter what career you've chosen, you can be sure that at some point you'll be called upon to speak in front of a group—even if it's just a handful of people.

What if your assignment is to persuade that group of people to support a worthy cause or to help them see change as a positive or to encourage them to act on a new idea or invest in a new product or just work better as a team? What will you say to get their attention?

What will your comfort level be? Will you be confident, relaxed, and self-assured? Or will you be self-conscious, anxious, and uneasy? Will you have the ability to positively influence them, to persuade or inform them, or to direct their behavior in some way?

An infant, even just days old, knows how to get what it wants. It screams until its needs, wants, and desires are met—then it's quiet. Business leaders, salespeople, educators—almost anyone functioning in our society today—needs to develop, to some degree, the ability to communicate their ideas, their feelings, and their points of view to others. Most of us, however, can't get away with doing it by screaming our heads off like the infant can!

The wonderful news is that to speak effectively in front of a group is a skill that almost anyone can learn. Once you begin to learn this skill, you can continue to improve, and you will improve immediately when you read this chapter and begin putting these ideas into action. Then the only screaming you'll hear is the cheering from your audience in approval of you!

WRIGHT

What are some of these helpful ideas people can learn, Joel?

WELDON

It begins with the realization that the ability to speak effectively is not a natural gift that only certain people have. You can develop your ability to speak with calmness and confidence, no matter how ineffective you may think you are now — because you're already an "expert" on speaking!

It's true! You've probably heard hundreds, if not thousands, of speakers, whether at business meetings and conventions, seminars, religious services, political events, webcasts, or on television and radio interviews. You've heard everyone from the athlete being interviewed after the big game to the politician seeking your vote, to salespeople selling their products. So you're already a speaking "expert" because if you think about it, you probably know exactly what you like and don't like when you hear someone speak!

Here's an exercise you can do to prove that point: Think back to some of the speakers you've heard and make a list of what you like and don't like when you're in the audience. Hundreds of people have done this exercise in my "Speak With Impact" classes. Here's a list of the top five positives and negatives they most often mention; see how these lists compare to yours. Let's begin with what doesn't work and turns an audience off (and these are not in any particular order):

Not being real and genuine

Giving a performance or a memorized, canned talk

Being boring and dull

Not connecting with the audience

Not making their message clear and easy to follow

Do any of those match your negatives? Chances are, they do! Now the turn-ons — the positives that you *do* like in a speaker:

Being genuine and credible

Having something meaningful to say

Being natural, relaxed, and confident

Having energy and enthusiasm
Using humor and interesting stories

Even if your list doesn't match up 100 percent to theirs, it's probably not very different.

WRIGHT

So if one of the keys is to understand that speaking before a group is a learned skill, what are some of the most important things one would need to learn?

WELDON

The preparation of your message is the first step. It begins with *knowing your audience*.

Suppose, for example, that you're an expert on safe driving, and you're going to speak to one hundred people for an hour on how to drive safely. What would you think some of your talking points might be?

WRIGHT

I guess I'd tell them to buckle up their seat belt, don't text message when they drive, don't dial their cell phones, and don't speed.

WELDON

Good, that's what most speakers would think they should include in their talking points! But wait! *Who's going to be in your audience?* Those points may not even apply to them! What if those one hundred people were professional racecar drivers and you're being brought in because there has been a rash of recent accidents on the track at one hundred and twenty miles per hour, and they want you to provide solutions for racecar drivers to drive more safely? Or what if those one hundred people were all repeat drunk drivers? What would *they* need to hear? Or what if they were all senior citizens over the age of eighty? Would they be texting? Can you see that knowing who the audience is in those three instances— elderly drivers, drunk drivers, and racecar drivers—would change what you would talk about drastically?

WRIGHT

Yes, I see what you mean. You're speaking of knowing ahead of time exactly who your audience is and what they need, correct?

WELDON

Absolutely! It all starts with your audience, and a concept I call "NFV." It's an acronym I developed years ago to help speakers understand their audience and make a real connection with them. The N stands for *Needs*, the F is for *Fears*, and the V is for *Victories*.

So when I say "Needs," it means, what does your audience *need* to be doing, thinking, and feeling, that they aren't doing now? If it's an audience of salespeople, maybe they need to learn how to sell value, not price, to sell the full line, or do more cross selling. Or if it's an audience of your employees, maybe they need to learn how to accept responsibility and carry their full load or to work better as a team and stop whining about things. You have to find out before you begin to develop your message—what does the audience *need*?

Then, what are their *fears?* What are they anxious about? Are they afraid of losing their jobs? Reducing their income? Is the competition getting more aggressive? Or is the future of the organization uncertain because of a pending merger? Those fears need to be addressed!

Next are the victories. What have been some of the recent things in the life of that audience that have been wins, achievements, and accomplishments that you can tie back to?

Once you know the NFV of the audience, only then can you start building the message that meets their *needs*, helps them overcome their *fears*, and reinforces their *victories!*

WRIGHT

That's a unique and wonderful concept, Joel. Is this the concept you use when you prepare for a speech?

WELDON

Oh, yes! Absolutely! In all of my thirty-five years on the platform, and the thousands of presentations I've delivered, each one begins with knowing my audience's NFV. As a result, no two presentations are ever the same. How could they be? If you're building your message for that day, for that event, and for that audience, based on *their* needs, *their* fears, and *their* victories, it's always going to be different. And that's really the starting point to prepare for any kind of message. It's the very thing that makes it possible for a speaker to connect with his or her audience in a positive way.

The next step is what I call "The Lesson of the Bus."

WRIGHT

That sounds interesting. What exactly do you mean by "The Lesson of the Bus," Joel?

WELDON

"The Lesson of the Bus" is another concept I've developed to help speakers connect with their audience, their listeners, or their prospects, as the case may be. Picture the scene. Most likely, at one time or another, you've been in a city or town that has bus service. Imagine that you're waiting at the bus stop. How do you know which bus to get on as different ones approach the stop? You simply look at the sign above the driver's windshield—that's what tells you the destination. It might say uptown, downtown, eastside, or westside, depending on where it's heading. You would simply wait until the bus comes along that's going where you want to go. It's pretty simple.

WRIGHT

It appears to be so, but it's amazing how many people visiting in a big city get lost by getting on the wrong bus.

WELDON

That's exactly the problem when it comes to presenting your ideas to people in an audience—they often get lost! In those first few minutes they may begin thinking to themselves, *"What does this have to do with me?"* Or, *"Why should I care about this?"* Or, *"This isn't interesting; it doesn't apply to me and my situation."* Instead of becoming engaged in the message, they tune it out and disconnect. They go somewhere else in their mind, because they feel like they're "on the wrong bus."

The solution is to make sure—right from the start—that your message is so connected to your audience that they grab a seat or a handhold on that bus and think, *"Oh, this sounds interesting! This is important to me!"* *"Oh, I do care about this!"*

"Oh, this sounds like it applies to me and my situation." Then you've got them "on the bus."

Sometimes there's another problem. Imagine that you're waiting at this big city bus stop, and a bus comes by at forty miles an hour, the door opens and the driver yells at you, *"Come on, jump on!"* No way! That's crazy! How could you jump on a speeding bus? You can't and you wouldn't. But how many times do we see speakers, even professional speakers, as well as corporate executives and salespeople, come roaring up on an audience full of energy and passion, without first creating enough interest to actually engage the audience so they want to be on that bus! Those speakers are like the bus driver speeding by at forty miles an hour and shouting at the audience, *"Come on, jump on board my presentation!"*

Here again, the answer is to use "The Lesson of the Bus" and it's made up of parts. The bus represents your presentation, your message, your speech. It's the body of ideas that you're presenting to your listeners. The sign on the bus represents your title and subtitle. It tells your audience clearly where you're going. They see the sign and it confirms the destination of the bus.

As the bus driver—the speaker, the presenter—you're in charge of and responsible for the journey. It's up to you to make sure that everyone is comfortable and understands where the bus is going before you start speeding off. It's up to you to take them to the intended destination and to arrive on time. Once the passengers (your audience) have seen the destination sign (your title and your opening comments) and it's someplace they want to go because you've determined that ahead of time, then you've got them "on the bus." Then you can gradually pick up speed and go twenty, thirty, forty, even fifty miles an hour and they're with you all the way!

So when you get up to speak in any situation, think of "The Lesson of the Bus" and as you're speaking and looking out at your audience, ask yourself these five questions mentally: *Did I get them on the bus? Am I going where they expected me to go? Am I taking them where they need to be taken? Are they comfortable and enjoying the ride? Are we running on time?*

When you answer *yes* to all of those questions, then your presentation is on its way to becoming amazing.

So ask yourself what you can do in your next presentation to get your audience "on the bus"!

WRIGHT

I see how knowing their NFV is what makes it possible to connect with your audience and get them "on the bus." It's also apparent that you've had a lot of life experiences, and it just begs the question: growing up, were you always a good speaker and tuned in to your audience?

WELDON

That's a great question and the answer will prove an important truth for this chapter. As a youngster I had very little confidence. I was an only child with no father, and even though my mother worked very hard, we were still poor.

Recently I attended my fiftieth high school reunion. There were over one hundred people attending from my class of about four hundred who graduated in 1959 from Far Rockaway High School in New York. Of those one hundred people, practically no one knew who I was. How could they? I never spoke up in class, I was extremely shy, and I was a loner.

Like many others, I had to start working when I was twelve. I caddied at the prestigious Inwood Country Club for seven years. In my senior year, Peppy, the caddy master, called me into the caddy shack and told me the members had a special award for me. I had been chosen to receive the caddy scholarship, which included four years of college—room, board, tuition—everything paid for by the members of the Inwood Country Club. He explained that each time the members played golf, they contributed to a fund, and then once a year they would select a caddy in need to receive a college scholarship. That sounds like a wonderful opportunity, doesn't it? If you had been offered that opportunity, what would you have done? Believe it or not, I turned it down! I didn't think I was smart enough to go to college—not smart enough to last four years—and I certainly didn't think I could be a professional at anything!

So I spent the next seven years working in the construction industry—banging nails, digging ditches, and working with my hands. At age twenty-five I got into sales—and failed miserably. I made only one sale after 1,200 sales calls in four months, and earned only $48!

Then I heard a recording called *The Strangest Secret* by Earl Nightingale, and it was a life-changing experience. If you haven't ever heard this amazing message, you need to. It's timeless. Recorded in 1956, it was given to me by my sales manager when I was failing miserably. That recording gave me one idea that was so powerful, it changed the rest of my life—it was the idea that we become what we think about. It made me realize so clearly that I had spent my entire young life— those first twenty-five years—thinking of all the things I couldn't do, and because I thought of all the things I *couldn't* do, I really couldn't do them! And suddenly I asked myself, what if I changed that? What if I started thinking about what I *could* do?

How about in your life? Have you been focusing on the wrong things? You too can change your focus.

It was that exposure to a spoken word message that showed me for the first time what an amazing effect the words we speak can have on our listeners.

Suddenly everything changed—I became a super salesman for that same company. In spite of those first few terrible months, by the end of that year I was number one out of over a thousand in the branch. They promoted me to Regional Manager, which meant I was hiring and training people and running meetings.

It was still very challenging for me to speak in front of a group. After conducting one of those meetings, a guy came up to me and said, "Joel, you really need to go to Toastmasters!"

"What's Toastmasters?" I asked.

"Come with me on Tuesday morning at 6:30 and you'll see how it can help you."

That Tuesday I went with him and joined the Tempe, Arizona, Toastmasters Club. It was 1969. I went every Tuesday morning at 6:30 for five years—didn't miss a meeting.

If you're not familiar with Toastmasters, check out their Web site: www.toastmasters.org. There are over 10,000 clubs all over the world. You can benefit so much from joining a Toastmasters Club in your area.

After five years I finally got up the courage to enter a speech contest in my Toastmasters Club. I won, and to my amazement I won at each level, all the way to the International World Finals, where I finished as one of the top three out of 60,000 members.

The event was written up in the *Arizona Republic,* the main newspaper of our state at the time, and soon people started calling and asking me to speak for their company. That's how my speaking career began.

The Independent Garage Owners of Phoenix were the first to hire me to speak in 1974 and they paid me $25. During that year I gave over two hundred and seventy presentations here in the Phoenix area, and through word-of-mouth, those led to many more. Today, over thirty-five years later, it's still word-of-mouth—they keep calling and I keep going!

So as you can see, my successful speaking career actually sprang from my *inability* to communicate. This proves the most important lesson about public speaking—it is a learned skill! It's not a natural talent! I'm sure some of the people you have interviewed in this book were gifted, they were gregarious, they were outgoing, and they were naturally confident. But that was not me, I was exactly the opposite! My speaking career is proof that people can learn this skill. By understanding this important steppingstone to success, they can transform their life—even with just one good idea put into action.

In my case it was Earl Nightingale saying that *"we become what we think about,"* combined with the training provided by Toastmasters. I am living proof that if I can do this successfully as a profession for thirty-five years, anyone can do it.

WRIGHT

That's such good news, Joel. Will you share an example of how learning these skills has become a steppingstone to success for one of your recent students?

WELDON

Yes, I'd love to share an example of that. Not long ago I got a call from a graduate who had completed our "Speak With Impact" class several weeks before. He's an executive with a worldwide drilling company that does exploration work for minerals (primarily precious metals). This is what he said to me:

"Joel, I think I've found the missing link in my career. Even though I have greater technical knowledge than almost anyone in my company, and even though I have excellent relationships with our customers, vendors, and employees, I seem to have been repeatedly passed over for the top positions. Now I understand that it's because I've been unable to communicate effectively in meetings, planning sessions, or even in budget reviews. It really has been the missing link!"

He went on to say that the tools he got and the concepts he learned in our "Speak With Impact" class have made it possible for him to connect so much better now with his listeners and to have a positive influence on them. Then he shared his big win. He had just spoken to sixty potential customers at a trade event—and gave the best presentation of his life!

"And just as important," he said, "I was so relaxed, comfortable, and confident. I began everything with the NFV concept. I knew my audience and I quickly 'got them on the bus'—and then I made their bus ride informative, fun, relevant, and effective."

As you can see, it is so vital to be able to communicate with confidence in front of a group, whether you're in sales, in a leadership position, in education or in civic work!

WRIGHT

Many people may be missing that important steppingstone in their career as well. What else might we need to learn in order to speak effectively, Joel?

WELDON

You'll want to learn some important delivery techniques. For example:

- How to read your audience
- How to stay connected to your audience
- How to use notes and prompts, and not memorize what you're going to say
- How to ask effective questions
- How to get people participating
- How to make stories memorable and tie them to your audience
- How to use visual aids and take-away materials
- How to stay on time
- How to use humor effectively
- How to use statistics for maximum effect

Then there are subtle little things—I call them "Polishing Points." They include things like:

- Understanding meeting room dynamics
- Why distance is death in a meeting room
- How to control the environment
- How to deal with difficult people in the audience
- How to evaluate your presentation

- How to prepare for radio and television interviews, webinars, and teleconferences
- How to think quickly on your feet when you're asked a question

As important as all these delivery techniques are, they are no substitute for having a carefully crafted message—a message relevant to your audience that they want and need to hear. Let me give you an example of what I mean by that.

Just supposing you were asked to speak tonight to fifty people, all of whom were going to lose their homes in the next ninety days. But you knew *three things* every one of those fifty people could do to prevent that from happening and you were invited to speak to them and share that information. How good a speaker would you have to be to influence that audience with those three ideas? That's right—the answer is you don't have to be a good speaker at all! You could fumble and mumble. You could even turn your back, sit on a chair, take off your shoes and socks and clip your toenails, and they would still pay rapt attention, hanging on every word you said, because what you're saying is so important to them!

Now, however, if you could say those three things in an effective way, that's enjoyable, that has humor, visuals, and stories—then you become amazing!

Unfortunately we've all heard speakers who have a great delivery, but nothing to say. They might have a wonderful voice, terrific stage presence, and magnificent visuals, but all that means nothing to the people they're talking to if their message is not relevant to them!

WRIGHT

What else do we need to do to maintain the connection with the audience and keep them "on the bus" so they don't want to get off?

WELDON

Your connection with your audience is really based on asking yourself this important question: *"So What and Who Cares?"*

As you review every point you're planning to make in your presentation, you must ask yourself, *"How does this relate to the audience and their NFV?"* If it doesn't relate, don't use it!

So many times we hear speakers say "This is my favorite story!" I feel like shouting out, "Then tell it to yourself! So what if it's your favorite story, how is it relevant to me—the audience!"

This leads us to another indication that you're maintaining the connection with your audience—you're becoming aware of how many times you say "I" and how many times you say "you."

We all know that old acronym WIIFM—*What's In It For Me?* Every salesperson and manager should know that, but how many times do speakers and presenters say "I"? *"I love this story,"* or *"I'm so excited about this,"* or *"Here's my favorite idea."* Don't do it! Instead, say something like, "Here's a story you'll love" or "You're going to be excited about this next idea" or "You're going to see how this example applies to what you're doing."

But listen to most speakers and you'll see how many of them give an "I" presentation: "I went to Europe, then when I got off the plane and I got my luggage, I went to my hotel. I checked into my hotel, and then I went to this restaurant." "I–I–I"—there are just too many references to the speaker—he or she says "I" far too many times and is not really connecting with the audience.

Now obviously, there's nothing wrong with telling personal stories when you speak, but why not make the listener part of the story? *"So come with me as my invisible partner to Europe. We're going to fly over together and when we land in Paris, we're going to pick up our baggage. You spot the bags first. Then we get into a taxi and we head over to our hotel. Then you say, 'Let's go to dinner,' so we go to this restaurant."*

By including the word *you,* even though I'm all alone, you—the listener and my invisible partner—are going on this trip. Now you're on the bus!

So no matter what the story is, you can engage your audience. Just become conscious of how many times you're saying *I,* versus how many times you're saying *you.* And realize, every time you use "I" there might be a disconnect with your listeners. Every time you use "you," you're strengthening the connection!

Try this next exercise: Write a letter to a customer or client—a lengthy five- or ten-page letter even—and never say "I" one time! It will help you develop the habit of eliminating the I's and focusing on the "you's."

WRIGHT

Wow, that's a lot to know! What about a company executive or even a salesperson who has to speak in front of an audience and knows he or she is just plain boring? Or the material the person has to present is really going to be boring. What can be done about that?

WELDON

We've all heard a boring speaker and if you think about it, what makes a boring speaker? Maybe the person speaks very slow or speaks in a monotone or the person has no energy or enthusiasm and is very, very serious. And maybe the person is speaking about a boring subject.

So if you're a boring speaker, what do you do? Someone might advise you to speed up your pace, to vary your voice, to act enthusiastic, to have a more exciting subject, or to add humor. That's one approach, but I think there's a better approach, because one of the things that makes speakers effective is being who they are, and let's face it, some people are just boring!

So there is another way—*don't change a thing!* Instead, brag about it! Yes, you can actually use your weakness as a positive by bragging about it!

Here's an example: I was speaking at a major company event and when I met the chief financial officer, he told me he was going to be giving a speech the next day and asked me for some advice. He told me he was boring. He didn't need to tell me that—I could tell. He said they called him Boring Bob, because he was so boring and everybody knew it.

Here's what I said to him: "Bob, you can prepare your audience for the fact that you're boring! Anticipate it—bring it up right away in your opening!"

What happened the next day was so amazing. I can still visualize Boring Bob and hear him saying these words: "Folks, it's going to take me about forty-five minutes to cover our financial outlook and review our past performance, and this is going to be tough on you because I am so boring."

At that point the audience chuckled. Then he said, "I'm so boring that sometimes I fall asleep listening to myself talk."

Now they were starting to laugh! "No really," he said, "I am so boring, that when I went on my first date with my wife, she slapped me—no, not because I was getting fresh with her—she thought I was dead!"

At that point the audience was roaring and clapping, and Bob now had them in the palm of his hand. Then he went on to say, "Okay, so now you know I'm really boring. But what I have to present is vital for you to know because it's going to affect your income both this year and next year. So I want to encourage you to force yourself to stay focused and alert, as I bore you with my forty-five-minute presentation."

Wow, he was so honest! He got them on the bus—and for the next forty-five minutes he was pretty boring—but he held the audience's attention because he used humor and bragged about his weakness of being boring. As a result, the audience was much more accepting of him.

I learned a great lesson myself by helping him that day—you can bring up any negatives before the audience even spots them, and with humor you can turn them into positives!

WRIGHT

I've heard you say that when someone prepares to speak, he or she needs to be able to summarize the entire message in one sentence. Is that true?

WELDON

Yes, that's absolutely true. That's what I call beginning at the end. Always start planning your presentation with the end in mind. What is it you want that audience to feel or think or do? What do you want them to learn or buy or consider or change?

An example could be "I want to inform my audience about the risks of stolen identity" or "I want this audience of my employees to be more customer focused" or "I want them to be more grateful in these difficult times for the good they already have."

Or if it's a charity event, "I want my audience to volunteer for a committee and contribute to the general fund."

When you have a crystal clear picture in your mind what that one sentence is, you can begin organizing your ideas step by step by step, point by point, or as I call them, building block by building block. Once you know the end—the result you want, based on the audience's needs, fears, and victories—you can focus your entire message on that objective.

When you finish speaking, your listeners will probably summarize your entire message in one sentence to an associate or friend who asks about it. So once you realize that fact, ask yourself, what do you want that one sentence to be?

WRIGHT

How would you summarize in one sentence, Joel, everything you've learned as a professional with forty years of studying public speaking? Can you put it in just one sentence of, say, twenty-five words or less?

WELDON

Yes, I can! "Speak to the audience about what they need, in an organized way that they can follow, and get yourself out of the way." I think that's less than twenty-five words—it's actually only twenty-three words!

WRIGHT

Well, Joel, it's been a pleasure talking with you today. But you still have two words left. Give us two more words, Joel.

WELDON

Here are two words to remember: *"You can!"*

ABOUT THE AUTHOR

For over thirty-five years, Joel Weldon has been sought after as a professional speaker, seminar leader, sales trainer, and executive speech coach. He's one of the elite group of speakers to have earned all four of the highest honors in the speaking profession: the Golden Gavel *"for his profound impact on corporate America,"* the Communication and Leadership Award, induction into the Speakers Hall of Fame, and "Legend of the Speaking Profession."

His business card and corporate logo is actually a heavy eight-ounce can that says: *"Success Comes in Cans, Not in Cannots!"* Over half a million people have that Can of Success. Most of them keep it on their desks!

JOEL WELDON
P.O. Box 6226
Scottsdale AZ 85261
800-852-8572
info@SuccessComesInCans.com
www.SuccessComesInCans.com

CHAPTER SIX

Negotiate Your Path to Success

An Interview with...

MARI FRANK

DAVID WRIGHT (WRIGHT)

Today we're talking with Mari Frank. Mari has been an attorney/mediator in private practice in Laguna Niguel, California, for the past twenty-four years. She's also a professor of negotiation and mediation, a professional speaker and trainer, an expert commentator for the media, and author of several books, including a textbook called *Negotiation Breakthroughs*. Mari is also the radio host of *Privacy Piracy*, a weekly one-hour radio show at the University of California Irvine on KUCI 88.9 FM and www.kuci.org.

Mari has appeared on dozens of national television programs including *Dateline*, *48 Hours, The O'Reilly Factor, Investigative Reports, NBC and ABC Nightly News, CNN, Geraldo at Large, CNBC, and The Montel Williams Show,* and she's been interviewed on more than three hundred radio shows. She has been featured in major newspapers and magazines such as the *Wall Street Journal, USA Today, Chicago Tribune, Los Angeles Times, The New York Times, The Washington Post,* and her many articles have been published in legal journals and numerous magazines.

Mari, welcome to *Stepping Stones to Success.*

MARI FRANK (FRANK)

Thank you for the opportunity to talk about steppingstones to negotiation success—my favorite subject.

WRIGHT

Mari, you've been an attorney for twenty-four years and you're a negotiation professor. How do you define negotiation?

FRANK

Negotiation is simply a process that we all use to bargain for what we want. We negotiate every day—with companies with whom we do business, with dealerships when buying a car, with our spouse as to what television set to buy or what channel to watch, with our kids to do their chores or when setting their curfew. The list of negotiations is endless. We engage in pact-making all the time.

Negotiation is both an art and a skill in which we *communicate with others to seek common ground to reach a mutually satisfying, sustainable agreement.* The *art* of negotiation derives from your natural ability to engage effectively with others to influence them to cooperate with you. The *skill* of negotiation involves a systematic understanding of the tools and the processes necessary to take the *"steps to success."* An accomplished negotiator will blend the art of negotiation with proven, conscious skills to arrive at valued and successful agreements.

The Latin origin of the word negotiate is *negotium,* which means "not at leisure or *not at ease."* When you strive to achieve an objective with another person, you probably won't be *at ease* until you reach a favorable outcome. Your success will depend on your positive skill-oriented approach, and your strategic efforts to fulfill your underlying interests and the concerns of all stakeholders.

To have a quality negotiation, all parties must be heard, understood, respected, and participate in fashioning the final agreement. When the parties believe the result is fair, there's commitment and follow-through. At the point when a quality deal is signed and the terms are fulfilled, the parties will then be "at ease" and finally have "leisure" time to relax and enjoy the result.

WRIGHT

You shared with me that over the years, you have developed a specific success strategy for reaching a mutually beneficial agreement. Please tell us about what you call "solutioneering."

FRANK

It's a great process for satisfying all parties and engaging them to achieve positive results. When people are pleased with the terms of their contract, follow-through is easy and no outside enforcement is necessary. As a long-time mediator, I'm thrilled when my clients are cheerful and relieved when they get a favorable agreement or resolve conflict with evenhanded results.

The "solutioneering" procedure I developed reframes the issues of non-agreement as *positive opportunities* to create enhanced solutions instead of points of discord. I guide all parties to collaborate, analyze, and jointly investigate the various perspectives until all the stakeholders understand each other's most important underlying interests. This approach engenders a safe, trusting environment to brainstorm workable, acceptable alternatives.

Instead of spotlighting arguments and differences, "solutioneering" focuses on common interests and desired objectives. Parties gain insight and clarity into all views. From there, the reciprocal promises made in the agreement are clear, effective, and mutually satisfying. When I guide clients through "solutioneering" to set forth deal-making or for conflict resolution, the result is joint commitment, contentment, and a continuing positive relationship. "Solutioneering" is effective in commerce and in personal situations. Contracts are improved and renewed, and companies flourish. In personal matters, marriages endure challenges, children learn to problem-solve, and friendships overcome misunderstandings. On the global level, diplomats use similar techniques to resolve confrontations, reduce conflict, and avoid wars.

WRIGHT

But aren't most negotiators just trying to get the best of their opponents?

FRANK

Thank you so much for asking that question! It's true that many people think that they are going to win if they can overpower their perceived *adversary* in the negotiation. We see it in business, when large companies take advantage of smaller vendors. We see it at home when one spouse rules the house without regard to the needs of the other spouse. We see it between consumers and governmental agencies and commercial entities when the consumer believes he or she has no leverage. Worst of all, we see this between countries when there is mutual suspicion, misunderstanding of perspectives, and an imbalance of power. In the global sense, war is the outcome of failed negotiations and imbalance of power.

Let's look at the result of a negotiation in which one party focuses only on his or her self-interest. This is a win-lose situation. How does the "loser" feel? Consider if you felt forced into a transaction that you knew (or you later learned) was unfair. Maybe it didn't meet your needs or you were deceived. If the negotiation winner is your boss, you may want to quit. If you stay because you have no choice, you won't be happy. Perhaps you'll be angry or resentful. This kind of response has led to insidious revenge and workplace violence.

If a business imposes an unfair agreement upon you, you may decide to sever that relationship; or if you are stuck in a contract, there will be future conflicts due to your lack of commitment. And if you feel angry enough you may complain to regulators, blog about the company online, or file a lawsuit.

At home, if your spouse doesn't engage in effective listening and "solutioneering" techniques and you constantly feel as though you aren't getting your needs met, how long will your marriage last? If you feel you "can't" divorce because of the children, will you just be miserable and find covert ways to get even?

If you live in a country where your basic needs aren't being met, consider how you might band together with others to revolt against your government or more prosperous nations. We've seen how "powerless" people try to gain control using piracy or terrorism.

If you're the winner in a win-lose negotiation, your triumph may be very short-lived. The defeated one will usually find ways to express his or her disappointment or anger. In either case, there will be negative repercussions.

Aside from lost business associations and destroyed relationships, unfair agreements may ruin your hard-earned reputation. If you take advantage of others in negotiations and disregard their interests or needs, your victory may be fleeting.

The possible short-term gain is never worth the long-term loss of future business, positive relationships, or your standing in the community.

WRIGHT

Mari, in the legal profession, you negotiate and mediate professionally. Isn't there a different approach to your "solutioneering" process when you are negotiating cooperative deal-making versus when you are resolving conflict after a dispute?

FRANK

Actually, the *steppingstones to success* for dispute resolution run parallel to the path that we navigate when parties are *not* in conflict. But you're correct that there are some dramatic, emotional differences. Anger and hostility create much greater challenges because trust is often destroyed. Trust is essential in any bargaining situation. When parties get together to start a business, enter into a contract, or get married, the emotional state is usually trusting, pleasant, and emotionally gratifying. The parties collaborate and share the goals of the partnership.

When clashes arise (which happens frequently even when parties are positive about a potential collaborative agreement), negative emotions destroy the good feelings. Suspicions creep up and trust is shattered. The parties divert from their intent to work together as a team. As hostility escalates, the parties deviate from the "steppingstones to success" and the "solutioneering" process. They veer off the path of cooperation and end up on thorny, antagonistic detours. When parties engage in angry cross-accusations and fail to listen, agreements are breached and promises are broken. To revive the pact, the parties must refocus on "solutioneering." Stop the escalation, calm the emotions, and return to focusing on interests.

When arguments surface, the parties must switch gears and immediately refrain from blaming and accusations. To renew trust and cooperation, they must cut through the conflict by clarifying misunderstandings, listening to each other's concerns, and apologizing for offending behaviors. The key to getting back on the collaborative track is to LISTEN, and the acronym below provides the steps to rehabilitate trust:

L—Let others speak freely.

I—Inquire using open-ended questions.

S—Satisfy others' need to be understood.

T—Treat everyone respectfully.

E—Empathize with the other party.

N—Never judge the other party's perspective.

Overcoming conflict through intense discourse and dispute resolution creates high quality settlements. The "solutioneering" process used to deflect conflict directs the parties back on the collaborative path leading to successful negotiations.

WRIGHT

So what makes a successful negotiation?

FRANK

The quick, easy answer is that a negotiation is successful when all stakeholders are pleased with the result. But actually, it's more complex. A successful negotiation is measured by how well the parties interact in good faith, share reliable and credible information, display an attitude of trustworthiness, listen to each other effectively, ask concrete open-ended questions, brainstorm options, select the best alternatives, and jointly arrive at a fair agreement that meets the parties' true interests.

Negotiation success depends upon each negotiator's expectations, perceptions, and needs at the particular time. What's valuable to one party may be of no value at all to the other party. If one business owner wants a long-term commitment, he or she may be willing to charge less for services than what would be required for a short-term deal. In this case, profitability over time is considered more important.

The other party may want to cut costs, so the length of the contract is not a high priority as long as the price is right. Thus, both parties' needs are met.

In a divorce situation, one party may be willing to give up future interest in a retirement plan in exchange for a lump sum payment up front. One spouse's interest in immediate financial liquidity outweighs possible greater income in the distant future. The spouse who is closer in age to retirement may wish to be assured of a larger income for retirement. In this scenario, parties achieve a fair exchange, but the desired outcomes are *very* different. Splitting up every asset equally might be "fair" under the law; however, it would not be a successful negotiation to simply divide all the assets and debts because the parties' underlying interests would not be satisfied. When each party's distinct needs are met and the parties are happy with the result, the negotiation is successful.

What one person finds agreeable, another person might find unacceptable. For example, you may be willing to pay more for the same brand and style of vehicle than someone else is willing to pay because you want a specific color and other options, which meet your needs. Style may be more important than price. You know that you will pay more, but because your interests are met, the negotiation is successful.

The assessment of the negotiation is also affected by the quality of the underlying relationships. You may get the price you want for a product, but if the salesperson is very difficult to work with, you may not deal with that company again. The success of your negotiation is contingent upon the quality of the relationships, as well as the merit of the deal.

WRIGHT

What steps to success must you follow to become an effective negotiator?

FRANK

I appreciate that you understand there are steps we all can take to negotiate successfully. Many people think that if they know what they want and they refuse to give an inch, then this stance makes them an effective negotiator. Some people have a natural talent for "schmoozing" to persuade people to get what they want. Charm may work at first, but after a negotiation has concluded, the agreement may fall apart if it isn't substantive. Some people just "shoot from the hip" in negotiations. However, without acquiring the conscious skills and tools of "solutioneering" effective negotiations, success will be hit or miss.

To be a superior negotiator, you'll need to develop your authentic negotiation *power*. I don't mean supremacy, control, or a means to strong-arm others. Instead I use the word *power* in negotiation to mean the ability *to influence* the other parties to want to collaborate with you for mutual gain. When you've set up an environment of positive relations, trust, and honest facts, you'll attain what you need out of the negotiations.

Your negotiation power is the capability to induce others to want to cooperate with you so that everyone will get their needs met. When you're in command of your negotiation skills you'll have the opportunity to cultivate lasting relationships and enhanced agreements. If relationships are nurtured with effective communication techniques, when misunderstandings arise (which is normal since we are humans and misperceive each other frequently), you'll have already cultivated an atmosphere of trust to facilitate the resolution of misunderstandings and challenging issues.

WRIGHT

So Mari, how do we achieve authentic negotiation power to influence others? And will that ensure that we get the best deal possible?

FRANK

There are six steps we must master to attain genuine negotiation power, and if we implement them, our success in getting a satisfactory agreement is assured. So let's talk about the six steppingstones to bona fide power in a negotiation. They are easy to remember using the acronym POWERS:

P = Preparation—You'll need to prepare using what I call the *"CPR method.* This approach focuses you on the issues of Content, Procedures, and Relationships to breathe life into your negotiation power.

O = Options—Consider alternative options that meet everyone's needs.

W = Worthiness—Demonstrate that you are to be trusted and test others for trustworthiness. It's important for negotiators to be reliable, honest, and credible.

E = Enthusiasm—Show your enthusiasm, your passion, and your commitment to a favorable agreement for everyone. It's important that the parties know that you care about more than just your own needs and that you are passionate, effective, and professional.

R = Relationships—Build bridges of mutual understanding, reciprocal respect, and effective listening.

S = Satisfying solutions—The result of all of the above creates satisfying solutions based on meeting the genuine interests of all stakeholders.

WRIGHT

Please clarify how the elements of POWERS give the negotiator the ability to be effective. Let's start at the top with P for Preparation.

FRANK

Preparation is a great place to start because it's your greatest strength in any negotiation. The party who does the most planning for the negotiation will be most influential and persuasive in getting what he or she wants. When I ask my law students if they would ever think of walking into the bar exam without studying and preparing themselves mentally, emotionally, and physically, they gasp at the thought of lack of preparedness. Clearly, without studying they know failure would be the result. But how many people walk into a negotiation and "wing it"? You'll set yourself up for poor results if you attend a bargaining session without preparing the content of the issues, the procedures you plan to use, and the process for building a congenial working relationship with the parties.

In order to ready yourself for any negotiation (whether it is with a business associate, your boss, your spouse, or anyone else), you must get organized, develop a strategy, do research, and prepare yourself physically and emotionally. Pre-planning is essential every time, in every negotiation; it doesn't matter how trivial the issue may seem, or how well you think you already know the facts.

To begin your plan, consider the following essential components: *Content*, *Procedures*, and *Relationship* issues. This strategy of "CPR" will enliven your negotiation power:

Content Issues—What are your own underlying subject matter needs?

What do you honestly want and why? What are the content issues of your proposal? Is it money, product, services, actions, business arrangements, loan approval, etc.? Does your proposal really satisfy your true interests? Are you bargaining for something that won't gratify you—even if you achieve it?

For example, before you purchase a residence, even if it's a fabulous price, will it be in a location that is easily accessible for work? Will the neighborhood and schools meet your kids' needs? What are the taxes, homeowner association fees, and other hidden fees? Have you talked with the neighbors about the community? What are the risks that might not be immediately visible? Research the surrounding area, find out all aspects of the home, city plans, etc., and what it would mean to be there. Your due diligence will reveal any potential problems that might exist.

What are the interests of the other parties?

What does the other party want or need? What are his or her motivations? In our previous example, why is the homeowner selling the house? What are his or her plans, problems, desires? What kind of relationship did he or she have with the neighbors? You aren't ready to make a viable proposal until you get the complete picture. The more you know about the other person's content issues before the negotiation session begins, the better prepared you'll be to achieve a favorable agreement. Find out who, what, where, why, and how for *each* content issue. That'll help you develop persuasive proposals to obtain your objectives. Educating yourself about your "adversary's" interests is a key to effective deal-making. Showing that you're knowledgeable and care about your adversaries will turn them into friends.

Never act on assumptions

Even if you find extensive information about the other party or parties before you negotiate—there still will be much you don't know. *Never* assume anything about the other party's goals without checking out the facts. The old adage is true that if you assume, you make an *"ass* (of) *u* (and) *me."* Voicing assumptions without knowing the facts is dangerous and often embarrassing. We've all learned from bad experiences that when we speak our assumptions, we may be perceived as foolish. (You'd be embarrassed if you were to ask a woman when she's "due" for her baby to arrive, only to learn she isn't pregnant).

We all try to categorize and organize data by making assumptions in our minds in order to process easily. But before you put your foot into your mouth, consider that your assumption *could be* wrong. Your sensitivity will show others that you are interested in their perspective when you ask polite, probing, open-ended questions. By listening intently to their answers, you'll gain keen insight into their concerns, needs, and negotiation approach. This knowledge gives you potential power to influence the parties' perspective.

Consider preparing these types of questions for those with whom you will negotiate:

- What is most important to you as we try to reach our agreement today?
- What would fulfill your expectations?
- How might we make this work for you?

- What are you most worried about?
- What do you feel is essential to make this mutually beneficial?
- Help me understand the basis for your proposal.
- What element of our proposal is most favorable for you?
- What specifically doesn't work for you and why?

You may not receive completely transparent answers, but you'll gain a better understanding of the other parties' intentions when you gently probe and ask for clarification.

What objective information will help you to be credible?

To influence another party, you'll need to be credible. Ask yourself what facts and objective criteria you must gather about the subject matter to be believable. What data will you need to present to be reasonable? What trustworthy opinions, facts, and written materials will help you to convince the other party of the fairness of your proposal?

For example, if you are going to ask a certain price for your product, ascertain the price of similar goods. If you're purchasing a vehicle, determine the various costs that are added to the invoice, and compare price and quality. If your "opponent" is better prepared, your bargaining position is weakened.

It's crucial to become knowledgeable before the meeting. The preparation of facts, figures, etc., will give you confidence and support your settlement suggestions. Be sure to verify the accuracy of your data before you present it so you won't be perceived as dishonest. Speak transparently and be willing to share facts and supporting documents in a non-aggressive manner. Your persuasive power will increase as you respectfully show the reasonableness of your offer and the quality of the information presented.

P-Procedural Issues—What procedures must be negotiated to set a collaborative approach?

Time, place, and environment all affect the process of your bargaining session. Who must be at the meeting or available by phone? Find out ahead of time who has the authority to make an agreement, and make sure all stakeholders are present at the meeting or at least available by speakerphone.

For example, if you are negotiating a customer service issue, you'll waste time unless you can get to a manager who has the authority to make a decision. Negotiate with someone who has the say-so to seal the pact.

How will you meet? What forum will you use?

Will you meet by phone, in a letter, e-mail, video-conferencing, or in person? The best negotiations take place in person since body language and facial expressions communicate true intent even better than words. Telephone is next best because you can hear intonation and inflection, and you'll have the opportunity to clarify misunderstandings immediately. Letters are more formal and are best used as a follow-up to an in-person meeting or phone conversation. E-mail or texting should generally never be used to bargain or resolve conflict. It's very precarious since it's not confidential, is usually accomplished in haste, and is very easily misunderstood.

If the negotiation will take place by phone, who initiates the call? What time will the call take place? Who will be available for the call? What documents must be sent to each other and reviewed before the phone conference? These issues initiate the negotiation process and are critical to set forth mutual accommodations. By initiating and organizing the procedural issues, you'll begin the negotiation process amicably and competently.

Who are the stakeholders?

Anyone who has an interest in the outcome should be part of the discussion and have a hand in designing the terms. If you make an agreement with only a few of the stakeholders, the other necessary parties will undoubtedly find fault because they didn't participate in the final outcome that affects them. Find out before you begin negotiations who will be directly involved in implementing the agreement. You'll need to hear everyone's concerns and challenges. If a deal is to be carried out by parties who are not at the negotiation table, be ready to work through struggles that will surface after the deal is made. It's far more efficient to engage *all* parties in the "solutioneering" process at the outset to address how the terms will be executed. When all affected parties are genuinely satisfied with the agreement, there will be commitment and better follow-through.

What environment is best for the negotiation to take place?

Your first issue to negotiate will be the place and time to meet. If you wish to have a cooperative negotiation, arrange to meet in a pleasing, comfortable location where the parties can openly share ideas in a private setting. A neutral place, like a restaurant, is positive for business deals. "Breaking bread" together enhances the communal collaborative approach.

For customer service issues, meeting in a quiet less crowded comfortable lounge offers privacy where the manager may be able to accommodate you without other customers hearing the discussion.

For family dispute resolution, a tranquil, comfortable room without distractions facilitates "solutioneering."

How will you be respectful of each other's procedural needs?

What time of the day will be most conducive to effective bargaining? If you are a morning person, you may wish to negotiate an early morning meeting for you to be most alert. For businesspeople, midmorning is often a good choice, before anyone is too tired or hungry. Sharing a meal together facilitates good feelings and joint decision-making. Cooperating regarding procedures sets a tone of collaboration for the remaining issues of the negotiation. If you're flexible and mindful of the other party's requests, it will increase the possibility of a good working relationship.

You'll learn a great deal about how the negotiations will progress just by how others interact regarding preliminary procedures and the agenda. If you perceive the other parties are not acting in good faith with regard to minor procedural issues, it's important to resolve those situations before the content negotiations begin. You may wish to consider not doing business with difficult people at all. If setting procedures creates more conflict during dispute resolution, you may wish to consider hiring a neutral third party to engage the parties in a guided "solutioneering" process so that disagreements can be resolved privately and quickly.

If you've negotiated mutually agreed upon procedures, you'll be more optimistic about future collaborations. It will set the tone for a successful conclusion for all involved.

Relationship Issues

Human nature is such that the more we like someone, the more we are willing to accommodate his or her needs. It's enjoyable to negotiate with pleasant people, and uncomfortable to deal with difficult people.

Consider what relationship issues you have with the other parties before you meet. Is the other party logical or emotional, straightforward or closed, shy or gregarious? It's important that you pay attention to the other party's style, culture, comfort zone, and approach. Being sensitive to the other person's feelings will set a respectful tone to interactions. Even if you are very prepared as to the subject matter, if you offend the other party with an approach that is perceived as offensive, you'll lose all credibility and negotiation power.

What must you find out about the other party in order to be informed and persuasive? If you're unable to learn much about the other party before you meet (by the Internet, references, phone conferencing, etc.), plan open-ended questions ahead of time to help you get at the information you need. Create questions that allow the other party to reveal his or her inner thoughts and desires. Inquire politely about family, hobbies, career, etc. Learn what you can about the "human side" of your negotiation partner.

When you better understand the other party, you'll suggest solutions that will be relevant to that person. Knowing what is comfortable for others helps you shape your proposals to put them at ease. Active listening will show you what motivates the other party. Each party has a distinct perspective, what is valuable to you may not have significance to the other party and vice versa.

To sum up how you'll attain successful negotiation power, you'll need to first and foremost focus on the P in POWER. It reminds you to *Prepare your CPR issues to breathe life into your negotiations.*

The acronym CPR will remind you how to prepare for a successful negotiation:

Content—What must you research regarding the subject matter of the negotiation?

Procedures—What procedures will be conducive to effective "solutioneering"?

Relationship—How can you best relate to the other party?

When you can answer the three questions above, you'll be prepared and empowered to influence the other party (or parties) to brainstorm mutually acceptable agreements.

WRIGHT

The second letter of POWER stands for options. Please explain how developing options for settlement leads to negotiation success.

FRANK

If you start negotiating with only one result in mind, the bargaining will end early. Negotiators who are inflexible and narrow-minded often are disappointed when they can't reach an agreement. Creating several alternatives before the meeting will provide you with contingency plans so you are ready for any objections or criticisms. You'll have a repertoire of resources to satisfy yourself and the other parties to carry the negotiation forward. Develop propositions that bridge the gap between you and the other parties.

For example, when families are setting up chores for family members to complete, each person may choose from a list of all the household activities that need to be accomplished. One option for agreement would be for each individual to have a turn to choose which chore that individual would like to take. Other options would be for each to pick the choices out of a hat, set up a rotating schedule, agree to team up to do chores together, or even pay each other to do chores they dislike. You are only limited by your own creativity.

When one negotiator comes prepared with several options for settlement, it inspires others to dream up possible solutions. Thus, the productive "solutioneering" process engages positive breakthroughs.

After brainstorming possible solutions, the next step is to focus on the most feasible suggestions. If the creative process falters, all it takes to renew "solutioneering" is for one party to ask, "How else could we make this work?" Entertaining options that incorporate the interests of all the parties creates a cohesive working group with a common goal. Adversarial parties transform into an innovative team to explore solutions. Nonjudgmental brainstorming leads to more imaginative and mutually satisfying results. When you initiate several ingenious options, you'll achieve powerful negotiation breakthroughs.

WRIGHT

So now that we have explored preparation and options, how does the W for *Worthiness* fit into the strategy for steps for success?

FRANK

Let me ask you to consider, if you don't trust someone how willing are you to negotiate a deal? Worthiness is the result of being trustworthy. If someone is dishonest or unreliable, he or she won't merit your time. It's critical to trust the people we do business with and it's essential to believe in those we love.

If we are buying a car, we want to know that the dealership and factory will be dependable and reliable so that if we have a problem it will be fixed immediately.

At home we must believe that our spouse is honest and faithful to us, otherwise we can't trust the relationship. When we place our hard-earned funds in a bank or with a financial advisor, we must first ascertain whether the bank and/or the advisor is responsible, honorable, and honest. Whenever we engage in any relationship, it's necessary to check out the other party's reputation, honesty, and integrity. We're foolish if we don't consciously trust incrementally, and verify the veracity and morality of the people with whom we are negotiating.

There are scammers and fraudsters who may take advantage of your good faith if you're not careful to seek out principled and respectable people to partner with. We must also safeguard our own reputations by being truthful, saying what we mean, and meaning what we say—and following through dependably. If we're misinformed or mistaken, we must admit we are wrong, and take responsibility for our actions. By apologizing when it's due and forgiving others' good faith mistakes as well, we increase our own credibility.

Worthiness in negotiations creates trust, which is vital to your negotiation power.

WRIGHT

So say we're prepared for the negotiation, we've developed options, and we have proven ourselves to be trustworthy. How will *enthusiasm* make a difference?

FRANK

Your enthusiasm and passion about your proposal and the negotiation is infectious. When you are animated, yet credible and calm, your eagerness will entice others into doing business with you. Your zestful, pleasing disposition will attract advantageous relationships. And when you demonstrate genuine interest in everyone's ideas, products, or manner of living, they will reciprocate.

Your enthusiasm must be authentic. If you're insincere, it will be evident.

If you believe in your product, service, or relationship, show your enthusiasm. All of us remember certain teachers in school who inspired their students. The instructor was filled with gusto and love for the subject matter and the students. The students were attentive, involved, and easily persuaded. Your passionate proposals and inspiring presentations will significantly influence the other stakeholders. Demonstrating your enthusiasm about the "solutioneering" process will make them eager to collaborate with you.

WRIGHT

Mari, you said earlier that the R in Powers is there to remind that us that positive relationships are key to a successful negotiation. What if we are engaging in just a onetime purchase? Is the relationship issue still powerful?

FRANK

Great question. I have learned over the years that we live on a very small planet. People you haven't seen in thirty years may suddenly e-mail you or bump into you while traveling. The Internet makes us very vulnerable if we cross another person. Even if we believe we may never see a person again, the quality of our interactions creates our reputation both on a personal and career level.

No matter whether we are dealing with a small hotel manager in a third world country, a long-term contractor, a former employee, or a vendor, when we build bridges of understanding and respect, we pave the way for future appreciation and mutual benefits. Whether cooperating to create profitable deals or lasting partnerships, pooling our intellectual and financial resources expands the scope of our influence.

By sharing perspectives, effectively listening, and showing that we understand others, we cross barriers and achieve committed agreements. Our positive associations, whether long- or short-term, directly and indirectly increase our power to influence others to engage with us in "solutioneering." Your short-term positive relationships may someday lead to future lasting profitable partnerships.

People remember relationships—good or bad and now, in the information age, they can easily affect your reputation with just a keystroke.

WRIGHT

So finally we arrive at the S—the last letter in Powers, which signifies the satisfying solution(s) that we strive for in our negotiations. So is every negotiation that ends with an agreement "satisfying"?

FRANK

If that were the case, we'd never have lawsuits for breach of contract! Indeed, the ultimate goal of every negotiation is a satisfying solution that is effective as to the subject matter and builds congenial rapport. Splitting the difference or just "cutting the baby in half" may leave the parties feeling that they've all lost. When parties give in to "just to get it over with," they may feel defeated, and later sabotage the contract.

To have a committed, satisfying agreement that is mutually fulfilling, there must be a real meeting of the minds. By consciously listening intently to each other with the goal of understanding, the parties will feel respected. If they ask probing, polite, open-ended questions, eradicate negative arguments, and focus on problem-solving, their success rate will soar. To attain the highest quality negotiated agreements, consider using the "solutioneering" techniques we've discussed to guide you expertly along the *steppingstones to success*.

ABOUT THE AUTHOR

Mari J. Frank is an attorney, mediator, author, professor, expert witness, radio show host, media commentator and Certified Information Privacy Professional. During her twenty-four-year law/mediation practice, she has successfully resolved thousands of disputes, both as an advocate and as a neutral facilitator. She is a certified mediator panel member for the Orange County, California, Superior Court, and she presently teaches negotiations, mediation, and conflict management at the University of California, Irvine.

Professor Frank has also taught negotiation and conflict management to corporate executives, law students, and thousands of attorneys as a certified trainer for continuing legal education for the State Bar of California.

Mari has authored dozens of published articles, training booklets, and a textbook on negotiation. She's been interviewed on *Dateline, 48 Hours, Montel Williams Show, the O'Reilly Factor, NBC, ABC, MSNBC,* and over three hundred radio shows. She has been quoted in *The New York Times, The Washington Post, Los Angeles Times, Chicago Tribune, US News and World Report,* and dozens more national periodicals. She hosts her own weekly radio show *Privacy Piracy* on KUCI, 88.9 FM, at the University of California and hosted a ninety-minute PBS television special.

MARI J. FRANK, ESQ., CIPP

Mari J. Frank, Esq. and Associates
28202 Cabot Road, Suite 300
Laguna Niguel, California 92677
949-364-1511
Mari@MariFrank.com
www.MariFrank.com
www.kuci.org/privacypiracy
www.identitytheft.org

CHAPTER SEVEN

Discover Your Inner Resource

An Interview with...

DR. DEEPAK CHOPRA

DAVID WRIGHT (WRIGHT)

Today we are talking to Dr. Deepak Chopra, founder of the Chopra Center for Well Being in Carlsbad, California. More than a decade ago, Dr. Chopra became the foremost pioneer in integrated medicine. His insights have redefined our definition of health to embrace body, mind and spirit. His books, which include, *Quantum Healing, Perfect Health, Ageless Body Timeless Mind*, and *The Seven Spiritual Laws of Success,* have become international bestsellers and are established classics.

Dr. Chopra, welcome to *Stepping Stones to Success*.

DR. DEEPAK CHOPRA (CHOPRA)

Thank you. How are you?

WRIGHT

I am doing just fine. It's great weather here in Tennessee.

CHOPRA

Great.

WRIGHT

Dr. Chopra, you stated in your book, *Grow Younger, Live Longer: 10 Steps to Reverse Aging,* that it is possible to reset your biostats up to fifteen years younger than your chronological age. Is that really possible?

CHOPRA

Yes. There are several examples of this. The literature on aging really began to become interesting in the 1980s when people showed that it was possible to reverse the biological marks of aging. This included things like blood pressure, bone density, body temperature, regulation of the metabolic rate, and other things like cardiovascular conditioning, cholesterol levels, muscle mass and strength of muscles, and even things like hearing, vision, sex hormone levels, and immune function.

One of the things that came out of those studies was that psychological age had a great influence on biological age. So you have three kinds of aging: chronological age is when you were born, biological age is what your biomarker shows, and psychological age is what your biostat says.

WRIGHT

You call our prior conditioning a prison. What do you mean?

CHOPRA

We have certain expectations about the aging process. Women expect to become menopausal in their early forties. People think they should retire at the age of sixty-five and then go Florida and spend the rest of their life in so-called retirement. These expectations actually influence the very biology of aging. What we call normal aging is actually the hypnosis of our social conditioning. If you can bypass that social conditioning, then you're free to reset your own biological clock.

WRIGHT

Everyone told me that I was supposed to retire at sixty-five. I'm somewhat older than that and as a matter of fact, today is my birthday.

CHOPRA

Well happy birthday. You know, the fact is that you should be having fun all the time and always feel youthful. You should always feel that you are contributing to society. It's not the retirement, but it's the passion with which you're involved in the well being of your society, your community, or the world at large.

WRIGHT

Great things keep happening to me. I have two daughters; one was born when I was fifty. That has changed my life quite a bit. I feel a lot younger than I am.

CHOPRA

The more you associate with young people, the more you will respond to that biological expression.

WRIGHT

Dr. Chopra, you suggest viewing our bodies from the perspective of quantum physics. That seems somewhat technical. Will you tell us a little bit more about that?

CHOPRA

You see, on one level, your body is made up of flesh and bone. That's the material level but we know today that everything we consider matter is born of energy and information. By starting to think of our bodies as networks of energy information and even intelligence, we begin to shift our perspective. We don't think of our bodies so much as dense matter, but as vibrations of consciousness. Even though it sounds technical, everyone has had an experience with this so-called quantum body. After, for example, you do an intense workout, you feel a sense of energy in your body—a tingling sensation. You're actually experiencing what ancient wisdom traditions call the "vital force." The more you pay attention to this vital force inside your body, the more you will experience it as energy, information, and intelligence, and the more control you will have over its expressions.

WRIGHT

Does DNA have anything to do with that?

CHOPRA

DNA is the source of everything in our body. DNA is like the language that creates the molecules of our bodies. DNA is like a protein-making factory, but DNA doesn't give us the blueprint. When I build a house, I have to go to the factory to find the bricks, but having the bricks is not enough. I need to get an architect, who in his or her consciousness can create that blueprint. And that blueprint exists only in your spirit and consciousness—in your soul.

WRIGHT

I was interested in a statement from your book. You said that perceptions create reality. What perceptions must we change in order to reverse our biological image?

CHOPRA

You have to change three perceptions. First you have to get rid of the perceptions of aging itself. Most people believe that aging means disease and infirmities. You have to change that. You have to regard aging as an opportunity for personal growth and spiritual growth. You also have to regard it as an opportunity to express the wisdom of your experience and an opportunity to help others and lift them from ordinary and mundane experience to the kind of experiences you are capable of because you have much more experience than they do.

The second thing you have to change your perception of is your physical body. You have to start to experience it as information and energy—as a network of information and intelligence.

The third thing you have to change your perception on is the experience of dying. If you are the kind of person who is constantly running out of time, you will continue to run out of time. On the other hand, if you have a lot of time, and if you do everything with gusto and love and passion, then you will lose track of time. When you lose track of time, your body does not metabolize that experience.

WRIGHT

That is interesting. People who teach time management don't really teach the passion.

CHOPRA

No, no. Time management is such a restriction of time. Your biological clock starts to age much more rapidly. I think what you have to really do is live your life with passion so that time doesn't mean anything to you.

WRIGHT

That's a concept I've never heard.

CHOPRA

Well, there you are.

WRIGHT

You spend an entire chapter of your book on deep rest as an important part of the reversal of the aging process. What is "deep rest"?

CHOPRA

One of the most important mechanisms for renewal and survival is sleep. If you deprive an animal of sleep, then it ages very fast and dies prematurely. We live in a culture where most of our population has to resort to sleeping pills and tranquilizers in order to sleep. That doesn't bring natural rejuvenation and renewal. You know that you have had a good night's sleep when you wake up in the morning, feeling renewed, invigorated, and refreshed—like a baby does. So that's one kind of deep rest. That comes from deep sleep and from natural sleep. In the book I talk about how you go about making sure you get that.

The second deep rest comes from the experience of meditation, which is the ability to quiet your mind so you still your internal dialogue. When your internal dialogue is still, then you enter into a stage of deep rest. When your mind is agitated, your body is unable to rest.

WRIGHT

I have always heard of people who had bad eyesight and really didn't realize it until they went to the doctor and were fitted for lenses. I had that same experience some years ago. For several years I had not really enjoyed the deep sleep you're talking about. The doctor diagnosed me with sleep apnea. Now I sleep like a baby, and it makes a tremendous difference.

CHOPRA

Of course it does. You now have energy and the ability to concentrate and do things.

WRIGHT

Dr. Chopra, how much do eating habits have to do with aging? Can we change and reverse our biological age by what we eat?

CHOPRA

Yes, you can. One of the most important things to remember is that certain types of foods actually contain anti-aging compounds. There are many chemicals that are contained in certain foods that have an anti-aging effect. Most of these chemicals are derived from light. There's no way to bottle them—there are no pills you can take that will give you these chemicals. But they're contained in plants that are rich in color and derived from photosynthesis. Anything that is yellow, green, and red or has a lot of color, such as fruits and vegetables, contain a lot of these very powerful anti-aging chemicals.

In addition, you have to be careful not to put food in your body that is dead or has no life energy. So anything that comes in a can or has a label, qualifies for that. You have to expose your body to six tastes: sweet, sour, salt, bitter, pungent, and astringent because those are the codes of intelligence that allow us to access the deep intelligence of nature. Nature and what she gives to us in bounty is actually experienced through the sense of taste. In fact, the light chemicals—the anti-aging substances in food—create the six tastes.

WRIGHT

Some time ago, I was talking to one of the ladies in your office and she sent me an invitation to a symposium that you had in California. I was really interested. The title was *Exploring the Reality of Soul.*

CHOPRA

Well, I conducted the symposium, but we had some of the world's scientists, physicists, and biologists who were doing research in what is called, non-local intelligence—the intelligence of soul or spirit. You could say it is the intelligence that orchestrates the activity of the universe—God, for example. Science and spirituality are now meeting together because by understanding how nature works and how the laws of nature work, we're beginning to get a glimpse of a deeper intelligence that people in spiritual traditions call divine, or God. I think this is a wonderful time to explore spirituality through science.

WRIGHT

She also sent me biographical information of the seven scientists that were with you. I have never read a list of seven more noted people in their industry.

CHOPRA

They are. The director of the Max Planck Institute, in Berlin, Germany, where quantum physics was discovered was there. Dr. Grossam was a professor of physics at the University of Oregon, and he talked about the quantum creativity of death and the survival of conscious after death. It was an extraordinary group of people.

WRIGHT

Dr. Chopra, with our *Stepping Stones to Success* book we're trying to encourage people to be better, live better, and be more fulfilled by listening to the examples of our guest authors. Is there anything or anyone in your life who has made a difference for you and has helped you to become a better person?

CHOPRA

The most important person in my life was my father. Every day he asked himself, "What can I do in thought, word, and deed to nurture every relationship I encounter just for today?" That has lived with me for my entire life.

WRIGHT

What do you think makes up a great mentor? Are there characteristics mentors seem to have in common?

CHOPRA

I think the most important attribute of a great mentor is that he or she teaches by example and not necessarily through words.

WRIGHT

When you consider the choices you've made down through the years, has faith played an important role?

CHOPRA

I think more than faith, curiosity, wonder, a sense of reference, and humility has. Now, if you want to call that faith, then, yes it has.

WRIGHT

In a divine being?

CHOPRA

In a greater intelligence—intelligence that is supreme, infinite, unbounded, and too mysterious for the finite mind to comprehend.

WRIGHT

If you could have a platform and tell our audience something you feel would help them and encourage them, what would you say?

CHOPRA

I would say that there are many techniques that come to us from ancient wisdom and tradition that allow us to tap into our inner resources and allow us to become beings who have intuition, creativity, vision, and a connection to that which is sacred. Finding that within ourselves, we have the means to enhance our well-being. Whether it's physical, emotional, or environmental, we have the means to resolve conflicts and get rid of war. We have the means to be really healthy. We have the means for being economically uplifted. That knowledge is the most important knowledge that exists.

WRIGHT

I have seen you on several primetime television shows down through the years where you have had the time to explain your theories and beliefs. How does someone like me experience this? Do we get it out of books?

CHOPRA

Books are tools that offer you a road map. Sit down every day, close your eyes, put your attention in your heart, and ask yourself two questions: who am I and what do I want? Then maintain a short period of stillness in body and mind as in prayer or meditation, and the door will open.

WRIGHT

So, you think that the intelligence comes from within. Do all of us have that capacity?

CHOPRA

Every child born has that capacity.

WRIGHT

That's fascinating. So, it doesn't take trickery or anything like that?

CHOPRA

No, it says in the Bible in the book of Psalms, *"Be still and know that I am God"* — *Psalm 46:10.*

WRIGHT

That's great advice.

I really do appreciate your being with us today. You are fascinating. I wish I could talk with you for the rest of the afternoon. I'm certain I am one of millions who would like to do that!

CHOPRA

Thank you, sir. It was a pleasure to talk with you!

WRIGHT

Today we have been talking with Dr. Deepak Chopra, founder of The Chopra Center. He has become the foremost pioneer in integrated medicine. We have found today that he really knows what he's talking about. After reading his book, *Grow Younger, Live Longer: 10 Steps to Reverse Aging,* I can tell you that I highly recommend it. I certainly hope you'll go out to your favorite book store and buy a copy.

Dr. Chopra, thank you so much for being with us today on *Stepping Stones to Success.*

CHOPRA

Thank you for having me, David.

ABOUT THE AUTHOR

Deepak Chopra has written more than fifty books, which have been translated into many languages. He is also featured on many audio and videotape series, including five critically acclaimed programs on public television. He has also written novels and edited collections of spiritual poetry from India and Persia. In 1999, *Time* magazine selected Dr. Chopra as one of the Top 100 Icons and Heroes of the Century, describing him and "the poet-prophet of alternative medicine."

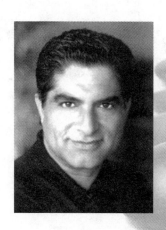

DR. DEEPAK CHOPRA
The Chopra Center
2013 Costa del Mar Rd.
Carlsbad, CA 92009
info@chopra.com
www.chopra.com

CHAPTER EIGHT

Transitions:
Alligator Slaying & Surviving Hurricanes

An Interview with...
SALLY A. DESTEFANO

DAVID WRIGHT (WRIGHT)

Today we're talking with Sally DeStefano. Sally DeStefano is a global management consultant, coach, and executive. Based in Dallas, Texas, she has experience leading transitions, coaching for leadership and career skills, implementing strategic vision and tactical plans, building high performance teams, and facilitating mergers and acquisitions.

Sally, welcome to *Stepping Stones for Success.*

Why are transitions so difficult for people?

SALLY DESTEFANO (DESTEFANO)

Transitions are difficult for us because they require leaving something familiar behind without the comfort of knowing in advance what we should do or where we should go next. The darkness that occurs between the time a door closes (an ending) and the next door opens (a new beginning) frightens us because our usual frames of reference are obliterated in this space.

Being lost in the dark is a primal fear experience that we prefer to avoid. If a door slams shut on us, we want to shine a bright light in this unfamiliar place so we can travel quickly through the area "between the doors," see the right exit, and escape the unknown, having spent as little time there as possible. We want the lantern to show us the way out, not necessarily to enlighten us about new possibilities. The lantern we want is a tool for escape, not one for discernment. We too often try to rush transitions—we want to arrive at a new destination quickly without painfully stumbling around in the dark as we learn a new way of being. The concept of taking time to transition is especially challenging in the U.S. culture of immediate gratification and staccato time-frames.

Transitions are a normal part of life but they usually feel anything but normal. For many people, transitions are akin to the fearful alligator under a childhood bed—the monster waiting to chomp off an arm or a leg once sleep takes away consciousness.

An advertisement promoting candid adult communication with children about scary natural disasters, such as hurricanes, features a young boy who whispers in hushed, frightened words, "You can drown in your bed if you fall asleep." People facing sudden, life-altering changes over which they have no control may feel a lot like this young boy, thinking that if they aren't careful or wakeful, they'll succumb to some form of death—death of the person they know or death of a way of life or death of a relationship.

People in transition darkness often are so fearful of what might happen that they can't function effectively. They figuratively lie frozen in bed, afraid to close their eyes or to look under the bed to see if a monster really is lurking there. They may not ask, "What do I need to do to make my life better or to survive in a way that works for me?" "Should I take the alligator on or move to another bed?"

In some cases, the most productive thing to do is to fight the alligator. In others, finding another bed may be the best way to get a good night's sleep so you can take appropriate action the next day.

Whether a person fights the alligator or moves to another bed, change and the need for transitions cannot be avoided. Life constantly throws surprises, shifts in plot, and unforeseen barriers in front of us. We can't hide from alligators or hurricanes, and we can't avoid the necessity to transition when our circumstances change significantly. We *can* seek to understand what is happening and explore viable options for dealing with the new situation.

WRIGHT

Some people seem to move through transitions more easily than others. Do these people have a secret for dealing with change?

DeStefano

People who transition to new beginnings fairly easily during challenging times understand that embracing change as part of the normal life cycle works better than fighting change. They take time to reflect about their changed situation and explore different opportunities to move forward. They also know that forward movement requires letting go of the past and being open to a different future than they planned.

I am considered a high change individual. If work becomes routine, I change it rather than become bored with repetition or sameness. However, that doesn't mean I like sudden change that I don't create. I may consciously or unconsciously resist the need for transition because it isn't part of my current paradigm. Or I don't have the right perspective to deal with the fact that a familiar situation has changed or needs to be changed dramatically.

Even individuals with a high need for variety and challenge, with considerable tolerance for ambiguity, want to feel in control of their destiny. They prefer to make changes on their terms, not on someone else's terms. Therefore, when change is thrust upon people, they tend to resist. Resistance occurs even if the change would drive a transition that ultimately works better for the individual than the previous path. Yet we can't avoid change. It is ubiquitous, affecting each of us at different times and in different ways throughout the phases of our lives.

Too often we avoid transitioning to meet new realities until there is no other choice—transition or cease to exist. As we move through life, the same thought and behavior patterns that helped us in an earlier stage may no longer work. When extended resistance to needed adaptation occurs, people experience life problems and frustration. These individuals tend to blame their predicament on anyone and anything, and remaining in an angry, alligator-fighting mode instead of moving to another bed. Extended resistance also results in failure to seek out new ways of being or doing things, avoiding a transition that would re-energize life and result in more happiness than hanging on to old paradigms could ever bring.

When surrounded by change or faced with a clear need to change, you are at an important inflection point in your life. You must explore options or you could "drown in your bed."

WRIGHT

What do you mean by an "inflection point" and what does it have to do with transitions?

DESTEFANO

An inflection point is a place in time where a previously ascending curve either starts to descend or to jettison into another ascending arc. Andy Grove, former Intel Corporation Chief Executive Officer, characterized inflection points in business as those times when significant changes in markets, culture, or political direction drive a reaction that either results in deterioration of an enterprise or transforms it into a different business with an exciting new future.

People have multiple inflection points in their lives. These points are critical times when they either reinvent themselves or fall into the backwaters of life. Which way the new direction takes them depends on factors that may change each time they go through an inflection point. As William Bridges and other psychologists indicate, though, human behavior in change situations tends to follow patterns based on previous experience or their personality profile.

For example, if during past inflection points a person was able to travel through the point of no return and on to the next life cycle by using persistence and hard work, he or she will tend to try that approach first when faced with an inflection point, which is another way of saying experiencing a new transition cycle. Furthermore, if one sees the glass half full rather than half empty, she or he is likely to use optimism to navigate through the dark space between an ending and a new beginning.

However, some transitions are so traumatic—so completely different from any previous situation—that familiar strategies and tactics simply don't work. In these situations, the most confident, perseverant, optimistic person finds confusion instead of the usual result from previously successful approaches.

Real pain accompanies the shocked disorientation of being deposited in unknown territory where familiar behavior has no sway. During the recession of 2008–2009, millions of Americans lost their jobs through no fault of their own. Many of these people were blind-sided, unaware that their world was about to be turned upside down. A significant number were without sufficient financial reserves to weather even a short period of unemployment. What reserves some may have saved, disintegrated as the housing market continued to dive, financial institutions failed, and unscrupulous people like Bernie Madoff bilked thousands of their life's savings.

A friend resigned her job right before the crash, unaware that shortly she would be thrown into a market flooded with millions of talented people scrambling for the few jobs still available as companies shed workers like dogs shed water after a bath. After months dragged on with little or no income, her constantly ringing phone was unanswered because she knew the calls were from bill collectors. Her garbage collection service was discontinued and she worried about paying for electricity. She ate breakfast bars for inexpensive meals and car pooled to a temporary part-time job, which paid only a fraction of her previous salary.

Over age fifty, my friend was faced with the prospect of losing her home, filing for bankruptcy, and moving across country to live with an elderly father in cramped quarters. Her sense of self-worth was diminished, yet she had to keep up the appearance of confidence in order to be considered for opportunities. Nothing that my friend did in the past to overcome adversity worked in the current situation. She had previously lost her husband but recovered financially from that shock by moving into a smaller home and cutting expenses to make ends meet. This time, though, the past transition strategy wasn't working because she couldn't sell her home nor could she pay for it. If the bank foreclosed on her home, my friend couldn't afford to pay rent. Furthermore, she had rescued ten dogs from various abusive situations; nobody would take a renter with ten dogs.

My friend is only one of countless people around the world who are coming to grips with a painful new reality. Things we thought were important become not so important in a permanently different situation. There is no going back to the way things were, and the way out of the present darkness is unclear until a new direction is adopted and pursued with commitment.

WRIGHT

I understand that you experienced quite a transition a number of years ago. How did that affect you?

DESTEFANO

What is happening to my friend and so many others reminds me of a troubling dream that I had several years ago when I was going through a difficult transition. My husband and I moved to a ranch we owned in Montana following an extended illness that required me to give up my career of over twenty-five years. Because everything familiar was left behind, I felt lost between worlds, uncertain about the new but quite certain that the old was a thing of the past.

During that time, I had a number of symbolic dreams, including one that depicted desperate conditions for thousands of people who descended upon our ranch, trying to escape the destruction of the cities they had lived in and the lives they had led prior to some unidentified catastrophic event.

These shocked people had scrambled to the country hoping to find a way to survive. Their cars sat abandoned on the highways, gas tanks empty. The city refugees shivered in the cold, barren Montana winter, killing wild animals for food and camping next to a stream. They chopped down the few cottonwood trees that clung to the creek, burning the scarce wood for warmth that would not be possible once the last tree was destroyed.

In my dream, I saw these pitiful people gradually transition from their desperate condition to become like the Crow Nation natives who had camped next to Big Timber Creek over two hundred years prior. As these former city dwellers learned new ways to work together and to find sustenance, more options became clear to them. Somehow they survived the winter; spring brought new food and creativity to their struggle to survive in a radically changed world.

I believe this dream was not only symbolic of my need to leave behind an old way of being and embrace a new way of living, it was perhaps also a precursor of widespread future changes. Our way of life in this country is changing dramatically, and thousands of us may someday find ourselves scrambling for survival and learning new ways of being, as had the people in my dream.

WRIGHT

Are you forecasting a dismal future for us?

DeStefano

I don't tell this story to share a doomsday scenario. Rather, the symbolic message is simple—by necessity we need to find new ways of being to address situations that differ significantly from anything we have experienced in the past. Although transitions are a normal part of the life cycle, we likely will need to completely transform at some point in the future. Travel through the confusing, disorienting period between past and future will require new patterns of behavior—ones that we can begin to develop before the transformational inflection point is upon us. We can practice dealing effectively with everyday ambiguity. We can make many small adjustments to our lifestyle that will help us get in shape for a future starkly different from the present. We can embrace incremental transitions while finding simpler ways to be happy in the world and with each other.

Wright

What does living simply have to do with transitions for people who need to get through a difficult time?

DeStefano

When our material things are taken away or when survival is a priority, we find how little we need.

Another Montana insight occurred when my plans to develop a tourist lodge had to be put on hold due to economic conditions following the dot.com bust and later, September 11, 2001. When my husband and I moved to Montana to recover my health, we thought we could develop a thriving business on the land that was originally purchased for retirement. Because stock values from our investments fell precipitously, furniture and building materials we brought to Montana sat for seven years in two large storage containers. Meanwhile, we lived in a 900-square-foot, two-room dwelling that served as residence, office, and auxiliary kitchen during large events that we conducted at our ranch.

Over the seven-year period we lived in Montana, we learned how little we really needed to survive and to thrive in a more natural environment than the large metropolitan area from which we had moved. Seven years later, when the two containers of furniture and building materials were opened, I was astonished to see the things that had been put out of our consciousness. We hadn't needed any of them!

Patrick Lencioni, a well-known global management consultant and highly regarded motivational speaker, has started what he calls the "simplicity project." I've known Pat for many years, having hired him to work in my organization when he was in his early thirties. He is an unusually creative and insightful individual who has transitioned many times throughout his life, stating to me in the early 1990s that he was a great believer in William Bridges' perspective on making successful transitions.

Pat has transformed his priorities from the complex life of a road warrior consultant to a champion of balanced family life, spiritual commitments, and simplification. Pat realizes that we need to value our families above our work, honor the spiritual side of our existence, and learn to live simply in spite of a non-simple world.

Sometimes the most transformational change we can make in life is to walk away from complexity and embrace simplicity. If we lived more simply, we would not need such high compensation in this country, which is negatively affecting our competitive position in the global economy. We can give up unnecessary luxuries and downsize our footprint.

I'm not advocating the cap-and-trade policy touted by some politicians. What I am saying is that if we could transition to a simpler life, we would not require so much wealth and material trappings.

I am an owner of too many things and take up too much space. I don't need all of it, yet it's difficult to get rid of the collections of a lifetime. I know that some of my stuff—maybe most of it—interferes with being able to move around freely and quickly transition to another way of life. The thought of moving the stuff of success is daunting! I recall earlier years when I could pack all my possessions in a Volkswagen and move to wherever I needed to go, simply and quickly. Now, as I consider the possibility of having to relocate to find work, I dread having to deal with all the stuff I've collected. Like my friend with ten dogs, I can't imagine leaving our four horses behind; but I don't need four horses, three carriages, and all the related paraphernalia. Unlike Montana, where we had a hayfield and significant grazing available to support horses, having these animals near a large metropolitan area doesn't mean we can ditch the cars and drive a buggy to work. Hay is more expensive than gasoline.

Most of us have toys—cars, vacation homes, electronic devices, clothes and accessories, hobby activities. Do we really need all of this? Burdened with this stuff, how difficult will it be to transition to another way of life when necessary? I think of people I met when Hurricane Ike tore through south Texas in 2008, leaving many homeless, escaping with only the clothes on their backs. In a frenzy to help, I went through our closets and other areas of our home, easily packing up things that we possessed but didn't need.

In another hurricane-related situation, I encountered a fascinating, wise woman on a flight that took me through New Orleans. She was returning to celebrate Thanksgiving with her mother and sister, who were finally able to move back into their southern Louisiana home three years after Hurricane Katrina's devastation. Her comment was, "We found out what we didn't need. We will never be the same, but we are grateful for family and friends. While it's very special to be able to move back into our homes, we have learned that very few things are needed for survival and happiness."

Talk to any natural disaster survivor, a cancer survivor, or someone who has survived a job loss and you will understand how relatively easily we can transition away from nonessentials.

WRIGHT

Layoffs trigger major transitions for many people. I know you have been involved in your share of layoffs. What was that like and what advice do you have?

DESTEFANO

What this amazing Louisiana African American woman and her family learned from Hurricane Katrina is not an easy lesson for people confronted with job loss. They have not lost everything, but they are afraid they could lose the life they have known.

During a twenty-week period, five hundred fifty people laid off during the 2008–2009 recession journeyed through my career transition workshops. Ironically, over the course of my career I had coordinated layoffs that profoundly affected approximately the same number of people. When you are the person delivering a layoff message, rarely do you see precisely how this significant loss affects individuals, even though you know it does.

The first time I led a layoff, I had recently built a human resources organization from the ground up for a rapidly growing company. Unfortunately, the company encountered rough financial waters. This situation resulted in the need to eliminate jobs that had previously been added to support anticipated growth which had not occurred. I fretted about how this layoff would affect people. But nothing prepared me for the gut-wrenching result of an early morning call from my boss, the Chief Executive Officer.

"Sally, you have to eliminate twenty positions from your department." I was living on a sailboat at the time, and I almost fell down the companionway as I heard his words over my cell phone. After ending the call, I stumbled to the head, where I immediately threw up. Despair came in waves as I continued to eject everything from my stomach. However, I couldn't reject my responsibility for delivering the distasteful message to people whom I'd recently convinced to join my team. I sobbed and sobbed, all alone on my boat, ironically named the *Honah Lee*. Any illusion of the land of milk and honey was about to be shattered for twenty of my people and for many others who depended on the company for their livelihood. Within hours I was delivering the awful message.

Although I'm fairly certain that nobody died as a result of this layoff, I'm equally certain that lives were changed by it. Layoffs never became easy for me over the years, and I always went through a throw-up stage when I learned I had to implement a layoff. Layoffs should never come easy for those who make or deliver that decision, any more than the decision to go to war should be easy for decision-makers and implementers of that life-altering event.

Nobody can depend on an employer for one's financial stability and future. The concept of life-long employment is dead. You can't transfer financial responsibility for your well-being to someone else—employer or government—without becoming slave to an institution that cannot and will not protect you if its survival is at risk. We need to be prepared for job transition at all times in our lives.

WRIGHT

Have you ever been laid off?

DeStefano

I had never been laid off until reorganization resulted in elimination of my job in late 2008. On the day the corporate representative arrived to communicate to people being affected, I found myself throwing up once again, with a new twist—as the terminations were communicated to my colleagues, I took multiple long walks around my company's facility, sometimes letting a deep, anguishing noise escape from my soul. No spring chicken and the sole wage earner, I was frightened about the future. I faced a transition that all people who lose a job experience, each in their own way.

I started this transition with frenetic activity without setting aside reflective time to consider options. Instead, I dove into the deep end of the pool and swam to various perceived safety points. I should have taken time to reflect, to experience what William Bridges calls the "Neutral Zone." Instead, I began thrashing around in the darkness, banging into multiple walls trying to find a quick way out of my situation. I felt like a bird flying repeatedly into a window that appears to have a desirable world on the other side. After "banging my beak" on various windows, I realized that I wasn't making progress. I was painfully bumping from one window to another, eroding valuable energy without finding an escape from my predicament. Worse, I was losing confidence and self-respect, mired in fear about the future and worried that material obligations would "drown me in my bed."

WRIGHT

So you were laid off for the first time in your life and found it difficult. What did you do?

DESTEFANO

Someone who believed in me threw a life raft into my dark sea, and I started helping hundreds of laid-off people go through the initial stages of their career transitions. As a part-time, temporary project consultant for a large consulting firm, I was making less than half of my previous income and traveling three times the distance to earn it. Yet the work became a healing discovery process for me.

It was fulfilling to apply my knowledge and coaching skills to help others, and I lost my discomfort with public speaking. I found ways to re-energize the workshop content to fit the unique needs of different groups and individuals. People's feedback validated my value as an educator and group facilitator and encouraged me to share ideas by writing about transitions as well as talking about them. My own transition began to dawn. I developed a perspective where it was no longer mandatory for me to get another vice president job in a corporate world that was spewing out people over age fifty at an alarming rate. I began knocking on different doors as the transition from an old to a new paradigm unfolded. I also found inspiration from the people I met in my workshops.

One of the discussions at the beginning of each workshop elicited people's response to the question, "What were your feelings when you found out that your job was being eliminated?" People talked freely about their feelings, some more brashly than others. Approximately one-third acknowledged they were relieved when they were told their fate. A frequent comment was, "At least now I can quit worrying and start exploring something new and more meaningful." Several individuals stated they had been unhappy with their jobs but hadn't actively sought alternatives because at least they knew what they had ... and the dark space between where one door closed and another opened was not a place they wanted to enter voluntarily.

One group elected to discuss what they dubbed "contingency thinking," or exploring possibilities from a new perspective.

A senior financial leader explained he had decided to learn air conditioning and heating from a friend who had a thriving enterprise and needed a business partner.

A woman with twenty-nine years experience in the restaurant industry described herself as "definitely not ready to retire." She decided to channel her organization skills into the public education system.

An immigrant technologist talked about a used tire business he wanted to restart after having sold a similar business the last time he was laid off.

About 15 to 20 percent of the participants described themselves as "wide open; I don't know what I want to do next."

One undecided individual was angry and frustrated that he didn't have a clear direction in mind. He was seeking a silver bullet delivered on a silver tray. This young man was fighting the darkness between what he was doing for a living and whatever his new direction would be. He was very impatient with the ambiguity of his situation and angry that he had not found a solution. Even though his old employment was not yet ended, he wanted a new path laid out before his last day of work. Unfortunately, his transition probably would be lengthy because the intense anger he harbored was interfering with positive forward movement.

Another man in his fifties acknowledged that he was having problems with his ego because he had lost a very senior position and was being recruited for a "lesser job, one I did earlier in my career." We discussed how he could bring great value to the role in a much different way than he had as a younger professional.

Looking at an opportunity from several perspectives can be quite helpful to people in transition. Contingency thinking requires quality time in the Neutral

Zone, that ambiguous space between an ending and a new beginning. However, making sure that you experience sufficient Neutral Zone time is difficult for most of us because our society tends to be action-driven, not thought-driven. Recognizing when to think and when to act is important to all transitions. I learned this reality from personal experience by bumping into false windows and bending my beak in the process.

WRIGHT

A lot of unemployed people would say they can't afford to spend time in the Neutral Zone. It's too much like examining your navel, don't you think? What do you do there?

DESTEFANO

Being in the Neutral Zone without fighting or angrily banging on doors provides time to reflect on possibilities that exist at the intersection between a person's interests and abilities. If one has properly closed the door on preoccupation with his or her past, this time also allows reflective examination of future possibilities without burdens from the past. It's difficult to give up familiar ways of making a living or a professional identity that may be more about position than substance. Think about it: How many people are employed to do something they can do well but have no real interest in doing? How many try to follow their interest but don't have the skills to excel at it or there is no market for it? For someone experiencing job loss, the Neutral Zone provides time to do the following:

1. Reflect about your true interests and what you really need to be happy.
2. Articulate your abilities as demonstrated by your previous accomplishments in all aspects of life, not just work.
3. Identify what activities are your strengths (those things that include both interests and abilities).
4. Determine what market exists for your strengths.
5. Plan how to find the right place for yourself in that market.

Once you give yourself time in the Neutral Zone to accomplish these five things, it is easier to transition or commit to a new direction—to engage in an inflection point that carries you to new opportunity. Sometimes you can go through this process alone. Often, it helps to have a guide or guides to assist you. Most importantly, you need to acknowledge that an end has occurred, but it is not *the end*. You are embarking on a new adventure that may be the most satisfying experience of your life.

What if you don't have much time to spend in the Neutral Zone because you have bills to pay and a family to feed? At particularly challenging times like these, you may need to find multiple streams of income while you work your way through the five steps of navigating a career transition. Having more than one way to put food on the table may be a future trend that works for larger numbers of people than those who traditionally have lived on a single source of income, or two, if married.

When I was living in Montana, I found that many people there use more than one job to keep them afloat in this beautiful but difficult place to earn a livelihood. Life in America is changing, and earning a living may become more challenging than it has been in the recent past. Having multiple income possibilities and more than one perspective may be your path out of the Neutral Zone after a loss and into a transitioned state of being.

Exploring alternatives is not a theoretical or purely meditational exercise. It requires disciplined research and analysis, truthfulness about self and situation, and the courage to take unprecedented action. Being in the Neutral Zone allows time for examination of the unfamiliar and for planning a new, effective course of action. The goal of being in the Neutral Zone is not to find the old door that closed and to reopen it—the objective is to identify the new door that takes you from confusion into a new clarity and direction.

WRIGHT

What hopes do people in transition have?

DeStefano

Negotiating transitions means that you won't "drown in your bed" in spite of a hurricane of changes thrown across your path. You can cast off your old safety blanket and find a new bed. You probably will feel lost for awhile as you ponder and explore new possibilities. You have not died—you have passed through one of life's inflection points. Transitions can lead to a happier, simpler future if you kill the alligator of your fears and step courageously into a new life . . . or a new way of being in life as it has become for you. The past is dead, but you will live on to enjoy a brighter future by engaging in successful transitions, one step at a time.

No challenge is too great for you to conquer, the fearful darkness of being lost will become the light of a new direction, and you will transform to become someone better than the person you left behind in the past.

ABOUT THE AUTHOR

Sally DeStefano is a global management consultant, coach, and executive. Based in Dallas, Texas, she has experience implementing strategic vision and tactical plans, leading organization and change management, building high performance teams, facilitating mergers/acquisitions, and coaching for leadership and career skills. She has worked in telecommunications, software, hardware, semiconductor, hospitality, retail, and higher education environments. She worked for fifteen years as a vice president or senior vice president, eleven of which were spent as the top corporate human resources executive. She has spoken to large groups on various leadership topics and lives outside Dallas with her husband and four horses.

SALLY A. DESTEFANO

Perspectagon,™ *LLC*
Argyle, Texas 76226
940-464-7673
www.perspectagon.com

CHAPTER NINE

Bully to Leader:
Three Phases to Personal Transformation

An Interview with...
FRANK A. DILALLO

DAVID WRIGHT (WRIGHT)

Today we are talking with Frank A. DiLallo, author of the book titled; *Peace2U: Three Phase Bullying Solution* and creator of *The Peace Project*; an audio stress management program. Frank is the founder and director of Counseling & Training Services, providing consultation services to schools on prevention and intervention solutions to bullying and other obstacles interfering with academic performance. He is a frequent public speaker and trainer on a variety of topics.

Frank, welcome to *Stepping Stones to Success*. You are associated with innovative solutions to the bullying problem. What led you to developing the *Peace2U* initiative with schools?

Frank A. DiLallo (DiLallo)

First of all David, I would like to say that I am honored and grateful for the opportunity to contribute to this book. I am glad you asked this question because I would like to share how my personal and professional history converged leading to the development of *Peace2U* and *The Peace Project*.

Bullying is a serious concern for schools and in the workplace and I'm passionately committed to actively seeking solutions to this end. Working directly with bullying incidents for many years, I'm acutely aware of the national, as well as international scope and gravity of the problem. Bullying is a human rights violation with physical, emotional, social and legal consequences on a global scale. This epidemic has major implications for individuals, families, schools, communities, and the workplace—seriously undermining student achievement and work productivity. Bullying is not going away anytime soon and if there was ever a time in our history for innovative solutions, the time is now.

Wright

Were there any events in your life that influenced your making a commitment to bullying solutions?

DiLallo

Definitely! I'd like to highlight some significant events in my life—so significant, in fact, that focusing on solutions to the bullying problem has become my personal and professional mission.

Wright

Please do.

DiLallo

As a young boy, I realized early on I was physically stronger than most kids and had a lot of natural athletic ability. Of course it's only human nature to move toward what brings us pleasure—so I did what I was good at and became positively addicted to sports. This was such a double edged sword though. On one hand, I gained confidence from my "body smarts." On the other hand, my athletic prowess made me one-dimensional and led to a lofty sense of pride and at times feelings of superiority.

A downside to competitive sports is it creates and reinforces a myopic lens of "better than/less than." An intense need to be better than—win the game, always requires an opponent—a person or team to be less than—lose the game. The baneful truth of this dubious attitude is; who I am as a person gets wrapped up in the outcome—when I win I feel good, when I lose I feel bad—so the goal becomes; win at all cost! When locked into this precarious position there is usually a price to pay for all involved. The most successful coaches go beyond emphasizing winning and teach important virtues and life skills such as; teamwork, cooperation, focus, determination, perseverance and humility—win or lose.

I was recently at an airport terminal waiting to catch a flight to a speaking engagement for a leadership weekend involving high school youth. I was thinking about this "better than/less than" concept and wondering how I was going to incorporate it into my presentation. It's amazing when we ask for guidance what appears. I couldn't help but notice a teen passing by wearing a t-shirt embossed with; "Our Sport Is Your Sports Punishment." Not having an opportunity to ask her about the origins of the shirt, I'm not certain she really subscribed to what her shirt actually said. For all I know, she was just wearing it to cover her body. However, if she didn't believe what the shirt undeniably conveyed, she probably would've experienced enough dissonance about the shirt to make it uncomfortable to wear in public.

WRIGHT

Are there any implications to this "better than/less than" attitude beyond sports?

DILALLO

Absolutely! The residual effect of this attitude didn't originate with sports and isn't isolated within athletic competitions. Having a better than/less attitude is a form of oppression. Oppression of individuals and groups is pervasive and continues to be prevalent even in our "civilized" world today. A majority of students are actively involved in competitive sports, making this skewed lens operable in the school building and beyond. A competitive edge often includes a strong sense of entitlement that is easily transferred from sports to other areas such as academics, relationships, and social status. An imbalance of power is an unfortunate byproduct of sports and in life—a setup for rampant disrespect and bullying behavior among youth and adults.

To add to this, our culture creates its own limiting beliefs—defining a person's worth and success via status, position, title, rank, speed, and amount of assets. The arrant truth is a caste system filled with disparity and human division. These divisions cause power structures creating social elevation for some—while reducing the dignity of the human spirit for others. In this disparity there is an illusion of better than/less than. This illusion holds the deception of separation among people causing anxiety and mistrust.

The woeful reality is that youth mimic these divisions and act out these power structures. Certainly the social media and "pop culture" have a profound impact on youth establishing their own unique subcultures in schools and beyond. As students define their own popular social norms, a large percentage of their peers feel ostracized.

Popularity is about power and control. If a group or person is perceived as "popular," paradoxically some other group or person ends up being "unpopular." Any personal or social action that discourages, disempowers, disenfranchises, or oppresses another person or group is a lose/lose. The illusion of better than/less than is always a lose/lose. Bullying, is also about power and control—better than/less than and is a lose/lose.

True success can never be established based on better than/less than. Pure success always has roots in a win/win position, whereby everyone and everything is considered in the equation. I mentioned heading to a leadership weekend for teens. When I arrived I was inspired by a t-shirt a teen was wearing embossed with: "Teamwork Divides the Task and Multiplies the Success!" I want to believe he wore the shirt because he believes in what it conveys.

WRIGHT

What was school like for you growing up?

DILALLO

If I were a young boy today, I have no doubt I would have been diagnosed with Attention Deficit Disorder. As with many children diagnosed with ADD/ADHD, I was easily frustrated and struggled with the traditional academic setting. Having a difficult time focusing, sitting still, and connecting with anything of academic interest made it difficult for me to get motivated in school. Early in my education, I did just enough to get by and had low scores on achievement tests. I felt very discouraged and didn't experience much success academically. I really struggled making a connection to my thinking and seriously lacked confidence in my cognitive abilities. These were all strong signs that I was underachieving—creating a painful chasm between me and academic success.

Attention problems and boredom left me to my own devices and many unrefined ways to stay stimulated. As a result, I engaged in what would be considered today to be bullying behavior. Naturally, students and adults at times, vehemently reacted to my behavior. Consequently, I experienced some very disturbing interventions, mostly reactions from grade school teachers and a principal. These interventions seriously affected my early learning and reinforced a contemptuous tone for my negative attitude about school and toward authority.

WRIGHT

Did your bullying extend into high school?

DILALLO

Not really. Through high school and even into postsecondary education, I never thought much about my behavior or how it affected others. My bullying had morphed into being intensely focused and highly aggressive in competitive sports. Aggression in most any sport at this level is of course encouraged and considered acceptable behavior. I have noticed over the years that this intensity and aggression is expected at a younger and younger age by coaches and parents. The attention I received for athletic achievements from family, school, community, and the media for aggressive play—an incessant need to win was intoxicating. The latter was culturally reflected back to me as "healthy" and/or a "winning attitude."

WRIGHT

Was there anything positive that came out of your participation in sports?

DILALLO

I'm glad you asked this, because I need to be reminded that there is an upside to sports as well. The catch-22 in all of this is that participating in sports was positive—an extremely important avenue keeping me involved in school. I was able to channel my energies and hone some positive attributes from my involvement. If it weren't for sports—from primary grades all the way to college—I have doubts about whether I would've even remained in school.

I'm thankful for my participation in sports and for my parents who encouraged and supported me every step of the way. I also had some wonderful role models as coaches who were instrumental on many levels. I am eternally grateful for the positive influence sports had on my life and the hopeful optimism I received from all those I met along the way.

WRIGHT

Weren't sports motivation enough for you to do well in school?

DILALLO

Yes and no. I only did the bare minimum—mostly so I could meet eligibility requirements. Sports did pull me through in spite of my disdain for school. It's also human nature to move away from things that bring us displeasure. Being an unmotivated learner and disinterested in studies, was a setup for failure in college. The primary reason for my being in school and even going on to college was to play basketball. I rode my athletic accolades through high school and was recruited to play college ball. Naively, with an intense focus on my game and chasing stardom, I ended up landing in the academic dumpster my freshman year.

After a year and a half of competing with many other former high school stars, I became disillusioned with the idea of playing college basketball. For the first time I was struck with the flip side of the superiority coin and became painfully aware of how inferior and insignificant I felt. Similar to an addict hitting bottom, the withdrawal from the feelings of superiority or high were agonizing and a major source of confusion. Letting go of a significant part of my identity was so excruciating, I even felt suicidal at times.

This was a pivotal moment in my life. After spending a period of time grieving lost dreams of being in the NBA, I made one of my very first life changing decisions—saying "goodbye" to my illustrious basketball career and making my college education a top priority. Although painful, it was one of the best decisions I ever made.

WRIGHT

What resulted from your momentous decision?

DiLallo

Well, like a fish out of water, I was in new territory and for the first time had to learn how to learn. The upside to being involved in sports most of my life was having the ability to take the same successful discipline I learned as an athlete and apply it to my academics—long hours, hard work, determination and perseverance. Along with this formula I also drew inspiration from an uncle, several high school teachers, and my college advisor. I even had the wherewithal to see a therapist who was instrumental in helping me sort through my confusion.

The culmination of self-examination and surrounding myself with support helped me shift focus. I became fascinated with the counseling profession and immersed myself in psychology, sociology and social work. I even landed my first "real job" in the field, all while continuing my undergraduate work. The really exciting discovery was how textbooks "came to life" when I could connect them with a relevant experience.

Wright

It's often said when a door is closed another one opens. Was this true for you?

DiLallo

Amazingly so! Once I made the decision to let go of my basketball dreams and commit to pursuing a counseling degree, a new vision began to magically unfold. Committing to something sets an intention that fuels the determination to realize successful outcomes. By making a commitment to my education, I managed to be the first in my family to graduate from college. Two years following the completion of my undergraduate studies, I completed a graduate degree in counseling—graduating with honors.

Although I wasn't sure what aspect of counseling I wanted to pursue, I was absolutely certain I didn't want to be a school counselor. Because of my early grade school history, I developed an aversion toward school and couldn't imagine myself working in an academic setting. As a result, the first twelve years of my career were focused on agency and private practice counseling—steering clear of anything even remotely connected to schools.

Wright

What kind of clientele did you serve in agencies and private practice?

DiLALLO

I frequently worked with preteen and teenaged clients and bullying issues often surfaced during sessions. The complaints around bullying from my young clients were always from a victim perspective. As a therapist, I was able to be present for them, but could not relate to being a victim of bullying as a student in school. As a result, being in a "helper" role kept me unconscious about my own bullying behavior.

I reached a point working in full-time private practice where I began to question my effectiveness, especially with teen clients. This was another confusing point in my life. I mistakenly envisioned a counseling career in private practice as the ultimate point of arrival—a destination rather than just a part of the journey. I grew restless and the experience of conducting therapy became mundane and repetitive. I had a feeling that there was something more for me to do—a bigger arena if you will. Although it doesn't feel good, I think it is important to recognize confusion as a necessary "stirring" inside— a helpful catalyst telling us we are ready to make a change or take a next step.

At an impasse in my career, an unexpected opportunity came to me—definitely unsolicited—a request to present stress management skills to middle school students. The timing was curious, because I was attending trainings and reading extensively on stress related disorders. Up to this point in my career, I avoided doing presentations, primarily because requests came from schools. Although I didn't quite jump at the chance, I agreed because of my interest in the topic. I also knew it would get me out of the office and force me to do something out the routine.

WRIGHT

How did the presentation go?

DiLALLO

To my surprise, the presentation went exceptionally well. I was excited to witness students responding and engaged in the process. This was my first awareness that I had something personally and professionally to contribute to schools. The feelings were very gratifying. So much so, I began to accept any and all requests to present at schools—with students, educators and parents. Presenting became experiential learning for me and I found it to be exhilarating. Coming away with positive experiences from schools breathed new life into me!

WRIGHT

Sounds like you discovered a new niche in presenting to groups.

DILALLO

I have to admit being in front of an audience is similar to being in an athletic competition—from the performance anxiety to the thrilling attention from an audience. The only difference I can see is the amount of sweat! When you engage with an audience it's very exciting—meaningful and rewarding too! Accumulating positive interactions with administrators and teachers began to quell my monsters around education. I was intrigued by my own enthusiasm about schools—in particular my exuberance around presenting to schools and the healing contradiction it presented for my early school experiences. This energizing curiosity was the impetus behind my taking a risk to apply for a counseling position at a local high school.

WRIGHT

Wow! That must have been a huge step for you.

DILALLO

It was a huge leap! I even subjected myself to a long arduous process of multiple interviews with administrators, teachers, counselors and board members— all people involved in education. Talk about anxiety provoking! I persevered though and was offered and accepted the position. My responsibility was to direct the school student assistance program. Similar to employee assistance, the basic premise is to afford students an opportunity to confidentially confide in a trusted adult and/or one of the many support groups offered. Having access to these support services increases the likelihood a student will improve his/her academic, social and extracurricular performance.

Accepting this position was indeed a huge contradiction to my certainty early on about not wanting to be in a school setting. However, remaining open to the path I noticed an amazing transformation occurring in me. To this day I believe avoiding schools was a way to not revisit a dreadful grade school experience. Working in a school was an opportunity to help students and collaboratively with teachers, administrators and parents. This vantage point increased my awareness and gave me insights from multiple angles I had never considered before. It was also a wonderful opportunity to rework my early angst around education.

WRIGHT

You were able to turn your negative school experiences into a blessing.

DiLALLO

That's the gift David—to turn negative or tragic life experiences into blessings. For much of my life, education had been my nemesis. Entering the field of education was providential and opened my heart and mind to many healing blessings—truly becoming my saving grace. Had I not gotten out of my comfort zone, I'm not sure I would've been in a position to receive such grace. Moving toward education, instead of away from it, empowered me to release my resentments and forgive—myself and others. Working in agencies and private practice for many years, little did I know that entering the field of education would become the antidote to my educational nightmares. Just like getting bitten by a poisonous snake, the only way to save the persons life, is to go back to the same snake for the antidote.

Divine intervention led me to the field of education, despite my resistance so long ago. The gift is becoming a lifelong learner with a "beginners mind"—staying open to wonder and curiosity and "trying on" new and different experiences. As a result my career has successfully evolved from agency counselor, to private counselor, to school counselor, to schools consultant.

As a schools consultant for the last twelve years, 80 percent of the calls I receive are from principals, teachers, and parents requesting assistance with bullying concerns. This volume of calls is a body of evidence regarding the enormity of this problem. Professionally responding to bullying incidents has also given me the opportunity to look at my early bullying behavior. This internal discovery process to reconcile personal bullying transgressions and heal early educational wounds has been challenging to say the least—but very rewarding. The results of my making a commitment to this remarkable journey, is a personal atonement and in the process I have created *Peace2U*.

WRIGHT

Would you be willing to share more about being a bully growing up and how educators responded to your behavior?

DILALLO

Sure. I think this will help you better understand how some of the events in my life became a critical foundation for the bullying initiative. It's not a pleasant thing to admit, but in my youth I would've been considered a bully. I don't recall anyone ever referring to me as a bully or labeling me as such—possibly because the awareness and language was not as prevalent. Although it's difficult to think of myself this way, I'm certain my behavior growing up was nothing less than that of a bully. As a kid, I humiliated, teased, taunted, and used physical aggression repeatedly in an effort to feel better or "better than"—to gain power and control over my environment and others. My actions were not necessarily conscious at the time, but did serve a purpose—operating as a maladaptive release or "feel good" behavior.

Bullying can be considered an obsessive-compulsive behavior, in which specific repeated behaviors or actions serve a genuine purpose. Of course, the purpose is immediate gratification, making the behavior self-serving and highly maladaptive. As with any obsessive compulsion, the behavior usually continues as long as the person finds secondary gain, i.e., satisfaction, enabling support, feels better, power, control, attention in the process, etc. Today, after years of reflection and support— a lot of uncovering and discovering—I consider myself to be a recovering bully.

WRIGHT

Were there any school related incidents that stand out for you?

DILALLO

Most definitely. During elementary school, I vividly recall incidents of my bullying other students and getting punished harshly for them. One incident involved my hitting other students for no apparent reason during recess on the playground in fifth grade. A student had obviously told the supervising playground teacher about it. The teacher summoned me over with her intense, angrily focused voice and intimidating eyes and asked if I hit Joey. I proudly replied, "yes" and before I could give a justified explanation, she retorted with a strike to the left side of my face with her rolled up leather gloves held tightly in her right hand. Her corporal "sting" left a lasting impression. I never could quite grasp the value of such a consequence. Hitting as a consequence to hitting is never a positive step toward resolving objectionable behavior or bringing about acceptable behavior.

On another occasion during recess, I hit a female student who was pitching in a game of kickball. I was the last player up and primed to kick a homerun—feeling confident I would drive in the winning run and sure of becoming the playground hero. Well the pitcher nixed my grand plan, because she held on to the ball until the bell rang. Both the fifth grade teacher and the school principal confronted me about hitting JoAnne. Emphatically, I admitted to the behavior saying, "Yeah, and the next time she doesn't pitch the ball, I'll do it again!" In my best ten-year-old thinking, I felt justified and a sense of entitlement about hitting my classmate. I felt angry because she was not playing fair. Plus, she obstructed my path to "victory." Someone had to teach her a lesson!

I was paddled, a forgotten number of times, by the school principal for this incident—another corporal "sting" that made a lasting impression. I suspect the reflexive punishment was a well intended form of consequence in an attempt to get me to change my behavior. The interventions however, didn't help me conclude a need to change anything about myself. Bullies have difficulty accepting responsibility—it's never about them. The problem is always about another person or group—an "I'm o.k., you're not o.k." position. The interventions with me were unsuccessful because they only strengthened my disdain for school. I internalized the incidents only to silently ask myself why I was getting paddled by the principal for something someone else did.

WRIGHT

Their response was harsh. Is it hard for people to find a soft spot for bullies?

DiLallo

I think it's true we have trouble seeing past the immediate behavior. Needless to say, my bullying behavior was not met with much sympathy. None of the teachers or principal inquired about any of the possible causal factors surrounding the behavior. As human beings we are often quick to judge "wrong" behavior without really knowing—without really listening or trying to understand the underlying causes.

An eye for an eye approach did not help me verbalize what was going on in my life or in my inner world. Gandhi said; "an eye for an eye makes everyone blind." I don't think I could admit or take responsibility for my behavior at ten, because the interventions gave me a reason to turn a "blind eye." Even if teachers did take the time to understand what was going on with me, bullying behavior should not be tolerated. Meaningful consequences should be imposed if the bully has any chance of taking responsibility or realize the impact the behavior has on others. As professional educators we must come to understand bullying as a dynamic. The behaviors and roles involved in this dynamic are clues—red flags—keys to unlocking critical information. This information could possibly hold the potential for antidotal growth—not just for the bully, but for the target(s), the bystander(s), the family, and even the entire school community.

When youth or adults bully, it's because they want something—power, control, to feel better, meaningful attention, listened to, taken seriously, etc. They may also be trying to undo or redo something that happened to them that precipitated the present behavior. Any behaviors that denigrate, humiliate, or harm another—to make someone feel "less than"—is a cry for a human experience to fulfill certain needs. With a comprehensive and systematic view, we must look through a compassionate lens to truly see and understand the bullying dynamic. Effective responses along with appropriate consequences from teachers makes all the difference—yes, in the world!

WRIGHT

Please say more about the bullying dynamic and taking a comprehensive and systematic view.

DILALLO

Bullying by nature is insidious and students tend to keep what I call "Covert Contracts"—the result of all three roles converging in a mysterious and inconspicuous way. The thrill is in going underground with this behavior and flying under any watchful radar. This is what makes the bullying dynamic so pervasive and dangerous.

Bullying always involves at least three roles—bully, target (victim), and an active or passive bystander. Wherever there is a bully, there is at least one target and possibly many other active and passive bystanders. An active bystander gains satisfaction by instigating a situation, but the bully enacts the offending behaviors. Active bystanders also keep the flames fanned on any bully initiated behaviors. The passive bystanders see what's going on, but have no intention of getting involved. Passive bystanders keep a code of silence and take no responsibility for not speaking up. It's not uncommon for the three of these roles to be interchangeable.

THE BULLYING TRIANGLE

WRIGHT

With the school situations you shared, how could adults been more effective?

DILALLO

One of the keys to an effective response is to eliminate punitive punishment. At ten, being hit by authorities did not give me useful tools or help me gain the confidence I needed to handle life situations appropriately. It only made me fearful, angry, and recalcitrant—a stance that made me feel entitled to take things out on my classmates. What I needed, but didn't know at the time, was help in making a connection between my behavior and how the behavior is a violation of my classmates' personal wellbeing—a human rights violation. I also needed healthy modeling and guidance toward a menu of alternative approaches to dealing with interpersonal and intrapersonal struggles.

A second key to effective response is for professional educators to take a serious look at how they respond to bullying incidents. The old expedient ways of dealing with bullying cannot be an option. As educators and even parents, it's critical that we control our own visceral reactions. Depending on the default button on our judgmental control panel, we often want to "teach the bully a lesson" or "have the victim stop being a tattletale" and everything in between. In doing so we neglect to understand there is more to bullying than meets the eye. A negative pervasive ripple is caused when we react to student behaviors— modeling for them inappropriate ways of handling difficult situations. An effective teacher response is imperative in breaking the bullying cycle. When students "push our buttons" it's good to use a supportive sounding board or even get professional help. We must remember it's o.k. to ask for help.

A third key is for educators to ask the right questions. If the educators in my life intervened properly they would have discovered my bullying behavior didn't originate on the playground. A simple but significant interventional question to ask a child who exhibits bullying behavior is; "Who is or has treated you this way?" I guarantee that 99.9 percent, if not 100 percent of the time, a bully's behavior originates from being a victim of the same or very similar treatment. Carl Jung said; "The healthy man does not torture others— generally it is the tortured who turn into the torturers." A person identified as a "bully" most likely learned this behavior from someone else. In fact, bullies will often mimic similar offending behavior targeted against them. Much of bullying is direct or indirect retaliation to behaviors that have been perpetrated on them—displaced aggression.

Asking the right questions and truly listening, could lead us to a more compassionate response. Please do not misunderstand me here. I am not suggesting we get soft on bullies. We do need to employ appropriate corrective discipline designed to help the bully take responsibility. When we ask; what, why, when, where and how questions we are giving students the opportunity to gain insight, awareness and change behaviors. When we take a look at the bigger picture we are in a better position to understand the underlying causal factors and better determine an effective corrective and formative course of action. This parallel response will give the bully meaningful skills for a lifetime and will more likely ensure social and emotional responsibility.

WRIGHT

Are you willing to share with us where your bullying behavior originated?

DILALLO

Much of the early origins of my behavior and attitude were modeled by my Dad. My father has many talents—cement mason, musician and a good joke teller, to name a few. He also is a veteran of the U.S. Army and served as a Sergeant in Korea during the Korean War. I think his war experience contributed to his being somewhat militant in his fathering. Dad had an angry side to him that made me fearful at times growing up. I don't resent or fault him now, because I know he was the best father he knew how to be at the time. It wasn't until I had four children of my own that I could understand and empathize with the overwhelming responsibility of fathering. Keeping in line with the theory that this behavior occurs in cycles, one could also ask my father the same question, "Who is or has treated you this way?" I am confident he would share his behavior did not originate with him either.

I am very fortunate, because my father and I have worked through our personal history together creating new ways of relating based on mutual respect and love. I am at peace with my father and have forgiven him. I feel very blessed he is alive today and I really enjoy being in his company when we are together.

WRIGHT

I am happy for you and your father that you have a good relationship today.

DILALLO

Thank you David, I appreciate you saying so.

WRIGHT

So, what I hear you saying is that all bullying has a history or story behind the immediate behavior. I also hear you saying we need to pay attention to our responses to bullying, possibly more so than the bullying itself.

DILALLO

Well said David! A percentage of calls I receive from principals and parents are regarding teachers who mishandle or mismanage students in their classrooms. I understand there is a lot of frustration in educating children. However, humiliating or demeaning a student in any way—physically or verbally—doesn't encourage steps to success or promote leadership potential. We can't apply age-old remedies that never worked to an age-old problem that continues to exist in a society that is constantly evolving, and expect to achieve positive results. Holding on to archaic methods of dealing with bullying only disenfranchises people, schools, places of work and possibilities. We must being willing to let go of what we know doesn't work!

Although the school incidents I shared with you were early in my life, it wasn't until later in life that I felt the effects. The power of the seeds educators' plant and the attitudinal harvest these seeds yield for future learning are tremendous. This realization for me was one of the sparks that ignited a passionate flame—a desire to positively influence education and the learning process by working toward eliminating bullying behavior.

WRIGHT

I can understand your concern about the negative consequences regarding any teacher that might verbally mistreat a student, but corporal punishment is a thing of the past, isn't it?

DILALLO

I wish that were true David. Although I share my story with you decade's later, but corporal punishment by some educators are still relevant today. According to the U.S. Department of Education 2006 Civil Rights Data Collection, there were over 220,000 uses of corporal punishment in public school districts in the United States. From this projected number, its estimated corporal punishment was used with approximately 78 percent of males and 22 percent of the females.

With increasing academic standards, I often consult with teachers who are frantically trying to meet these rigorous standards. At the same time there are a percentage of students showing up to class with less free attention to learn for a variety of reasons. As a result, teachers have to take up valuable class time trying to manage their classrooms. This menacing combination of teachers and students feeling academic pressures, along with students' having less free attention, are a slippery slope of ambivalence, ambiguity and even chaos in the classroom.

During our "No Child Left Behind" era, children are in fact being left behind. About one-third of our students aren't graduating from high school—one-third that do graduate aren't going on to college and only one-third who do graduate from high school go on to college. The current academic standards are much too data driven and as a result we are not effectively educating children on how to learn or in practical life skills. Our country has to take a serious look at reforming a broken educational system if we want to increase performance standards and compete globally.

Just like our educational system, the bullying problem requires innovative approaches that empower schools, families and communities to higher standards. With old and new forms of bullying continually on the rise; educators, parents, and students are faced with enormous learning and performance challenges. Innovative approaches must include effective yet meaningful corrective and formative approaches. There is also a necessity for cutting edge professional development and a willingness on the part of educational systems to "try on" new approaches.

WRIGHT

Was there a particular "a-ha" moment that led you down this anti-bullying path?

DiLALLO

Undeniably. There was a very remarkable event in my life that touched me to the core. My first real awareness of a personal energetic charge or "a-ha" moment around bullying was when I attended one of my initial educational trainings on classroom management over twenty years ago. The presenter discussed the bullying dynamic and played a song by singer/song writer, Lee Domann, titled "Howard Gray."

While listening to the lyrics about boys involved in a bullying triangle, I felt a strong personal connection to the story and flashed back to my own history of being a bully in grade school. At that cathartic moment, I sobbed and felt a deep remorse and responsibility for how I had treated others in my past. I consider this moment to be a spiritual breakthrough that heightened my awareness around bullying and the pain experienced by all involved—target, bystander, and bully.

I have been using the "Howard Gray" lyrics in my presentations with students for over ten years. I have since had several opportunities to speak with Lee on the phone about how much his lyrics have inspired me and still do today. In fact, the Howard Gray song was my inspiration for writing; The Code of Silence—a poem about my involvement in a middle school bullying triangle. I would like to share it with you if I may.

WRIGHT
    Please do.

DILALLO
THE CODE OF SILENCE
It was an ordinary day not much different from all the rest
Eric, Tommy, and Frankie in seventh grade, taking a different kind of test
Tommy is tall, thin, and picked on by most of the class
Eric, short, stout, lots of hot air and a voice full of brass
Frankie is tall, strong with less brain and more brawn
Always trying to prove he's better than, trying to make everyone his pawn
The three boys find themselves in the restroom at Guy Middle School
Eric standing in the corner playing it so calm, so cool
with his arms folded and leaning back against the cold block wall
Frankie and Tommy standing in front of an unfriendly bathroom stall
Suddenly tension mounts and Eric shouts in a loud sarcastic tone
"We should hit Tommy and do whatever we can to make him moan!"
He shouted even louder, "We don't like Tommy, we don't like his kind!"
The tension was high and like a puppet possessed, Frankie lost his mind
He began to hit Tommy in the upper right arm; he hit him with all his might
Tommy stood stiff trying not to flinch even an inch, not wanting to show any fright
Eric got louder and louder, "Hit him harder!" he yelled, while counting every blow
Just like a movie director this active bystander was surely running the show
"We don't like odd numbers," as he counted along with hit number five
"We don't like even numbers," taunting and provoking to keep this insanity alive
Tommy didn't do anything, he never fought back; he never even muttered a word
Why didn't he do something to stand up for himself? How strange, how absurd
Somehow, some way, this frightful bullying triangle came to a screeching halt
Three boys in a restroom, just an ordinary day, who would you say is at fault?
Three boys casually walking out of this nightmare and back to class just shows
The code of silence, not telling, is so very strong, because no one else knows
The bully, bystander, and target will forever keep this shadowy secret and shame
All three boys will never forget the damage done; they will always feel the pain
Many, many years have gone by and you would think this would all just go away
But every decision we make and how we treat another is always here to stay

Every hurtful action, every hurtful word, leaves a lasting imprint on others
Why not treat everyone with respect, dignity; like equal sisters and brothers?
Just like an etching in granite, what kind of impression do you want to make?
We only have one life to live, so treat yourself and others well for God's sake
Everyone deserves our very best, no matter what their beliefs or color of their face
Treat others with kindness, love, and respect, because we are all one in this human race

WRIGHT

That was very powerful! I am very touched. Thank you for sharing it with us.

DiLALLO

You're welcome. Thank you for listening.

WRIGHT

I'm curious. Does bullying always impede the learning process?

DiLALLO

Bullying does not have to become an impediment to learning. In fact, we can use the bullying dynamic as a teachable moment—a wonderful opportunity to teach new skills and learn critical life lessons. We cannot expect students to know how to effectively handle the multitude of life circumstances thrown at them. However, we must be equipped to creatively and effectively handle the myriad of difficult situations that show up in and out of the classroom—to teach and prepare students for what lies ahead. This requires specific training for educators, students and parents to work together to help each other. Part of this training should be to incorporate practice opportunities in relevant life skills to effectively make them "stick" for students and adults. Practice makes perfect!

WRIGHT

What solutions would you suggest to help educators positively address the bullying phenomenon?

DiLALLO

As I researched available programs, I could not find anything that effectively addressed bullying the way I envisioned. Some efforts take a top down approach— meaning there is a heavy reliance on policies and procedures to deter bullying behavior. Other approaches are highly informative for adults and helpful in identifying bullying behavior, but lack student involvement. I found programs that do involve students to be weak on skill building and often only emphasize a rigorous reporting mechanism. Many of the existing programs seem to hold biases, placing heavy emphasis on one of the three roles instead of addressing the dynamic of the entire bullying triangle.

Aspects of all of these elements are important; however bullying cannot exist with one person and cannot be remedied by focusing on any one role. It is not uncommon in the bullying dynamic for the roles to be interchangeable. The bully, target, and bystander each have a responsibility in this "3-D" exchange between the roles.

Peace2U: Three Phase Bullying Solution was developed out of a need for effective response with the schools I serve and beyond. Drawing on my personal and professional experiences, I wanted to develop a program that would immerse students in a process that was both practical and meaningful.

Over a ten-year period my response to bullying has evolved into three sequential themes or phases. Each phase contains a host of skill sets essential to transforming the bullying dynamic and creating a positive school climate.

The key phases are as follows:
1. Leadership (social responsibility)
2. Interpersonal Skill Development (supportive peer relationships)
3. Intrapersonal Skill Development (building internal assets)

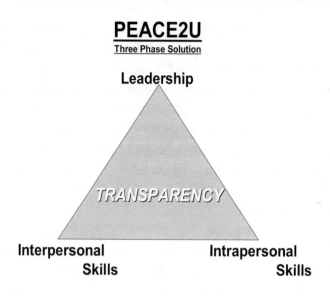

PEACE2U

Three Phase Solution

Leadership

TRANSPARENCY

Interpersonal
Skills

Intrapersonal
Skills

WRIGHT

Will you describe each of the phases for us?

DiLALLO

I'd be glad too. Phase One sets the bar on what it means to be socially responsible, with an emphasis on positive leadership. Leadership is introduced as simply how we treat ourselves and others—the Golden Rule. When we frame leadership in this manner, I believe we are all called to do the right thing. If we treat each other with dignity and respect, we all have the power to positively influence our environment. With practice this concept translates from creating the school of our dreams—to having the life of our dreams and an even more expansive vision of being a positive influence in the world.

The initial lessons in this phase explore the "leadership myth"—the faulty belief that leadership is about position, title, status, rank, and what is "popular." If students or adults hold this belief, one of the consequences is a community of disenfranchised people who give away their power to others. Assuming a degree of "better than/less than" exists in every organization or institution, a proportionate level of passivity and inaction also exists. Unless students and adults come to believe they have influence over their environment, they will passively accept the way things are and/or blame others—teachers, principals, work supervisors, etc. This phase empowers those engaged in the process to shift from a faulty belief about leadership to perceiving themselves as leaders with the power to influence their environment.

WRIGHT

What's an example of a skill building activity in Phase One?

DILALLO

One of the very first challenges is an exercise I developed called: "Who Me? A Leader?" When asked to stand if they are a leader, usually only a small fraction of students' stand up. When asked why they are standing or sitting, student responses are very telling about their perceptions of what it means to be a leader. Students stand describe being on student council or in athletics. Some don't even know why they stood up. Those sitting don't stand because they aren't on student council or an athlete or because they are more comfortable sitting. I take the latter both literally and figuratively. It's easier to be a follower.

What I have found over the years is that students rarely volunteer positive leader qualities or characteristics they can identify in themselves. There responses are usually around position, title, status, rank or popularity. The leads very nicely into a brainstorming session of positive qualities and characteristics around leadership. Most groups come up with twenty to thirty or more words describing what it means to be a positive leader. Out of thousands of leader words compiled over the years, the top five are: Courageous, Sense of Humor, Trustworthy, Respectful and Responsible.

The exercise continues by taking the student generated list and contrasting it with a list of words and feelings students describe regarding how they treat each other. This simple exercise reveals a startling discrepancy between the current reality—how students currently treat each other, with the positive leader words—how we all want to be treated. This revelation produces the necessary dissonance and dissatisfaction with the current state—creating enough requisite tension to make it very compelling for students to want to make a change. During this phase students begin to realize how they treat others has a rippling effect in the classroom, school, community, and in the world.

Students are actively involved in Phase One with a number of experiential processes to unmask the bullying dynamic through role-play scenarios. The latter are counterbalanced with Positive Behavior Rehearsal—practicing constructive responses to real-life bullying situations they may face. A very powerful part of this phase is when two real stories: "Howard Gray" and "The Code of Silence," are shared with students. These revealing stories of two separate bullying incidents, describe the long term consequences of bullying. The objective is to sensitize students to how bullying has a rippling affect that continues to swell even after the incident.

At the end of the session, students are again asked to stand if they see themselves as leaders. All students usually stand the second time around with the understanding that they are taking a stand to create a new reality with each other. A sense of unity is activated, along with a positive collective norm for a higher standard of expected behavior—a higher purpose. A profound shift happens among students when they become witnesses to the collective transformation. It's very exciting to see this unfold during this phase.

WRIGHT

What is the central theme of Phase Two?

DILALLO

Phase Two establishes a safe classroom milieu to help build bridges between students. Students experientially learn essential interpersonal skill sets and how to hold each other accountable for commitments made during the process. Helping students safely identify what's getting in the way of their being supportive and affirming with one another is a major objective. With a series of trust-building exercises, a safe container in the form of a circle is established preparing students to make amends and build positive relationships with each other in real time.

This interpersonal experience transpires in an exciting communal process, which I think is what sets this program apart from any other anti-bullying program on the market.

WRIGHT

Describe how the process builds safety?

DiLallo

One of the first activities during this phase is called a "Safety Check." It's a process establishing a simple baseline marker around physical, mental, emotional, social and spiritual safety in the classroom. Students are guided to look at how safe or unsafe they currently feel—Current Reality— and to imagine how safe they could actually become with each other—Desired Result. Students are asked to silently determine a personal number on a continuum from zero being the least safe to ten being the safest. The number chosen is their best representation of how safe they feel with their classmates.

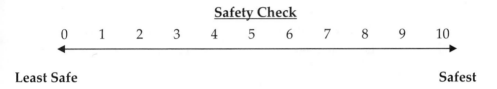

Safety Check

| 0 | 1 | 2 | 3 | 4 | 5 | 6 | 7 | 8 | 9 | 10 |

Least Safe   **Safest**

When students are asked to reveal their number, usually the full range from zero to ten is represented in the room. The contrast of high and low numbers is a stark realization for students. The bottom line is glaringly apparent—not all students are a "ten" on the continuum. This exercise alone creates enough dissonance and tension to motivate participants toward resolution.

Students are encouraged to look at how we often act as if we are all on individual islands—not needing anyone. Being responsible to others causes us to shift to a deeper understanding that we are all on the same planet. We cannot exist separate from each other. In spite of our differences, we have a choice to live in harmony or disharmony with each other on our relatively small planet.

The Safety Check is used again at the close of the phase two session. Students redo the Safety Check by juxtaposing their baseline number with a new number that often emerges as a result of the phase two experience. As students reveal their new number—which is usually anywhere from 1-5 or more points toward the goal—it clearly demonstrates they collectively have the power to create a new reality. It is very common for students to make a personal shift toward the ideal ten, even with vicarious involvement in the process. This very simple marker has a profound impact and creates a language and new norm of safety and accountability among students.

WRIGHT

What's the goal of Phase Two?

DILALLO

There are a number of goals in this phase, but the first goal is to use the process to; "help myself and others get to a ten." This helps students build in a way to measure personal and community successes. When we feel safe physically, mentally, emotionally, socially and spiritually we can also thrive in all of these areas as well. The process helps students shift from "my success is your loss" or "your loss is my success" to "my success is your success" and "your success is my success." Another goal is to increase social and emotional intelligences. The ultimate goal is to build community, which results in raising student confidence in making harmonious choices in their relationships with each other and beyond.

WRIGHT

Does the process include a way for students to work out conflicts with each other?

DILALLO

This is my favorite part of the process. One critical ingredient I found lacking in most programs is a constructive and healthy way for students to work out conflicts or repair relationships. I conducted peer mediation trainings for many years and although there are many useful skills, I found the process to be lacking for schools. In mediation you have two disputants and two mediators who can never truly resolve the conflict, because conflict doesn't only impact two people. There are many more bystanders aware of the conflicts, who are either actively or peripherally involved.

To single out any one of the roles or place any two of the roles together to "work it out" is splintered and incomplete at best. It is essential for each role to be involved in the process in order for this shadowy dynamic to come to light. I borrowed the most useful elements from mediation and designed what I think is a much more powerful approach called "Clear Talk." The success of this reparative approach occurs in the context of a communal experience.

Diffusing or transforming the bullying dynamic needs someone from the triangulation to courageously step up with a desire for change. Usually one of the roles will initiate taking a risk to step into the circle. This step is a huge leap for transparency. When risks are taken that model this kind of leadership, students will also start to take risks to support one another. As a result a positive peer culture begins to emerge.

Phase Two creates a laboratory experience for students to safely practice leadership and interpersonal skills. The safe container supports and encourages honesty, openness and courage to transform existing peer abuse. Shifting the responsibility to the classroom community creates transparency to help eliminate Covert Contracts. The bullying triangle is always lose/lose/lose, so the ultimate outcome must be a win/win/win. The bullying dynamic cannot exist in an atmosphere of trust, integrity, and accountability. The Phase Two process establishes the necessary conditions essential for a positive school climate to foster and grow. The sustainability of this community shift depends on the mutual benefit for each role to exit the bullying dynamic.

WRIGHT

Is there a problem getting the bully and victim in the same room?

DILALLO

There are many experts who would say to not get the victim and the bully in the same room. I would agree a bully and victim should not be isolated in a room with each other. However, the reality is they are most likely in the same room or rooms with each other all day. Short of transferring to another school and recreating a similar dynamic; targets need support, tools and other resources. A target is capable of learning how to deal with these situations—and must if they are to feel any power of influence over their environment. The reason I prefer to use the term target rather than victim, is a target has choices and can acquire the necessary skills to not become a victim.

The Phase Two process has safely had students who were considered very passive demonstrate awe inspiring courage for other students. This process has also successfully had identified bullies voluntarily step forward to make heartfelt amends with targets and bystanders. A profound shift occurs when a bully—who has a lot of influence in the class—models positive leadership qualities. I have even witnessed bullies weep with remorse. When this happens it is a miracle to behold. Teachers, administrators and students are profoundly affected by this communal experience.   I feel honored and blessed to have witnessed many of the transformations that occur for adults and students.

WRIGHT

What is Clear Talk?

DILALLO

Effective communication is an essential social emotional skill set that cannot effectively be learned from a book or from role plays. Clear Talk is an exciting five-step communication process that occurs in real time in Phase Two—making it safe for students to communicate within a structured and meaningful approach. Engaging in a real time process is an incredible way for students to integrate a lifelong skill. Although Clear Talk is an essential communication tool all students can learn, it is not necessarily the five steps that make the process so powerful—it's the communal experience that unfolds as a result. During the process students become more aware of and responsible to others. The result is existing divisions begin to melt away, trust increases, and relationships are strengthened.

WRIGHT

Will you give us an example of what the five-step process looks like?

DILALLO

I'd be happy to. The process begins when a student invites another student to enter the community circle to do Clear Talk. The safety created in the beginning of the process prepares students to take this step. There are one of two ways the initiating person can enter the circle: One, they have harmed this person and want to make amends or two, this person has harmed them and Clear Talk is an opportunity to make him/her to feel safe with this person—help him/herself and others progress to a 10 on the safety continuum.

Let's say the "target" asks the "bully" into the center of the circle to do Clear Talk. The five-step process is as follows:

One: "Thank you!"

The target thanks the bully for his/her willingness to step into the circle. Manners are important, but this first step goes beyond manners and sets an intention or spirit of gratitude, honor and respect—not blame. Part of this step is to teach about the sacredness and dignity of every human being.

Two: Data

What happened? The person initiating the process reports the facts around something or some things that happened between the two parties causing the conflict.

Three: Feelings

How do I feel about what happened? We often do not discuss our feelings openly, mostly out of self protection. Managing and reporting feelings is an important step toward building social and emotional intelligences. Five basic feelings are introduced as possible options to share with the listener—mad, sad, glad, afraid, and ashamed.

Four: "My [your] behavior said_____."

Although subjective in nature, this is an important step toward building observation skills, as well as giving and accepting feedback.

Five: Wants

The way I treated you or how you treated me is not working. In this step I state how I want to be treated or how I will treat you from this day forward. When we can clearly identify and state behavioral specifics about ways I want and don't want to be treated, follow through by both parities is more likely.

During "Clear Talk" the person invited into enter the center of the circle actively listens. When the speaker is finished, the listener goes through each step paraphrasing the speaker. Paraphrasing one step at a time makes listening very manageable. The listener can "Clear" with the speaker if need be and the process maintains the same sequential structure without deviation until both parties are complete. Most Clear Talks only take a few minutes, but have long lasting results.

Clear Talk can be measured by juxtaposing the original Safety Check number with a new Safety Check number following the completion of the process. Students around the circle are both actively and passively involved in the process—directly practicing and/or vicariously learning communication tools, how to give supportive feedback and how to hold their peers accountable. The communal process helps jump start a common vision for the school of their dreams.

WRIGHT

Will you share a success story with us in utilizing the five-step process?

DILALLO

David, the stories I am privy to when students use Clear Talk to get through difficult situations are what touch my heart's core. The power and healing difference I see this process making is what fuels my mission.

I have many success stories, but there is one in particular I would like to share with you. A student (Brent) entered the circle to do Clear Talk with one of his classmates (Jake). As he was going through the five-step process, I noticed Brent kept saying "we" treated you (Jake) this way. I found myself interrupting Brent, with some frequency, about owning his behavior and encouraged him to use "I" statements instead. As the process unfolded, I realized that, although it was important for Brent to own his behavior, his persistently using the pronoun "we" was significant as well.

When both Brent and Jake indicated they were "complete," I asked them for permission to take their Clear Talk process a step further. Both boys agreed. I said to Brent, "I noticed you said 'we' a lot when you shared the data (Step Two) of how you treated Jake and you probably noticed how much I interrupted you." He agreed. I then turned to the circle and asked that any student who believed he or she had ever mistreated Jake to please stand behind Brent. I suspected one or two students would probably stand behind him but I was wrong. All but four of the thirty students present stood behind Brent.

I have students use a "talking stick" during Clear Talk. I placed the stick on the ground to visibly represent the "invisible" line drawn between Jake and the rest of the students standing behind Brent. I then asked the students if they were aware of the division they had created between themselves and Jake. Students were aware of isolated incidents (covert contracts), but for them to visually experience the culmination of their actions was profound. I asked Jake how he felt being on the other side of the line—disconnected from his peers. He admitted feeling empty, sad, lonely, depressed, angry, and even suicidal at times.

As Jake shared this, many of the students on the opposite side of the line began to cry. This is the very first time the students collectively felt the enormity and gravity of the situation and how they were all directly responsible for another person's pain.

I asked the students what needed to happen in order for them to make this right with Jake. The students decided they would each do Clear Talk with Jake. Of course this took a while, but they may have saved a life—or at least a lifetime of pain. When each student finished, they all spontaneously circled around Jake as a gesture of support and said, "We've got your back!"

Witnessing the students make a shift from division and exclusion to a new social norm of inclusion and acceptance was nothing short of a miracle. They had in fact, co-created a new reality together. One of the female students commented with joyous surprise that before this she just accepted the negative treatment of Jake as "just the way it was going to be all year and nothing would change it." Following up with Jake in the next session, he was all smiles and said things had radically changed for the better.

WRIGHT

What an incredible transformation for these students!

DILALLO

It truly was a magical moment.

WRIGHT

What's involved with the third phase of your program?

DILALLO

The third phase acknowledges the accelerated speed or our world and how it discourages healthy human interaction. This cultural pace has become normative and easy for us to get out of balance. It's as if we are rushing around like hamsters on a treadmill—very busy, but where are we going? We can become irritable, agitated, less tolerant, impatient, mean, nasty, rude, angry, frustrated, and so on—all red flags that we are doing too much. The consequence of an accelerated pace is the tendency to disconnect from ourselves and push others away with our intolerance.

With the increase in technology, social emotional learning is more important than ever before. As we interact with our technology, we interact less with each other. One could argue that technology is actually increasing opportunities to interact with others. On the surface this is true; however, it cannot replace the biological need for face-to-face contact. The more time I spend looking at my computer screen, iPhone, or BlackBerry, the less time I spend looking in your eyes and interacting on a human level. This is wreaking havoc in our relationships. As a culture we are consuming a tremendous amount of cognitive information on a daily basis, but emotionally we are bankrupt when it comes to connecting on a face-to-face and heart-to-heart level in our relationships. A crude analogy would be a person who drinks a lot of beer or eats a lot of junk food will feel full, but lacks proper nutritional value with this kind of fullness.

Taking care of our intrapersonal life and listening to our heart is more critical today than ever. When we don't listen to our heart or take care of ourselves, we are more likely to take our imbalances out on someone. How we treat ourselves and others causes either a positive or negative ripple to happen in our environment. The direction we take and the kind of ripple we make is our choice. When we follow a healthy inner regimen, we are more likely to treat others well.

Unfortunately, our culture in many ways does not support the notion of slowing down, let alone taking a look inside. More awards and accolades are given for ones busyness than for being mindful of one's inner life. Looking inside is not a popular or common approach in a culture based on external rewards and immediate gratification. Success is frequently defined by our culture in terms of wealth and outward appearances.

WRIGHT

Do you think this accelerated pace and technology has anything to do with cyber or techno-bullying on the rise?

DILALLO

I'm afraid so David. Technology for the most part is relatively safe and efficient. Evolving into a global society, the world only gets "smaller." Rapidly expanding technologies bring us in closer contact with one another 24/7. As we pour large chunks of time into a growing field of electronic social networking, such as Facebook and Twitter, we become techno-hermits—lack human face-to-face connection. Not seeing facial expressions desensitizes us to each other's emotional responses during electronic interactions—making it an easy and "safe" way to lash out at others. This ever present downside brings the potential for cruelty, deception and harm which can take technology to dangerous levels.

I have intervened on a number of situations where students have set up hate websites or used technology in other ways, such as sexting to seriously harm others. Youth naively don't understand that once they click "send" they can never take it back. Interestingly enough, I recently became aware of a situation where technology was used by two female students to avoid having to work out a conflict face-to-face. The counselor became aware of the conflict and invited the two girls into her office to work it out. The girls said they couldn't work it out face-to-face, but if the counselor would let them go into separate rooms they could text message each other and work it out that way.

Technology is presenting some very complicated moral and ethical challenges. As experts diligently work to figure out proven approaches to address bullying behavior, old and new forms of bullying continue to rear their ugly heads. Technology has morphed bullying into new extremes and at levels so severe, even a single incident can collaterally involve an unprecedented number of people.

WRIGHT

What skill sets or techniques are encouraged in this phase?

DILALLO

Phase Three is an experiential opportunity for students to find a peaceful place inside themselves. The process is packed with stress management techniques and other exercises. The objective is to help us learn how to slow down our inner world and take time to look inside. The world is probably not going to slow down anytime soon—so while the world continues to accelerate developing these skills is essential to our wellbeing.

I included an audio CD titled *The Peace Project*, a stress management CD—as an accompaniment to assist facilitators during this phase. This CD was not designed to start an anti-war movement or teach students to become "peace activists." Phase Three is not about exploring our outer stratosphere—it's a mission headed in a much different direction—exploring the inner stratosphere, encouraging students to become "inner-activists."

As we take daily steps to journey inward, we discover our true nature and the unique treasure trove of gifts and talents we are all born with. By taking these courageous steps inward, our authentic gifts become positively visible, touching and transforming those around us. The journey inward is what it truly means to be a bold and successful leader! By teaching students how to pause, we are helping them learn more about how to lead a balanced life—giving them essential tools to become positive leaders in creating a safe school climate and a safe world.

Intrapersonal skill development is cause for pause. Adults and youth need time to relax, reflect, unwind, and do nothing, which is almost unheard of today. Taking care of our inner life is a lifelong adventure and *The Peace Project* and *Peace2U* offer a number of "inner-activities" to help. Students come to realize when they go to a peaceful place inside; it is easier to be compassionate with themselves and others. Effective well-adaptive approaches can happen in unlimited ways however, phase three concentrates on progressive relaxation, reflection, visualization, positive affirmations and a variety of thought and heart provoking exercises.

WRIGHT

How did *The Peace Project* come about?

DILALLO

The Peace Project CD was inspired by the tragic, unfortunate, and preventable string of school related shootings and other violence, most notably, Columbine High School. Just one year before the April 1999 tragedy. I was transitioning into my current consulting position from the position at the high school. Being immersed in a high school setting for eight years, I could only imagine what it would be like for students, teachers, administrators, parents, and emergency responders to have gone through such a horrific ordeal.

After feeling depressed for several months, I decided my state of mind was not helpful for me or schools. I shifted my question of "Who is going to do something about this?" to "What can I do to help the situation and make a difference?" Looking back, I realized that by reframing the question, I allowed myself to be open to different results—a new focus and more productive results.

Following a period of reflection, it occurred to me that I could make an audio recording based on feedback I received from hundreds of presentations on the stress topic. *The Peace Project* audio CD became on culmination of practical information and practice—a stress management tool for youth and adults.

I knew producing the CD had the potential for mass appeal and signification, but I really didn't think at the time it would have much impact. Initially, I was only interested in two things: 1) Shaking my own feelings of helplessness about school violence, and 2) Making some kind of contribution toward eliminating the problem—no matter what size audience. To my surprise, when *The Peace Project* was released in July 2001, two months prior to 9/11, it took on a life of its own. Hundreds of students, educators, counselors, and parents in the United States and around the world are using the CD with great success.

WRIGHT

What is the basic premise behind the audio CD?

DiLALLO

Stress affects every aspect of our lives—ranging from mild to severe. When our stress is high and unmanaged we are likely to be impatient, irritable, easily frustrated, "short-fused," cranky, irritable, grouchy, and so on. I believe there is a link between stress and a whole host of maladaptive coping strategies. Maladaptive coping is an ineffective attempt to get immediate relief through the use of alcohol or other drugs, cutting, cavalier sexual experiences, bullying behavior, and any other behavior that is a health or safety risk to self or others. When our stress is unmanaged and we are out of balance and our performance suffers.

The CD provides a variety of helpful techniques in hope that one or more of these techniques will become a life skill. Practicing the techniques with some frequency will help with leading a more balanced life. By managing our stress and being in balance, we are more likely to be patient, respectful, compassionate and loving, resulting in a positive ripple within and around us. We are also more likely to get to peak performance, even "flow."

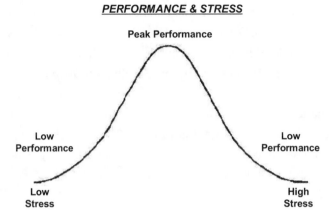

PERFORMANCE & STRESS

Peak Performance

Low
Performance

Low
Performance

Low
Stress

High
Stress

WRIGHT

What are your hopes for the future of education?

DILALLO

My hope is that educators continue to explore this incredible frontier of using technology to enhance old approaches and create new approaches to learning. These are some exciting times, to say the least. If we only focus on this direction, however, I fear more dehumanization and desensitization is on the horizon. The key is to balance technology with a conscious awareness of how critical face-to-face connection is to the human condition.

Mindful awareness of our humanity will give meaning and purpose to technology. The challenging frontier of technology also brings about other new and exciting challenges with regard to how we teach social emotional literacy and social responsibility. These explorations are vital to the human spirit. I want to feel confident in my lifetime that I have contributed to this vital and delicate balance.

WRIGHT

I have no doubt your efforts are contributing to a more peaceful planet.

DILALLO

Thank you David.

WRIGHT

Your lifelong philosophy is that success is more of an inward journey. Will you share with us what your own personal marker is for success?

DILALLO

David, I appreciate your asking this question, because just like the word "love," I think the word "success" has become watered down—trite, and has lost significance and meaning.

I'm successful by being mindful of my humanness—I cannot exist separate from you. I'm successful by living my life with passion and strive to exemplify what it means to be a positive leader, firmly upholding such virtues as; cooperation, patience, tolerance, kindness, and compassion. Success is when I am mindful of my relationships and my responsibility to consider others in everything I say and do. I'm successful when I know with confidence that everyone has a personal life story and it is our collective stories that connect us all and give us meaning. I'm successful when I do what I can to build bridges where there are divisions and work toward being a catalyst to shift to a worldwide community of stories in a shared effort to heal and help meet the needs of all people. I'm successful when I can daily look inward and search for truth—finding a deeper and a more spiritual meaning to answering the questions; Who am I?, Why am I here? and Where am I going?

My life is filled with deep gratitude and many blessings when I remain focused and connected to what's most important—maintaining balance in mind, body, and spirit. This includes a daily regimen of prayer, meditation, exercise, and proper diet. My relationship with my wife, four children, extended family, and close friends and meaningful work are what nourish and sustain me. My relationships help me expand beyond my limited thinking and deepen my faith in a good and gracious God. I pray that *Peace2U* **Solutions** are worthwhile contributions toward creating a peaceful and harmonious world.

Again David, I am deeply honored to have had this opportunity to share some thoughts and ideas in this forum. Many blessings on this book and all those who have so generously contributed their time and talents, as well as all those who choose to read it. Peace2U!

WRIGHT

Thank you Frank for sharing your expertise with us. Peace2U as well.

ABOUT THE AUTHOR

Frank A. DiLallo founded Counseling & Training Services, providing counseling and consultation services to schools with bullying and other obstacles to academic success. He is author of the book titled: *Peace2U: Three Phase Bullying Solution* and creator of *The Peace Project*; an audio stress management program.

For thirty years, Frank has counseled individuals, couples, groups and families. He has also conducted countless professional development trainings for educators and counselors on a variety of topics.

Frank is dedicated to eliminating bullying behavior and is in demand being called upon to prevent or intervene in schools. He is a frequent public speaker and trainer in both public and private sectors.

Frank received a B.A. in sociology from Adrian College in 1980 and a M.Ed. in Guidance & Counseling from the University of Toledo in 1982. He holds licensure in Ohio as a Professional Counselor and Independent Chemical Dependency Counselor and is certified as a Prevention Specialist II.

Married to Michelle and father of three sons and a daughter, Frank wants all children to do well. He enjoys time with family, hiking, and being a lifelong learner.

FRANK A. DILALLO
Counseling & Training Services
peace2usolutions@yahoo.com
www.peace2usolutions.com

CHAPTER TEN

How to be Heard and How to Listen:
Conversations with Your Aging Parents

An Interview with...

MAUREEN & LARA OSIS

DAVID WRIGHT (WRIGHT)

Today we are talking with Maureen and Lara Osis. They are a mother-daughter creative team from Calgary, Alberta. Maureen is both a Registered Nurse and Marriage and Family Therapist with multiple decades of experience helping families and seniors achieve healthy, balanced aging. She is the co-founder of ElderWise™, a company designed to help Boomers help their aging parents find resources and guidance to solve health, housing, and financial issues. Lara is a writer and editor with over ten years' experience helping ideas crystallize from the brainstorming stage to the finished page. Working together, Maureen and Lara have developed numerous presentations, handouts, and the book, *Your*

Aging Parents. Their recent endeavor was to create a road map for Boomers trying to have sensitive and difficult conversations with their senior parents. This led to the development of SMART conversations, a framework for discussing those hot button emotional issues.

Maureen and Lara, welcome to *Stepping Stones to Success*.

How did each of you develop your interest in "aging?"

MAUREEN OSIS (MAUREEN)

As a young child I did not have many older people in my life. I had only one grandmother who was not very healthy. I observed the respect shown to her by my parents and their willingness to be supportive.

But when I was fifteen our dear neighbor, Minnie, had a stroke. This was long before rehabilitation programs existed. It was also before the days of home care. So Minnie was living in an Auxiliary Hospital when she and her husband decided that a better quality of life was called for. Not having any family of their own, they met with friends and neighbors and designed a plan. I became part of that plan. Minnie's husband was semi-retired and worked from five PM until 9 PM. Several evenings a week after school, I would go to their home, help Minnie with supper, visit with her, and do my homework.

During my homework time, Minnie tried to ask questions about the subject I was studying and we used a variety of means to communicate. We often watched game shows on television and she would try to find the words to answer the questions. We devised a kind of sign language and slowly she learned to speak again. Bette Davis said, "Old age ain't for sissies," and I have to agree with her. Through Minnie, I witnessed her personal strength and determination to regain as much independence as she could.

Later in my work as a gerontological nurse, I met many older adults who survived personal losses and witnessed major changes in society at large. They experienced multiple changes in their bodies and they coped with those changes. They adapted to chronic health problems that developed over their lifetime. And through all of that they found ways to deal with a youth-oriented culture all around them—a culture that can make them feel obsolete, although they still have many gifts to give and a life still in progress.

LARA OSIS (LARA)

There is no way to grow up around my mom and not develop a passion for the two sides of the senior's coin—the unexpected joys of being around people who really will say exactly what they are thinking and have had so many life experiences to comment on, and the flip side of being a generation that gets marginalized, mocked in lots of ways, and told in subtle and not so subtle ways, your time is up. We are a culture that fears death and wants to live as long as possible, yet no one seems to want to get old because we think there is something inherently wrong with being old.

Unlike my mother, I had the great benefit of growing up with many members of my grandparents' generation in my life. They were present at family events and we were included in their lives—they were all so different from each other that I never saw them as a "posse of old people" who were all the same. We had everything from a retired rancher to a world-traveling former home economics teacher and a Catholic priest. I know it sounds like the start of a promising joke, but it was also a great way to connect to individuals from another generation.

WRIGHT

How did you develop your interest in helping the generations to connect and communicate?

MAUREEN

As a nurse, I observed so many situations where family members were disconnected and unable to deal with crises (e.g., Mom had a stroke or Dad was diagnosed with Alzheimer's disease). I realized that these families needed to learn new ways of talking to each other that would help them to work together for mutual support.

As a marriage and family therapist in private practice, I work with older adults and their families. Sometimes colleagues ask me, "Why do you work with old people? Do they ever change?" Far from the stereotype of curmudgeons set in their ways, I have found many seniors have a surprising adaptability to new challenges.

I think that Jim's story shows that seniors still have the ability and insight to change themselves. Jim was a ninety-year-old widower who came to see me.

When I asked him why he'd come for counseling, he said, "My wife died and I had a terrible realization."

"What was that?" I asked him.

He told me that he was the father of two sons. "I have a great relationship with the one son and a terrible relationship with the other." Jim told me he always had an easy time dealing with his younger son, but a terrible time getting along with the eldest son. He paused a moment and then continued, "I never worried about it before my wife died because she got along so well with our firstborn. Now that she's gone, I'm seeing that this isn't right." He nodded his head, "I need to repair this before I die. So I'd like to talk to you about counseling and see what I can do."

I talked to Jim a bit about the process of counseling and we discussed the value of some sessions together. I think it's only fair to see if people have a reasonable expectation of what counseling can do for them and how long it may take, so I asked Jim, "Do you think it will take very long for you to do this work?"

"Well it better not," he said looking a little surprised, "I don't even buy green bananas!" I couldn't help but laugh—who else but someone who has seen ninety years could sum up a situation quite like that?

After two sessions together, Jim decided he would try a meeting with his oldest son. At our next session, I was eager to ask him how things had been between them. "Well," he said, "we are on the road to a new relationship." And he smiled.

In my time as a nurse and now as a therapist, I have seen that older adults are very adaptable. Just think of Jim's willingness to come for counseling when he is part of a generation that thought therapy meant you were "crazy." Think of his willingness to admit that he played a role in his negative relationship with his son. He didn't even try to hide behind the adage, "Father knows best." Jim took responsibility for needing to change and to heal his relationship with his son.

LARA

I would say I have a profound interest in people. I am a close observer of human nature and find people in general endlessly fascinating. I also find myself frustrated by the way misinterpretation, strong unrecognized feelings, and patterns of behavior can set people up for major relationship trouble. Time and again we run our relationships based on assumptions and illusions about what we think of as coded messages from other people. We might think, "Well, she said this, but what did she really mean?" And I think family relationships are the hardest hit by these assumptions—especially when you have one generation, the Boomers, feeling responsible for another generation, their parents, when neither generation feels comfortable with the idea of the one being dependent on the other.

WRIGHT

What gaps exist between grown children (i.e., the Baby Boomers) and their aging parents?

LARA

The common reaction to the term "generation gap" has been to think of parents and their teenagers. But now there is a new generation gap and it is between adults who are fifty to sixty and their parents who are seventy to ninety years old. A generation gap exists because members of different generations have different values about authority, meaning of work, participation in family life, as well as divergent tastes in fads of music and fashion. More importantly, there are significant differences in their attitudes and societal expectations.

Gaps in attitudes:

Seniors think people should save rather than spend money and many do not even have a single credit card, whereas Boomers think life is too short to live without the things credit cards can buy.

Gaps in Societal Expectations:

Society is quick to praise a senior doing well and quick to judge a Boomer when something goes wrong. Frequently people will say, "It's so amazing—he's ninety and still living in his own home." But what they may not know is that the senior has the help of several family members to be able to stay there. And if a senior has a health crisis, Boomers frequently hear, "Why didn't you take care of that?" or "Why didn't you make him go to the doctor?"

These two generations also have major differences in their beliefs about communication. Seniors might have been raised with the adage that "children should be seen and not heard." Thus they learned that the opinions of elders mattered the most. In contrast, the Boomers grew up with a voice that rang loud in society. Whereas their parents might not want to "air their dirty laundry," Boomers believe that anything can be talked about.

WRIGHT

Maureen, what do you want Boomers to know about the senior generation?

MAUREEN

Boomers don't know what they don't know about aging. If you have no experience in the healthcare field or have not spent time with many different seniors, you probably do not know what is normal and what is not. When a parent is having problems, it may be difficult to understand what is happening and what should be done.

One part of my work is devoted to helping the public become more informed about aging. Disease and illness are not inevitable with the aging processes. I want Boomers to be informed about the myths of aging because these stereotypes may lead to uninformed decisions or conflicts between the generations.

One myth is that seniors living in their own homes are taking too much risk. However, most seniors are both willing and able to live on their own and safely make their own decisions. What Boomers need to do is to try to accept that their parents may choose to live with some degree of risk in their daily lives, and that this is okay.

WRIGHT

Lara, what do you want seniors to know about their grown children?

LARA

Boomers are feeling pressured from so many sides. In many cases they are still helping their own children, even in adulthood. Young adult children are living at home for longer periods of time and some are becoming "boomerang kids"—they get launched and then need to return to their parents' home. The economic affect of education, a divorce, single parenthood, or physical and/or mental health problems are reasons that young adults are relying on their parents.

Boomers are still working and trying to find a work/family balance in uncertain economic times, with one eye on a retirement date that, I am sure, feels like it's moving further away rather than getting closer.

I wish seniors could understand that some of the frustration Boomers express is not out of disrespect but out of deep concern. Boomers are very worried about their parents' health and safety, and seniors could listen for that concern and not take it to mean they are being told what to do.

Seniors should never discount the affect their comments can have on their Boomer children. Anything from complaints to compliments can land with great weight on overtaxed Boomers. Seniors could try expressing frustration with the situation rather than with their family members, and remember to express the gratitude they are feeling—it's good for both parties to hear what's going right, not just what's going wrong.

WRIGHT

Maureen and Lara, you have developed a model for open communication in families to bridge the generation gap. Tell us more about having a "SMART conversation."

MAUREEN

The aim of a SMART Conversation is to talk about a difficult subject with honesty and respect to achieve the outcome of serving everyone's best interests. There may never be a perfect time to have one of these difficult conversations; finding both the best time and the right approach can make a difference to "being heard."

WRIGHT

Maureen, what is the first principle of a SMART conversation?

MAUREEN

Set a goal before you *start* the conversation:

What do you want to talk about? What is the problem? For whom is it a problem? What is the best outcome you hope for following the conversation? Is the goal realistic?

And one important thing to remember is that if your goal is to get your parent to do what you want (e.g., quit driving) then you are not very likely to reach that goal. Set a more realistic aim, such as exploring your parent's ideas and trying to get your ideas across as a first step.

After one of my presentations, an audience member came up and said, "So I guess I can't *make* my parents do anything." And that pretty much sums it up. But here are some things that you can do. You can:

- Be clear about your intentions at the outset.
- Know something about the topic—for example, the facts about the risks of older drivers.
- Be specific. Talk about one topic at a time.
- Share the goal: you want to talk *with* your parents, not *at* them.

WRIGHT

Lara, after you have set a goal, what should you do next?

LARA

The next principle is as follows:

Manage your emotions:

Sometimes in talking to our parents we can feel like a kid again. Old issues may resurface. When you feel your parents' health or safety is at stake you may find it impossible to stay calm. You may also want immediate action and think the conversation should be a short one and not give it enough time.

If you have tried to have these talks in the past and they degenerated into fights, you may find yourself reluctant to try again. And when you do talk about health or housing or finances and you don't get the response you want you may feel disappointed, frustrated, or annoyed.

So here are a few tips:

- Try to find mutual interests within the topic.
- Break down the conversation into several parts. Perhaps talk about less contentious issues first or start with something that is meaningful to both of you. This will keep the tension level lower from the beginning.
- Talk to another family member or close friend beforehand to explore your emotional reactions prior to the "real" conversation. Notice how the comments affected you and the other person.

WRIGHT

Lara, you say that the third principle is to accept differences. This sounds like it might be hard to do.

LARA

Accept Differences:

There's a popular expression, "do you want to be right or do you want to happy?" It's the same with any difficult situation where people have very different opinions. But the bottom line is, what are you committed to? Do you want to keep your arms folded across your chest and say, "I know I'm right"? Or are you willing to find common ground and possibly a new solution—one that maybe you hadn't even thought of, once you can accept that your parent may never see things the way you do.

If you want to achieve the goal that you set, you must be prepared to respect different opinions and different styles of managing change. For example, sons and daughters often want parents to move closer—long distances can increase the worry when parents are older or left alone. But seniors might not want to uproot and move to a new community. Friends might be more important for their social wellbeing.

To accept differences requires that you really listen—it requires that you hear someone saying something you don't agree with. This takes energy. Suspend your own judgments when listening. Try to understand your family member's needs, hopes, and fears.

Usually, when we talk about something that is important to us, we want the other person to agree. You might have to agree to disagree—at least for now.

It's common to notice that people do not hear each other, particularly when they are expressing different points of view. Here are some ways to listen actively:

- Show that you are paying attention and make eye contact while listening.
- Pay attention to what is said and what is not said.
- Watch non-verbal signs; watch body language and facial expressions.
- Ask open-ended questions. Yes or no answers won't give you enough information.

WRIGHT

So, you have set a realistic goal, calmed your own emotions, and are prepared to accept differences between your opinion and that of the other person. What is next?

MAUREEN

Next is the R in SMART and it is as follows:

Recognize Responsibility:

Older adults have been making their own decisions for many, many years. When adult children take on more responsibility when parents develop health problems or become frail, it can be tempting to take over—to think that you are "parenting your parents!" And by the way, although I understand the seduction of this way of thinking, when I hear people talking about role reversal it drives me crazy.

Parenting is about helping a developing child to learn to understand the world and to acquire the skills to thrive in that world. It is about helping them learn new things and become functioning members of society. This is not the role for a grown adult with aging parents! Even when a parent has dementia or cognitive problems, you do not become their "parent." You do accept greater responsibility for them (e.g., their safety, financial management, etc.) and you might feel like you are taking care of a child, but it is not your role to discipline them as you would a child or control them "for their own good." Seniors are still autonomous individuals and should be free to make decisions—to the best of their ability.

Many Boomers fear that making any mistakes with their parents' care might have serious consequences. This is not a helpful image to have in your brain and heart when trying to navigate the new waters of helping an aging parent. Boomers need to remember that all they can do is their best.

This brings us to the last principle:

Take time and take turns.

Don't wait for an ideal time, but be ready to talk when an opportunity presents itself. You might also be able to promote an opportunity to talk about a specific topic. Try:

- bringing a newspaper article to read together,

- watching a movie together—and talking about the way the characters managed to handle the situation,
- sending a note ahead of your visit and asking to talk about a specific subject.

Be ready for a casual chat rather than an intense debate. A more casual conversation can allow you to hear more about what your parent is thinking and feeling.

Limit the time—not everything will be resolved all at once or immediately.

Mirroring can also be helpful. Listen to your parent then repeat back what you have heard to be sure you understand. This does not mean you are agreeing with what was said.

Take turns. Be sure to listen as much as you speak.

WRIGHT

Maureen, tell us about situations in which a SMART conversation doesn't work.

MAUREEN

If your parent has acute or chronic mental illness or incapacity, this will complicate the process. If you are too exhausted yourself, you are less likely to be able to listen or willing to accept differences of opinions. Also, there is a continuum of willingness and ability among people. Some people are not willing, while others may not be capable of having a meaningful and respectful conversation. If this happens to you, my advice is do not face it alone—seek professional help.

In summary, a SMART conversation is a process not an event. The goal of a SMART conversation is to talk about a difficult subject with honesty and respect. The outcome is to serve everyone's best interests.

A SMART conversation is based on five principles:

S   set a goal
M   manage your own emotions
A   accept differences
R   recognize responsibility
T   take time and take turns

WRIGHT

How have you used your own advice as a mother-daughter team working together?

MAUREEN

Lara has taught me to appreciate differences—different ideas, values, and opinions. I have also learned that wisdom is not exclusive to those with a certain number of birthdays. Wisdom, in various ways, can occur at all ages and stages of life. Therefore, I have learned humility and curiosity about what I will learn from others, even those who are younger than I am.

Through observing my daughter communicating with others (e.g., with her grandmothers) I have learned more about SMART conversations for myself, especially to "manage my emotions." And if you met Lara, you would know that she models this with a remarkable sense of humor!

LARA

Victor Borge once said the shortest distance between two people is laughter. My mother and I laugh a lot. I think we are also conscientious about listening to each other. As I said earlier, really listening does not mean agreeing, but being heard is a step toward moving forward in any situation. Whether I'm right about making a change to an idea or she's wrong about the direction of a project, we really listen to each other! (Just kidding.) Genuinely, the word that comes to mind is respect. I highly respect my mom and her intelligence and integrity. And I always feel respected by her.

ABOUT THE AUTHORS

MAUREEN OSIS is a registered nurse and marriage and family therapist who has devoted her career to working with seniors and their families. She has been featured on radio, television, and has written many articles and books. Through humor, Maureen encourages audiences to new ways of thinking, supports them in self-reflection, and surprises them with ideas they can immediately put into action. Her topics include "Boomers and their Aging Parents," "Age Denying, Age Defying," "SMART Conversations," and "Wise Enough to say Yes, Strong Enough to say No."

LARA C. OSIS BA is a writer and editor living in Calgary, Alberta. She has had the privilege of working with her mother off and on since the age of fifteen and therefore has truly developed an understanding of family dynamics over time, through firsthand experience, and through the diverse projects on aging and bridging the new generation gap to which she has contributed.

MAUREEN OSIS
Osis Consulting Services Ltd.
59 Glamorgan Drive SW
Calgary, Alberta, Canada, T3E 4Z3
403-246-3178
Fax: 403-246-1770
maureenosis@shaw.ca
www.maureenosis.com

LARA OSIS
403-246-3178
laracosis@shaw.ca

CHAPTER ELEVEN

Develop a Disciplined Life

An Interview with...

Dr. Denis Waitley

DAVID WRIGHT (WRIGHT)

Today we are talking with Dr. Denis Waitley. Denis is one of America's most respected authors, keynote lecturers, and productivity consultants on high performance human achievement. He has inspired, informed, challenged, and entertained audiences for more than twenty-five years from the boardrooms of multi-national corporations to the control rooms of NASA's space program and from the locker rooms of world-class athletes to the meeting rooms of thousands of conventioneers throughout the world.

With more than ten million audio programs sold in fourteen languages, Denis Waitley is the most listened-to voice on personal and career success. He is the author of twelve non-fiction books, including several international bestsellers. His audio album, "The Psychology of Winning," is the all-time best-selling program on self-mastery. Dr. Waitley is a founding director of the National Council on Self-Esteem and the President's Council on Vocational Education. He recently received the "Youth Flame Award" from the National Council on Youth Leadership for his outstanding contribution to high school youth leadership.

A graduate of the U.S. Naval Academy Annapolis, and former Navy pilot, he holds a doctorate degree in human behavior.

Denis, it is my sincere pleasure to welcome you to *Stepping Stones to Success!* Thank you for being with us today.

DENIS WAITLEY (WAITLEY)

David, it's great to be with you again. It's been too long. I always get excited when I know you're going to call. Maybe we can make some good things happen for those who are really interested in getting ahead and moving forward with their own careers in their lives.

WRIGHT

I know our readers would enjoy hearing you talk about your formative years. Will you tell us a little about your life growing up in the context of what you've achieved and what shaped you into the person you are today? Do you remember one or two pivotal experiences that propelled you on the path you eventually chose?

WAITLEY

I believe many of us are redwood trees in a flowerpot. We've become root-bound by our earlier environment and it's up to each of us to realize that and break out of our flower pot if we're going to grow to our full potential.

I remember my father left our home when I was a little boy. He said goodnight and goodbye and suddenly I became the man of the family at age nine. My little brother was only two, so I had to carry him around as my little shadow for the ensuing years. To this day my kid brother has always looked at me as his dad, even though there is only seven years' difference between us. He'll phone me and ask what he should do and I'll tell him, "I'm your brother, not your father!"

Our dad was a great guy but he drank too much and had some habits that took a firm hold on him. He never abused me and always expected more from me than he did from himself. I had a push-pull—on the one hand, I felt inadequate and guilty when I would go to succeed but on the other hand, Dad kept feeding me the idea that he missed his ship and I'd catch mine. The only thing I could do to get out of that roller coaster impact was to ride my bicycle twenty miles every Saturday over to my grandmother's house. She was my escape. I would mow her lawn and she would give me such great feedback and reinforcement. She told me to plant the seeds of greatness as she and I planted our "victory garden" during World War II. She told me that weeds would come unannounced and uninvited—I didn't need to worry about weeds coming into my life, they didn't even need to be watered.

I said, "Wow! You don't have to water weeds?"

"No," she replied, "they'll show up in your life and what you need to do, my grandson, is model your life after people who've been consistent and real in their contribution as role models and mentors."

She also told me that a library card would eventually be much more valuable than a Master Card. Because of my grandmother reading biographies of people who'd overcome so much more than I was going through, I thought, "Wow! I don't have any problems compared to some of these great people in history who really came from behind to get ahead." I think that was my start in life.

I went to the Naval Academy because the Korean War was in force and you had to serve your country, so the best way was to run and hide in an academy. If you earned enough good grades you were put through without a scholarship or without money from your parents. Since my parents didn't have any money, it was a great way to get a college education.

I became a Navy pilot after that and learned that if you simulate and rehearse properly you'll probably learn to fly that machine. But much of it has to do with the amount of practice you put into ground school and into going through the paces. As I gained experience being a Navy pilot, I eventually decided to go on and get my advanced degree in psychology because I wanted to develop people rather than stay in the military. I pursued a program where I could take my military and more disciplined background and put it into human development. That's basically the story.

I earned my doctorate, I met Jonas Salk, and Dr. Salk introduced me to some pioneers in the behavioral field. Then along came Earl Nightingale who heard just a simple taped evening speech of mine and decided that maybe my voice was good enough, even though I was a "new kid on the block," to maybe do an album on personal development, which I did in 1978. It surprised me the most, and everyone else also, that it became one of the bestsellers of all time.

WRIGHT

Being a graduate of Annapolis and having been a Navy pilot, to what degree did your experience in the Navy shape your life and your ideas about productivity and performance?

WAITLEY

David, I think those experiences shaped my life and ideas a great deal. I was an original surfer boy from California and when I entered the Naval Academy I found that surfer boys had their heads shaved and were told to go stand in line— everyone's successful so you're nothing special. I found myself on a team that was very competitive but at the same time had good camaraderie.

I realized that I didn't have the kind of discipline structure in my life that I needed. I also discovered that all these other guys were as talented, or more talented, than I was. What that shaped for me was realizing that the effort required to become successful is habit-forming. I think I learned healthy habits at the Academy and as a Navy pilot just to stay alive. To perform these kinds of functions I really had to have a more disciplined life. That set me on my stage for working more on a daily basis at habit formation than just being a positive thinker only.

WRIGHT

In our book, *Stepping Stones to Success,* we're exploring a variety of issues related to human nature and the quest to succeed. In your best-selling program, *The Psychology of Winning,* you focus on building self-esteem, motivation, and self-discipline. Why are these so crucial to winning and success?

WAITLEY

They're so crucial they're misunderstood. I think especially the term "self-esteem" is misunderstood. We've spent a fortune and we had a California committee on it—we formed the National Council on Self-Esteem. What has happened, in my opinion, is that self-esteem has been misused and misjudged as being self-indulgence, self-gratification—a celebrity kind of mentality. We've put too much emphasis on the wrong idea about self-esteem.

Self-esteem is actually the deep down, inside the skin feeling of your own worth regardless of your age, ethnicity, gender, or level of current performance. It's really a belief that you're good enough to invest in education and effort and you believe some kind of dream when that's all you have to hang onto.

What's happened, unfortunately, is that we've paid so much attention to self-esteem it's become a celebrity and an arena mentality kind of concept. Most people are "struttin' their stuff" and they're celebrating after every good play on the athletic field, whereas, if you're a *real* professional, that's what you do anyway. A real professional is humble, gracious, and understands fans. I think that what we've done is put too much emphasis on asserting one's self and believing that you're the greatest and then talking about it too much or showing off too much in order to make that self-esteem public.

The real self-esteem has two aspects: 1) Believing that you deserve as much as anyone else and that you're worthy. Someone may look at you and tell you they see real potential in you. If you can feel that you have potential and you're worth the effort, that's the first step. 2) The second step is to start doing things to give you confidence so that when you do something and learn something it works out and you'll get the self-confidence that comes from reinforcing small successes. That combination of expectation and reinforcement is fundamental to anyone who wants to be a high achiever. That's what self-esteem is really all about—deserving on the one hand and reinforcing success in small ways to get your motor running and feel the confidence that you can do better than you have been.

Fears crop up and get in the way of our motivation. In my case I was afraid of success. Nobody had ever succeeded in our family and because they hadn't, I felt inadequate to be able to succeed. Whenever it would show up around the corner I would think, "Well, this is too good to be true for me—I don't deserve that." So I would feel a little bit doubtful of my abilities. When I would succeed, there would be an attendant, "Yelp!" I would feel because I would not believe I deserved what I had achieved.

I think fear is the thing that gets in the way of our motivation because we're all motivated by inhibitions and compulsions. You should be motivated more by the result you want rather than the penalty. That's why I've always said that winners are motivated by reward of success rather than inhibited or compelled by the penalty of failure. If you get this conviction that you're as good as the best but no better than the rest—I'm worth the effort, I'm not Mr. Wonderful, I'm not the center of the universe but I can do some things that I haven't done yet—and then apply this motivation to desire rather than fear, that is when self-discipline comes into play.

I'd have to say, David, I could spend the entire interview on self-discipline because I missed it as one of the most important ingredients in success. I've always been a belief guy, an optimism guy, a faith guy, and all the self-esteem things but I think, as time went on, I forgot the amount of discipline it takes for anyone who is a champion in any endeavor. I think I'm back on that track now.

WRIGHT

I can really appreciate the Flame Award you won from the National Council on Youth Leadership for helping high school leaders. I've got a daughter in college and I know how difficult and important it is. But in some circles, self-esteem has gotten a bad reputation. For example, in many schools, teachers won't reward high achievers for fear of hurting the self-esteem of others in the classroom. Many people feel this is not helpful to these children.

In your opinion, where is the balance between building healthy self-esteem and preparing kids and adults to cope and succeed in a competitive world?

WAITLEY

I think that there has to first of all be some kind of performance standard. A good example is the Olympic Games. The idea of the Olympic Games is to set a standard that you've tried to live up to in your own way as a world-class person, realizing that there can only be so many Olympians and so many gold medalists and so on. I think, on the one hand, it's really important to have standards because if you have a standard, then you have something tangible to shoot for or to measure against.

I think there's a problem, however, in that only so many people can be medalists and win medals at the Olympics. One of the reasons that the high jump bar, for example, is set so that everyone can jump over it the first time, is to experience the feeling of success that first jump produces. The feeling of success is working in the competitor before the bar is raised to world record height and to much higher standards than even the normal Olympian.

I'm one who believes in testing. It's difficult when you have a "No Child Left Behind" concept because many times today we're going pass/fail. We're moving people up through the grades regardless of their performance simply because we don't want them left behind and therefore feeling that they're not able to function simply because they can't compete with some students who've been given many more opportunities to succeed than others.

Having said that, I'd say that healthy self-esteem is gained by giving specific stair-step, incremental, bite-sized pieces; perhaps there needs to be several different standards set. Usually the grading system does that and the point system does that where you have someone who has a four point three grade average because of all the extra credits they're taking. Then you have those with a three point eight and then those who are just barely passing. Unfortunately then, what that does is enable only a few people to get into universities and the others have to go to community colleges.

What I will have to say, however, is that we in the United States have to be very careful that we don't dumb down or lower our standards for excellence in our schools. Traveling as much as I do, I have discovered information about this. For example, there are 300 universities in Beijing alone—just in one city in China. The way it goes internationally is that the public schools in Japan, for example, are much more competitive than the private schools. If you're in Japan going to a public school, you have to really perform up to the highest standards in order to ever think of qualifying for any kind of university. You'd have to go into a vocational school if you didn't compete in higher standards in public schools in Japan. The same thing is true in Singapore, China, and in the developing nations.

We have a situation brewing here where we've got global developing countries with really high standards in English, mathematics, engineering, and science. And we have educators in the United States who are more concerned about making sure that the self-esteem of an individual doesn't get damaged by this competitive standard. I think we have to maintain standards of excellence.

I wish we had kept dress codes in schools. I have found schools that have marching bands. A certain amount of uniformity not only encourages greater athletic performance but higher academic standards as well. The same is true globally. There's an argument that if you put kids in uniforms, you're going to limit their creative thinking. The truth is, if you can standardize the way people appear in their style, then you can focus more on substance—their experience, imagination, contribution, and their study. The core of an individual rather than the surface of an individual can be developed much better. It would be great if we could combine the more disciplined aspects of the developing countries with the more entrepreneurial, creative, free-thinking aspects of our society, which means we're critical thinkers (i.e., you throw us a problem and we'll try everything we can possibly think of to solve it). In the developing countries they'll use a textbook or an older person's experience rather than using critical thinking.

We're very entrepreneurial here in America, but I'm very much concerned that our standards are being lowered too much. If we're not careful, we're going to take our place in the future as a second-rate educational country and therefore forfeit the idea of being a technological and market leader.

WRIGHT

I also hear grumbling about motivation. I'm sure you've seen business people roll their eyes a bit at the mention of listening to "motivational" tapes or CDs. Some tire of getting all hyped up about change or sales goals, for example, only to lose their excitement and fail to reach their goals. Are they missing something critical about the nature or application of motivation?

WAITLEY

I really believe they are, David. I think they're missing the idea that what you *want* in life turns you on much more than what you *need* in life. Too often business managers even today focus on the hard skills because they say that the other skills are "soft skills." Well, there's no such thing as a hard or soft skill because you can't separate your personal from your professional life anymore. You get fired more for personal reasons—for being late, for your habits, for you hygiene, your behavior, your anger. This idea that technical training as opposed to motivation is the way to go is misguided.

I have found that employees are excited and are full of desire and energy because management listens to them, reinforces them, is interested in their personal goals, and is interested in keeping them inspired. That inspiration is what we remember. So, when we go to a meeting we remember how we felt about the meeting, not the specifics of the meeting.

I think this emotional component—keeping people's energy and desires foremost and doing a desire analysis of employees rather than just a needs analysis—is very, very important. I often think this is lost in the idea that we're giving a pep talk, or a quick fix, or a Band-Aid when, as Zig Ziglar has mentioned so many times, "Motivation is like taking a bath. You take a bath every day and you might say why take a bath—you're going to get dirty anyway." But the very nature of doing it, and doing it on a habitual basis, makes this positive energy continue to flow and motivation becomes habit-forming. I think you need a lot of it to keep these habits of excellence or else you'll just be running scared—you'll be afraid not to do well because you'll lose your job.

Believe it or not, we have a lot of employees in America who are working harder than they ever have before so they won't be fired. That's not really the way to go after a goal—constantly looking through the rear view mirror trying to cover your behind.

WRIGHT

If you don't mind, I'd like to change the focus a little to the topic of self-discipline. People seem to know what they should do and how they should change, but they just can't discipline themselves to take the necessary steps to do so. What is the secret to becoming a disciplined person?

WAITLEY

I think the secret is to get a team, a support group, a mastermind group because not only is there safety in numbers but there's accountability in numbers. When we are accountable to one another to maintain a certain standard of discipline, it's much easier to work out if someone else is getting up at six-thirty in the morning with you. It's much easier to have a support group if you're interested in maintaining a healthier diet, for example, because the temptations are irresistible to procrastinate and to fall off the wagon. That's why I believe you need a team effort.

It also has to be understood in an immediate gratification society that there is no "success pill" that you can swallow. There is no quick way to get rich and get to the top. There is this steady ratcheting to the top and that's why I think leaders need to say it's going to take us about a year to get any permanent change going. So, I think we should all understand there may be a little dip in productivity as we start this new program of ours—a little dip at first and a little uncertainty—but over time, over about a year, we're going to become like an astronaut or an Olympian. We need to engrain these ideas so they become reflexive. It takes about a year for an idea or a habit to become a reflex. This idea of being able to do it in twenty-one days is misguided. I don't think it takes twenty-one days to learn a skill. It may take twenty-one days to learn to type, it may take twenty-one days to begin to learn a skill, but it takes a year for it to get into the subconscious and take hold.

I think we have to learn that discipline is practicing on a daily basis for about a year so that it will become a habit—a pattern—that will override the old inner software program.

WRIGHT

I'm a big believer in the greater potential of the individual. I remember a fellow—Paul Myer—who helped me a lot when I was a young guy. He was in

Waco, Texas, with a company called Success Motivation Institute. You may know him.

WAITLEY

I know him very well. Actually, he's one of the icons and pioneers in this entire field. He and Earl Nightingale were the first ones to ever have a recorded speaking message other than music. Earl and Paul were pioneers in audio recording and I have still a great respect for Paul. I spoke for his organization some time ago.

WRIGHT

He personally helped me a lot when I was younger and I just really appreciated him. In your book and program, *Seeds of Greatness*, you outline a system for nurturing greatness. Will you give us a brief overview of this program?

WAITLEY

It's taken me thirty years to get this thing to where I want it. I wrote the book twenty years ago titled, *Seeds of Greatness*, and sure, it became a bestseller but so did *One Minute Manager*, *In Search of Excellence*, *Iacocca*, and every other book at that time. I have trouble keeping that thing pumped up.

Over the years I've found that *Seeds of Greatness*, for me, has been a system. What I've had to do is go back through all the mistakes I've made as a family leader. I knew I was a father and not a mother *and* father so I had to find a mother who was also a good clinical psychologist and who had worked with every form of behavioral problem. We put our efforts together so that we had a man and a woman as family leaders with clinical and other experience who could give parents or leaders of the day a certain track to run on where they could coach their small children and adolescents on a daily basis.

I provided a perpetual calendar that gives coaching tips of the day—what I call "sign on the day" and "sign off the day"—for parents to use to communicate with their kids. Then I had to put nineteen CDs together—audio tracks—that covered these "roots and wings," which I would call the "core values" and the more motivational or, if you will, ways to set your kids free.

The idea of parenthood should be to lay the groundwork, make it safe to fail an experiment, and then send them off on their own as independent, not codependent, young adults so they can reach their own destiny. I divided it into "roots of core values" and "wings of self-motivation and self-direction" and tried to balance the two so that whether you're from a blended family, or a single parent family, and whether you're structurally religious or whether you're spiritually religious, it would work, regardless of your personal core belief system.

I'm very happy that we've finally put together a self-study program that can be taught by the authors or by people who are licensed facilitators. It's something that a family leadership group could take and work on their own at their own speed by watching, listening, interacting with their kids, and using a combination of a written book, the audios, the DVDs, and this coaching calendar to maybe put it all together so that over a period of six months to a year they might be able to effect some changes in the way they interact with their kids.

WRIGHT

Sounds great! Before our time runs out, would you share a story or two about your real life coaching and consulting experiences? I know you've coached astronauts and Super Bowl champions as well, haven't you?

WAITLEY

Well, I have. I've been lucky to work within the Apollo program in the simulation area. I found that simulation prevents failure of the first attempt. In other words, if you're going to go to the moon and they're going to shoot you up a quarter of a million miles up and back in a government vehicle, you had better have your rehearsal down and really pat. The astronauts teach you that the dress rehearsal is life or death. The Olympians teach you that at the moment you go to perform, you need to clear your mind so you can remember everything you learned without trying—you develop muscle memory and reflex.

Twenty-one years ago when Mary Lou Retton was doing the vault, she needed a nine point nine five to tie the Romanian for the gold medal in women's all around gymnastics. I asked her what she was thinking about when she went to vault and she said, "Oh gosh, I guess what everyone thinks about—speed, power, explode, extend, rotate, plant your feet at the end. When the pressure is on I get better just like drill. 'Come on, Mary Lou, this is your moment in history!' "

I thought, "Wow! That's not what everyone thinks. What everyone thinks is, 'Thank God it's Friday,' 'Why me?' 'Don't work too hard,' 'Countin' down to Friday,' 'Looking to five P.M.,' 'Romanians are better trained, probably on steroids,' " So I get these stories of Olympians who have internalized this wonderful running the race in advance and simulating as well.

I guess the one story that I'll share is about a ten-year-old boy. In about 1980 this boy came to a goal-setting seminar. He told me that none of the people who had paid their money were really working on their goals. They were really thinking about what they were going to eat and golf. I gave him a work book and told him to go back and do what they were supposed to do and write down his abilities and liabilities, what he was going to do this year and next year and five years from now and twenty years from now. He got all excited because he thought it was this wonderful game that you can play called, Write the Future, or Describe the Future.

So he ran back and worked on the project and forty-five minutes later he astounded the adults in the audience by saying he was earning money mowing lawns and shoveling snow so he could go to Hawaii on the fourteenth of July to snorkel on the big island of Hawaii's Kona Coast. Then he said next year he'd be eleven going into the fifth grade and he was going to build models of what was going to be a space shuttle and he was going to begin to learn more about numbers and math. In five years he'd be fifteen and as a tenth-grader. He said he would study math and science because he wanted to go to the Air Force academy—he was all excited about that. I asked him what he was going to be doing in twenty years and he said he'd be an astronaut delivering UPS packages in space.

I forgot all about him and twenty years later, sure enough, I saw him on the *Today Show* as they showed a picture of an astronaut on a tether line pulling the satellite into the bay of the space shuttle. I thought, "My gosh! This kid did what I only talk about in the seminars." He was a living, breathing example of someone who was focused on this. I said to my family, "Look at what he did!" And they said, "What have *you* been doing for the last twenty years?" I said I was a goal tender. They told me I should be a goal achiever too.

WRIGHT

What a great conversation. I always enjoy talking with you. It's not just uplifting—I always learn a lot when I talk with you.

WAITLEY

Well, David, I do with you as well. You've got a great program and you do a lot of good for people who read and watch and listen. I think you give them insights that otherwise they would never get. I'm just grateful to be one of the contributors and one of the members of your global team.

WRIGHT

It has been my sincere pleasure today to visit with a truly great American, Dr. Denis Waitley.

Denis, thank you for taking so much of your time to share your insights and inspirations for us here on *Stepping Stones to Success.*

WAITLEY

Thank you very much, David.

ABOUT THE AUTHOR

Denis Waitley is one of America's most respected authors, keynote lecturers and productivity consultants on high performance human achievement. He has inspired, informed, challenged, and entertained audiences for over twenty-five years from the board rooms of multi-national corporations to the control rooms of NASA's space program and from the locker rooms of world-class athletes to the meeting rooms of thousands of conventioneers throughout the world. He was voted business speaker of the year by the Sales and Marketing Executives Association and by Toastmasters International and inducted into the International Speakers Hall of Fame. With over ten million audio programs sold in fourteen languages, Denis Waitley is the most listened-to voice on personal and career success. He is the author of twelve non-fiction books, including several international bestsellers, *Seeds of Greatness, Being the Best, The Winner's Edge, The Joy of Working,* and *Empires of the Mind.* His audio album, "The Psychology of Winning," is the all-time best-selling program on self-mastery.

DR. DENIS WAITLEY

The Waitley Institute
P.O. Box 197
Rancho Santa Fe, CA 92067
www.deniswaitley.com

CHAPTER TWELVE

The Journey from Hard-Headed
to Tough-Minded Leadership

An Interview with...

RAND GOLLETZ

DAVID WRIGHT (WRIGHT)

Today we're talking with Rand Golletz. As an executive coach, consultant, speaker, and author, Rand brings something unique to his profession. He's been a CEO, the Chief Marketing and Sales Officer of a Fortune 100 company, and the practice leader of a worldwide consultancy. Rand's value proposition can be summarized by saying, "He's been there and done that."

Rand works with corporate leaders and business owners to develop the characteristics of what he calls "tough-minded leadership." This is his second collaboration for Insight Publishing. The last, *Blueprint for Success*, was published in 2008. His solo book effort, *Redefining Type A,* is currently being edited for publication in 2010.

Rand, welcome—or should I say "welcome back!"? How have you been, what have you been doing and, more specifically for our readers, what have you been thinking about?

RAND GOLLETZ (GOLLETZ)

Actually, one thing that's been consuming me since we talked for the *Blueprint* book is helping organizations do a better job of leveraging their leadership strengths. That includes helping leaders identify and develop them into *über* strengths, accepting the notion that there's no such thing as a perfectly well-rounded leader (that's a difficult proposition, by the way). I've also been helping both companies and their leaders configure their strengths in ways that give them the best opportunity to win.

WRIGHT

So, if I heard you correctly, Rand, including what you're *not* saying, you think the traditional path to developing talent—identifying weaknesses and developing them into strengths—isn't the way to go. True?

GOLLETZ

Now that I've opened that can of worms, let's deal with the worms. First, I have created "rules" (if you will) for developing leaders that serve as the entry point for my discussions with prospective clients—leaders in large organizations. The rules comprise my governing beliefs about leadership development. Here's the first one:

You must accept that you are not equally and infinitely capable of all things.

WRIGHT

Okay, let's stop there, Rand. Are you saying that someone who is not a good people *manager* won't become a good people *leader*?

GOLLETZ

Not exactly. Here's what I am saying. Someone who's not a good people leader (and by the way, that category needs to be defined more precisely to have any hope of working with it) might become a better people leader than he or she is. But the likelihood of taking a guy like "Chainsaw" Al Dunlop—the CEO accused of driving Sunbeam into the ground—and turning him into Mother Teresa is slim.

So I'm not saying you shouldn't try to improve in areas of weakness, only that you will not get your best leverage there.

As a strategic matter, the quickest road to success is to apply one's strengths to opportunities that present themselves. That occurs when leaders make decisions about where to focus their company's resources—all of them, including time, talent, and money.

Leaders accepting that they're not capable of all things begins with how parents raise their children. Parents often drill into their kids' heads the notion that they can be anything they want to be. If they truly want their children to be the best they can be, that premise is simply untrue. At a fairly early age, kids telegraph what they're good at and what they love doing—and they're generally the same things, by the way. Unfortunately, parents and school systems do their best to turn kids with specialties into uninspired generalists.

Here's a fresh way to think about this: To be successful in business, you must at least have acceptable, baseline levels of capability in a variety of areas. You must know, however, where your strengths are. From there, you do your best to create opportunities to exploit your strengths while limiting the exposure of your weaknesses in critical situations. Therefore, my second "rule" is this:

You must understand your strengths and weaknesses in a precise and granular way. Knowing them starts with feedback.

WRIGHT

I've heard you say before that "feedback is the breakfast of champions." You're not telling me now that feedback is useless, are you, Rand?

GOLLETZ

No, I'm not, David. I want to convey that much of the feedback obtained in the interest of personal development today is a complete waste of time. Let me explain. Most of the companies I work with use a formal 360-degree feedback process with their executives. Some are "off-the-shelf" processes, some are custom-designed, and many combine the two. What's the problem? Many of these processes ask well-meaning but generic questions. What's the result? They generate well-meaning but generic answers.

WRIGHT

Can you give our readers an example of these questions and answers?

GOLLETZ

Sure. I recently worked with an executive who had been through a written 360-degree feedback process. In addition to having a "check-the-box" exercise for providing feedback, people also had ample opportunity to write in narrative insights. One of them wrote: "John (the leader) does not collaborate very well. Unless he learns this vital skill, I believe that his promotional opportunities will be very limited."

WRIGHT

I get the feeling you believe that the feedback wasn't very useful.

GOLLETZ

I'll go you one step better, David. It was completely useless! Here's why: It's imprecise and unactionable. The word "collaborate" is too lofty and too generic a word. When I think of that word, more specific words come to mind that describe collaboration—like "negotiate," "compromise," "influence," and twenty or thirty others. All are part of collaboration and would do a better job of describing the potential development opportunities for John than "collaborate." Each of those words can then be broken down into even more precise and finite descriptions.

WRIGHT

I didn't realize it was this complicated.

GOLLETZ

Here's what usually happens next: John approaches the feedback provider—we'll call her Jeri—to get to the heart of the matter. Jeri, by the way, is John's peer with whom he interacts frequently. In a tepid way, John asks Jeri to help him understand her comment. Jeri sweeps the sky with her hand as she says: "Oh John, don't worry. It's no big deal. I had to write something." Jeri either doesn't want to invest herself in John's development, or she doesn't want to upset him, or she fears a tacit, unspecific retribution, or a combination of all of the above.

So here's the scenario: John really doesn't want feedback that can give him heartburn. Jeri doesn't want to give him specific feedback that can give John heartburn. John feels obligated to develop a plan that will eliminate "collaboration" as a future development opportunity. John ends up looking through catalogues for a "collaboration workshop," or he calls someone like me to help him deal with this feedback—vague as it is.

WRIGHT

So Rand, let me pin you down. What would you do if you were called to help John?

GOLLETZ

I'd help John understand the importance of getting feedback and how to solicit feedback that's *relevant*. We don't have space to do that here, but this step is really important. After that, I'd have a conversation with Jeri and ask her two questions. "Jeri, when John isn't collaborating well, what is he *not* doing that you'd like to see him do and what is he *doing* that you'd like to see him stop doing?"

Those questions will elicit answers I can actually work with. Generally, I'd use her answers as jumping-off points for more questions that will get to even more detailed answers.

WRIGHT

I get it! So, as an executive coach, you deal in *doing,* therefore you must get feedback that defines specific actions. Am I right?

GOLLETZ

Exactly. As an expert paid by large companies to help executives develop, I can only provide a return on their investment if I nail down the issues in the form of actions—which brings me to my third rule:

You must understand that knowing what to do and actually doing it are not the same thing.

WRIGHT

That seems obvious to me, Rand. Am I missing something?

GOLLETZ

Here's what happens *a lot* (and I can't emphasize this enough). An executive at a Fortune 500 company—we'll call him Ray—had a problem delivering coherent presentations. His boss gave him books to read on the subject and had Ray attend a seminar that covered the precise material he needed. Yet when he returned to the workplace, he'd clearly made no demonstrable progress to improve delivery of his presentations.

Ray's problem wasn't that he didn't know what to do; he simply couldn't do it. The only way he could have improved was with practice, lots of repetition, critical feedback, and more practice. Ray was deficient in "skill" not "knowledge."

WRIGHT

So you're saying that, for many companies, sending people to classes tends to be the universal cure, whether the illness calls for it or not?

GOLLETZ

Exactly. It's the uncreative, ineffective way many companies deal with their executives' development challenges, which brings me to the next "rule":

To effectively develop people, companies and executives need to understand the differences among knowledge, skills, talents, and character attributes.

Let me use the example of a cardiac surgeon to illustrate this, addressing knowledge first.

WRIGHT

Have at it, Rand.

GOLLETZ

You are the aggregate of your knowledge, skills, talents, and personal attributes. *Knowledge* is the level you've attained learning concepts and facts; it's not performance, achievement, or success. You can acquire knowledge by reading a book or attending a seminar. In terms of business success, knowledge is necessary but insufficient.

Wouldn't you want your cardiac surgery performed by a physician who has actually performed the surgery you need and that he has not just acquired knowledge?

WRIGHT

Amen to that.

GOLLETZ

Skills are one's strengths at performing specific tasks. In the surgery analogy, the same intelligent physician has now had five years of surgery experience— actually *doing* the surgery you need. This might be a guy you'd trust with your heart.

WRIGHT

Yes, Rand. That would make a big difference to me!

GOLLETZ

Talents are inherent, genetic strengths. Wouldn't it be great if this physician had been born with great hand/eye coordination?

Personal attributes are characteristics of morality, character, and personality developed early in life. Courage, endurance, persistence, resilience, and integrity are some of these attributes. What if this physician has repeatedly performed needless, egregious bypass surgeries? Would knowing that make a difference to you?

WRIGHT

Absolutely!

GOLLETZ

So to deal effectively with your development challenges, you need to understand their sources and initiate the appropriate mechanisms for change. Most leaders don't do that, nor do most companies. Their automatic answers are either "send that person to a seminar" or "hire an executive coach."

Let me tell you something—plenty of schools conduct seminars and tons of executive coaches are ready, willing, and able to convince executives that their specialty can provide the solution. They claim that they deliver the "silver bullet" to fix the problem.

WRIGHT

This whole issue is a lot more complicated than I would have imagined. Is there more?

GOLLETZ

Of course! You have to add *passion* into the mix. As much as I hate that word because it's so overused, passion is really important in developing and deploying personal capabilities.

In my world, *passion* means zest and commitment. It's the fuel for the fire. We each excel at certain things, but for one reason or another they don't light a fire under us. Maybe we've done them for so long that they bore us.

Yet in the workplace, people come to us to tap into our knowledge, skills, and talents, not our passions. Back when I was a senior Fortune 100 executive, I can imagine what would've happened had my CEO asked me to do something and I responded with, "Well, it's like this, Bob, I don't really feel passionate about that kind of assignment, so I'll pass."

WRIGHT

So what's the answer then?

GOLLETZ

It's called *work* for a reason. We can't avoid all of the assignments that don't engage us emotionally. But here's what we can do. We can consciously search for jobs and assignments that play to our passions as well as our capabilities. We can assume the burden of self-direction that will result in career propulsion. We can *act* rather than *react*. We can limit our exposure to non-engaging work by stepping up to the plate for work that *does* engage us. We can volunteer, we can delegate, and we can view our performance and development as evolving out of self-management and self-direction.

WRIGHT

It sounds like that old "e" word — *empowerment.*

GOLLETZ

That, David, is a great point! Real empowerment comes from the decision to take the reins. Too many people assume that their careers are out of their hands — that when they show up at work, someone else controls their lives. "Empower me," they request. I say, "Empower yourself!" *Own your life.* No excuses, no blame, no victim mentality, no finger pointing. Stop whining and start doing!

WRIGHT

I know that your brand is all about "tough-minded leadership." Just what is that? When I hear it, I think of General Patton.

GOLLETZ

General George Patton was a tough-minded leader. Some people believe that he was also a hard-headed leader. But the difference between the two is huge.

I work with a lot of hard-headed executives who want to become tough-minded. I don't work with any who are tough-minded and want to become hard-headed. That's because hard-headed leaders are cold, inhumane, and remote. They don't engage people, seemingly because they lack the "empathy gene." They can't embody the concept that, while they might get people to do what needs to be done, tough-minded leaders can get people to *want to do* what needs to be done. The difference is not hair-splitting; it's enormous.

Here's my definition of tough-minded: "the ability, inclination, and discipline to face any situation with strength, determination, and equanimity." What do you think?

WRIGHT

Sounds good to me!

GOLLETZ

Tough-minded leaders are focused, persistent, resilient, empathetic, and courageous. They retain their confidence, seriousness of purpose, and sense of humor regardless of the situation.

Think of it this way: Leaders are confronted constantly with challenges that appear to be in conflict with each other. As a result, they have to:

- create quality while reducing cost,
- improve shareholder returns while attracting high-quality staff, acquiring profitable customers, and obtaining low-cost capital,
- align teams to achieve organizational goals without overly protecting personal interests,
- integrate patterns of competitive change into planning and execution,
- cultivate trust rather than mandate obedience,
- create a merit-based rather than politically based environment, and
- assert authority without impairing empowerment.

Unless a leader brings qualities of tough mindedness to the fore, he or she can't possibly accomplish what needs to be done successfully. I help leaders discover and apply these qualities to benefit their organizations, their constituents, and themselves.

WRIGHT

Who do you think of as being tough-minded?

GOLLETZ

Dwight D. Eisenhower because of his actions at D-Day. If you read about the way he balanced judgment, courage, humility, and humanity, you realize what an impressive man he was. In the same vein Winston Churchill exemplified that it's okay to be a late-bloomer—as long as you're not late for the flower show!

WRIGHT

Well put, Rand!

GOLLETZ

Pat Tillman comes to mind as well. This football player could have made additional millions in the NFL but chose to join the U.S. Army Rangers because he believed his life needed to stand for more—that his sacrifices up to that time insufficiently expressed his gratitude for his opportunities. He died in pursuit of this goal. What a staggering commitment!

How about Viktor Frankl? His book, *Man's Search for Meaning*, detailed his experience in a Nazi concentration camp. The only thing he had left was his dignity and his ability to choose his own attitude. He didn't allow the Nazis to take these away from him.

Many more come immediately to mind—Lincoln, Gandhi, Joan of Arc. They brought attributes of character—a critical dimension of leadership—to challenges for which they were specifically suited. Right place, right time, right strengths, right passion.

WRIGHT

I noticed, Rand, that you didn't include business leaders among those people you cited. Is there a reason?

GOLLETZ

Only that it would have been obvious to include Walt Disney, Thomas Edison, Steve Jobs, and Meg Whitman in this group. Tough-minded leaders come from all walks of life, many races, and both genders. That's the reason.

Also, I have a strong orientation to athletics and the military as examples of what I believe to be the paramount character attribute—courage.

WRIGHT

When you think of present-day tough-minded leaders, what people come to mind?

GOLLETZ

I'll invoke the names of three athletes.

The first, Tiger Woods, came from an interesting background. His dad, a Green Beret, used mind games to teach Tiger the focus and discipline he later demonstrated so abundantly on the golf course. His mom, a Thai Buddhist, taught him about equanimity and "being present." By the way, Hank Haney, Tiger's coach, said that Earl Woods (Tiger's father) was the best golf coach of all time—

and he didn't even play golf. Unless you've been asleep for the last decade, you've likely noticed that Tiger Woods is as tough as nails.

The example that I invoke most, however, is champion cyclist Lance Armstrong. There's focus and discipline, and then there's Lance Armstrong. The title of his book, *It's Not About the Bike,* says it all. He beat cancer. He won the Tour do France seven consecutive times. He retired to devote his time to the foundation he created. Now, in order to give his fund-raising efforts more attention, he's back training (harder than ever) and racing. Lance is "the man."

I also like to mention Andre Agassi, the tennis champion. He had a great career that temporarily hit the skids. His work with his coach, Brad Gilbert, brought him success in the 1990s that far surpassed anything he achieved as a highly acclaimed teenager in the 1980s. Andre's impeccable manners are what strikes people most. He's very much a "yes ma'am, no ma'am" guy noted for treating others with dignity and respect, no matter their place on the social ladder. He also insists that people who work for him comport themselves in a similar way. He not only "talks it," he "walks it." I find that characteristic impressive *and* unusual.

WRIGHT

Rand, as always, this has been enlightening and enjoyable. I've come to look forward to our exchanges.

GOLLETZ

Me too, David. One last thing—my book *Redefining Type A* will be available shortly. It comes directly from my life experiences, first as a corporate CEO and now as an executive coach for senior executives and those who aspire to be.

WRIGHT

Will you give our readers an overview?

GOLLETZ

Say no more! Here's the deal. Many leaders from all walks of life are stressèd, self-indulgent, over-baked, and neglectful of themselves and their families. They're hard-headed instead of tough-minded. *Redefining Type A* was created to be an admonition, a recommendation, and a prescription for leaders who embody those behaviors and want to change.

ABOUT THE AUTHOR

Many coaches and consultants who work with business leaders "talk the talk." Rand Golletz also "walks the walk."

Rand spent twenty-five years achieving major results working in large organizations. As the youngest officer in a Fortune 100 company, he led its sales development efforts. Later, as Senior Vice-President and Chief Marketing and Sales Officer of another Fortune 100 firm, he led the charge to establish a multi-billion dollar brand.

Rand's experience includes being CEO and COO for companies with hundreds of millions of dollars of revenue, as well as director and practice leader for the strategy consulting practice of a top-ten, worldwide consultancy.

Now an executive coach, strategy consultant, speaker, and author, Rand works with corporate leaders and business owners to develop and sustain the focus, discipline, and momentum required for them to experience professional and personal success. His latest book supporting this goal is *Redefining Type A*, to be released in 2010.

RAND GOLLETZ

Rand Golletz Performance Systems
P.O. Box 5305
Laytonsville, MD 20882
(301) 482-2598
www.randgolletz.com
www.redefiningtypea.com
rand@randgolletz.com

CHAPTER THIRTEEN

Choose Your Own Blueprint

An Interview with...

DEBORAH BAKER- RECENIELLO

DAVID WRIGHT (WRIGHT)

Today we are talking with Deborah Baker-Receniello. Deborah has her PhD in Counseling Psychology and BA in Business Administration. She is a graduate of Spencer Business Institute and Founder of DBR Life Strategies & Business Coach. She's a member of the International Coach Federation (ICF), Coachville, Women In Influence, Toastmasters, and the International Virtual Women's Chamber of Commerce.

Deborah's unique background as an entrepreneur selling her own professional services and her twenty-five years' experience in counseling and management give her a distinctive edge. She has worked closely with top-management, small businesses, teams, and solopreneurs with extensive experience in management, public service, communication, training, marketing, and start-up design and growth.

Deborah is the author of: Why It Works! The Science Behind Manifesting Everything You Desire, Play a Bigger Game! Proven Strategies to Design and grow Your Successful Small Business, 101 Great Ways to Live Your Life Volume 2, co-authored with Brian Tracy, Zig Ziglar, et al.

She also enjoys water-color and acrylic painting, gardening in her English Rose Garden, and dancing.

Deborah, welcome to *Stepping Stones to Success*.

BAKER-RECENIELLO

Thank you, David. It is great to be with you today. I have to admit to you, David, that today is a dream come true for me! My two most cherished role-models in life and business are Deepak Chopra and Jack Canfield. Dennis Waitley influenced me earlier in my development, as human potential and peak performance has driven me most of my life. It's been my dream to be associated with these mentors as a signpost in my own life, and here it is.

This is such a great project and most timely, especially in the time when we are witnessing the collapse of the old, rigid structures in our world today. Something new is birthing and I am very excited to assist clients be a part of it all. We have reached a point in evolution where we have the capacity to consciously co-create reality and choose our own blueprint for the future. With rapid change, we must be able to trust our own ability to sense what is happening around us and chose best responses. It's time for the world to stop being fearful. Our ability to grow our business, our career, and our income are directly related to our ability to master ourselves. Our life and businesses today require a new perspective and a new ethic.

WRIGHT

That's a revolutionary and ambitious vision! Where do we start?

BAKER-RECENIELLO

If you are to become the architect of your new design, you must understand the blueprint and how it works. Anytime you do anything, whether it's personal or in business, the human factor comes into play. Human beings are yourself, your employees, your customers or clients, your family, your team. All come together to define and contribute to your business success and mostly takes place at a subconscious or deeper level.

Science is now verifying this on many levels. Quantum physics helps us understand how the physical matter comes about and our role within it. Along with brain research, it helps explain how our beliefs and thinking creates matter and how we all reap what we sow.

WRIGHT

Deborah, I've heard some people say this is baloney. What is quantum physics telling us now and how does it relate to business?

BAKER-RECENIELLO

Principles of quantum physics have led to advanced technologies like lasers, transistors, and CAT scans; however, the principles of quantum physics are an essential component to what is happening around us.

Fred Alan Wolfe, physicist, stated in a recent interview with the Public Television series, Thinking Allowed, he said, "I'm talking about the fact that what one being does in some way affects everybody on the whole planet. It's not just separate beings all going their own ways. We are interconnected in ways that are very subtle and not easy to appreciate. In his book, Reality and Consciousness, Peter Russel, physicist, states: instead of trying to explain consciousness within the current super-paradigm, we need to accept that consciousness is as fundamental as matter—in some ways, more fundamental.

I met Theoretical Physicist Amit Goswami about seven years ago and his voice still echoes in my mind: *Consciousness is the ground of all being-ness!* He later related these tenants of quantum physics:

The atomic world is nothing like the physical world we live in. It's not really solid, but made of rapidly flashing packets of energy that can be either a particle or a wave (matter or energy). The view of our world is a vast oscillation of interconnected forces; a web of life, sea of infinite possibility. Consciousness and Energy is all that is, was, and will be. You can look at yourself as a tiny field interacting with larger energy fields all the way to the whole universe.

We communicate with our world outside the bounds of measured time and space; non-physical and non-local.

Quantum packets are defined as probabilities of existence and are multidimensional. They have intelligence, can make decisions, and respond to the observer. What you are looking for, or what you consistently focus your attention on, strongly affects what will happen in your life.

In other words, the field (which is what spirit is—a field of pure potentiality) is a continuum of all possible energy and information states that will subsequently manifest themselves as space-time events. Matter, your body and your experiences are space-time events. You are not your body, your experience, your joy, your family, or your business. You are the spiritual nature of energy acting through a body to create your reality. As Dr. Deepak Chopra states: *when we discover pure awareness, whether through insight, meditation, or a freak accident; we discover our essential nature is spiritual, non-material.*

WRIGHT

So quantum physics gives us a model for our spiritual and physical reality. What does recent brain research tell us?

BAKER-RECENIELLO

Brain research is telling us we don't have to accept things as they are. Our brains can change in moments due to plasticity in the brain. Our marvelous brain acts as a master architect. It knows all the angles, geometry, design, and layout and the master builder. The brain is an organ that functions in the now. It doesn't know time as past, present, or future. If you think it now, it's happening now, and can cause physical results within the body, now.

It takes the vision of your dream, your beliefs, and your emotion then translates it into a design or blueprint. Your vision (visualization with eyes closed, making a movie) is a mental blueprint and the brain transforms the vision into electrical stimuli (neurons firing). The charge is in the form of emotional energy, which fires chemical-constructs (hormones) and memory from the hypothalamus. This translates in physics as an oscillating standing wave.

Your dream then becomes a beacon in the ocean of potentials, like a flashlight. You may think you are alone in a darkened room, however, when you turn on a flashlight, others can find you. Other potentials (people, places, things, times, and events) will then rush to meet your expectations through the Law of Attraction—

like attracts like. Just as a coin has two sides that cannot be divided, thought, intention, emotion, and focus are the flip side of physical dreams.

WRIGHT

Could this be why it seems the elite, the most successful, and wealthy people are that way? Could it be that they know something most people don't understand?

BAKER-RECENIELLO

There's not enough time here today to go into much detail. This is the reason I wrote: *Why It Works, The Science Behind Manifesting Everything You Desire.* If you understood why it (quantum physics, brain functions, the biology of emotion, focused intention, and visualization) works, would you be more willing to give it a shot? With this, you begin to see that you can change your view of reality, write your own blueprint, and have your dreams come to fruition.

If you understand this you can open to new insight into your business. Most business people look at effects and not the cause. If you focus on "what is," you attract more of "what is."

Let's look at a very simple example: As a business owner, you can have an idea with a certain benefit in mind. If you communicate to multi levels of employees, you need to be very specific in your own thoughts and communication with specific detailed instructions.If your thoughts run contrary to the direction or communication, problems may occur. What are you thinking? You may verbally say one thing, yet think another. "Can it be carried out successfully? Will they follow instructions? Can it fail?" These thought can be transferred to others. Remember that in communication, only 10 percent is verbal. If you are not in total alignment with what you say, the communication can become confusing.

You can think of it like the flow of electricity. You have an appliance (you or your idea) that needs to plug into something bigger (an electrical socket or organization) to make it work effortlessly. What happens if the appliance has a frayed live wire? It jumps, flops, disconnects, and could cause harm.

WRIGHT

Now I begin to see that if your employees get a different picture about your idea, they could block your success by thinking totally differently to the original idea and it becomes frayed.

BAKER-RECENIELLO

You are beginning to see what effect you have on your business and all people involved. Leadership is more about responsibility in today's world and today's quantum paradigms. To be an effective role model, influence other people , help others grow, and create healthy and functional business systems, leaders must develop themselves first, because of their special roles and situations and because they touch the lives of others.

Organizations are for products and services. Organizations also are the setting where people spend a large amount of time. What if they brought their true essence and expressed it in everything they do and were encouraged to do so?

Let's look at the desired case from our other scenario. People interact, trust, feel respect, and are willing to listen. On an energy level, both or many energy fields are intermingling and becoming something much greater than they could have been alone.

Usually, what is felt after this interaction is empowerment and inner peace. When your batteries are fully charged, you can function in an entirely different manner. This is where creativity, new ideas, and innovation are born. This breeds success, leading to quantum leaps in the evolution of your business.

WRIGHT

As a leader of an organization, do you have any tips to become more aware of this?

BAKER-RECENIELLO

Focus on what will make a difference within yourself. Then you will affect positive change in your leadership, your organization, and the world because we are all part of the same oscillating energy field.

Here are some tips:

- Learn to speak with clear purpose, in a positive manner. Be responsible for honest and direct communications, maintaining integrity.
- Commit to focus on the present moment and make whatever your current task is the most important.
- Commit to follow your vision without wavering, stay the course.
- Own it—this involves accountability and responsibility
- Be flexible—change what you do to achieve the outcome you desire
- Strive for balance—create choices that provide meaning and fulfillment. Inner happiness comes when mind, body, and spirit are aligned.

Just imagine your business having leaders who understand, take responsibility, and have integrity and respect for others.

WRIGHT

Now that I understand quantum physics and brain function, I have a desire for a better life or business. What's the process of taking the dream to fruition?

BAKER-RECENIELLO

David, there is a specific process for bringing your dreams to fruition. And, it is critical to do this to achieve a satisfying life. This quote from Napoleon Hill says it all, *Cherish your visions and your dreams, as they are the children of your soul; the blueprints of your ultimate achievements.*

Define *your dream*? You may want an entirely new job or a significant career change. Maybe you are seeking a promotion or believe you deserve a raise! Perhaps you desire to start your own business. Sometimes you ignore your own dreams because of self-doubt, fear, or external complications. You can think of many different excuses to brush those dreams aside. Your world will become more exciting and you will begin to live a more passionate and meaningful life if you follow your dreams.

Our media is only too happy to supply us with stories of individuals who overcame tragedy, serious illness, and emotional upheaval to achieve success regardless of these obstacles. Though seemingly an inspiration, these stories also convey a paradoxical message—these miracles are indeed extraordinary and may seem out of the reach of ordinary people.

It is my experience, when I speak with leaders in any field and through coaching hundreds, that they are doing what they do because they have a sense of values and purpose that drives them. People's vision for the future captures their entire heart at the deepest level of their soul. Achievers are dreamers and doers!

WRIGHT

What do you need in order to have an extraordinary life, miracles each day, and your dreams come true?

BAKER-RECENIELLO

Get a rough idea of where you are now, and then begin to develop the vision of where you want to go. Clarity, focus, strategy, and then action are paramount in your successful life, career, or business. Most want to start with the action first. Let's begin with clarification by looking at values.

What are values? These are what matter most to you—that which is in your heart and soul. When you align yourself with your values, they act like a guide or compass. Then you can weigh future events by staying the course. You achieve greater satisfaction and you use them to build your plans of the future. Values help you build better relationships whether in your personal, career, or business lives. Allow yourself time to reflect on what you value most. Here are a few examples: creativity, problem-solving, flexibility, make a difference, structure, integrity, open communication, variety, respect, imagination, stability, family, spirituality, leadership, influence, power, caring about others, freedom, adventure.

WRIGHT

Now armed with our values, how might these contribute to our strategy of obtaining our dream? What is the bridge that propels us into action?

BAKER-RECENIELLO

Your life's purpose is embedded deeply within you. It is the reason that you believe you are here or why you have your dream. This purpose becomes the door that opens your passion and passion inspires you to get up in the morning and actually drives your daily life. To discover this purpose ask yourself what do you do naturally or with little effort. Is it making things, designing things, painting, music, writing, crafting, etc? Ask yourself what do you enjoy doing so much that you lose track of time? Another question is what have you accomplished in life that made you feel terrific? Still don't know? Ask ten people you know to tell you what they think you are good at or what talent do they see. Your purpose is your inspiration.

Know *why* **you are doing this.** What is the most important thing about this purposeful dream? What will it do for you to fulfill your dream? And most importantly, what is your role? How do you make a difference? This process is referred to as your mission. A mission statement is usually meant to define internal motivation. Motivation leads to passion and passion with purpose leads to fulfillment.

Are you ready to create your vision? Knowing what you just discovered, answer this question. The extraordinary factor now comes into play. You are so far ahead of the game; congratulate yourself. Take your values, purpose, mission, and create that vision.

Ask yourself, if you had an all powerful genie appear to give you all the time, money, resources, and contacts—everything you needed and you wanted to design your life, career, or business—what would it look like in ten years? Make it as wild as you like. Most people play the game of life and business too small. Here is your chance to play a bigger game. More detail is available in my book, Play a Bigger Game! Design and Grow Your Successful Business. If you and I had a conversation in three years, tell me what has happened and how your life has changed.

You could ask yourself: What would my life be like if this dream happened? Then, what would my life be like if it didn't?

WRIGHT

How do I rev it up? Let's focus on how to strategize this vision into action.

BAKER-RECENIELLO

Here is where the ultra-ordinary happens. Take your newest, most powerful and highly leveraged knowledge, and set your goals to truly inspire and motivate you based upon your values, purpose, and vision. What would your vision look like in ten years? Then moving backward in time, what would it look like in three years? Set out your plan of action with making your goals *smart*—Specific,

Measurable, Attainable, Relevant (aligned), and Time-based. It is also important to realize that if you have a bump in the road, just recalibrate yourself or your goals. Be Flexible. There are no mistakes, only learning. The ultra-ordinary know this secret and persevere.

Once your vision is in place, *create a support team.* This can be family, a buddy, a mentor, a coach, your business team, or your peers. Make sure this support team believes in you. Be specific in how you want to be supported.

WRIGHT

What kinds of businesses would be good start-ups for those interested in starting or growing their business?

BAKER-RECENIELLO

As I mentioned at the beginning of this interview, *now* is a great time to be in business. Energy is the essence of life. Every day you choose how you are going to use it by knowing what you want, what it takes to reach that goal, and by maintaining focus.

Don't let fear paralyze you. Look for the opportunity to fill a need or problem you can solve—anything that brings people together instead of separating them will flourish. Think cooperative, not competitive. What would happen if two or more visions come very close and merge into something fantastic? Whether that is one individual or an enterprise involving thousands acting together to make the world better in some way—ecosystems, business systems—think globally, revolutionary progress, products, or services.

No business can possibly expect to be all things to all people, and any that try will likely find business dwindling due to others who specialize to better meet the needs of that customer segment. Each segment has its own set of common characteristics and unique needs and preferences.

The key question for most is *how do I find my own niche?*

The key to finding a fabulous niche is to identify where your passions and strengths lie. This allows you to package a solution to your targeted market's biggest unmet need or problem!

- Look for a need or problem that you can solve.
- Identify the targeted audience with this need or problem.

- Do they know they have the problem? If you have to educate, it'll take longer to succeed.
- Can you reach them easily?
- Can they afford to pay you?

Test your product or service. This is a step that most business owners and entrepreneurs miss. Create a package, program, sale, product, or service to try out your solution. Gather testimonials and take the opportunity to learn more about your niche. It is better to test and learn than to fall flat on your face. Think about it: sometimes you need to destroy something in order to create something new. Nature does it all the time—earthquakes, tornados, drought, dying animals turn into oil, decaying matter to natural gas, great pressure on coal produces diamonds, a baby being born.

- Get your business fundamentals together.
- Create your systems.
- Create your team.
- Have fun.

WRIGHT

What if you already have a business and it is stagnant?

If you are looking for ways to grow or reinvent, here are a few ideas:

- Review what has worked successfully in the past and what hasn't. Evaluate possible outcomes of multiple scenarios.
- Interview your clients; use surveys. They know what they want.
- Look at your systems.
- Don't be afraid to swap out or modify a previous proven business model for a new model that reflects the changes in the business environment.
- Realign wayward practices with their mission and original goals.

For more detail, check out: *Play a Bigger Game! Proven Strategies to Design & Grow Your Successful Small Business.*

I work with clients who have a desire to change, achieve their goals, and commit to an action plan for success. Usually they are forward thinking, willing to learn and grow individually, and develop their business. My clients understand that people are important and systems run a company.

WRIGHT

Deborah, how can readers get a copy of your books and other information products for themselves?

BAKER-RECENIELLO

The quickest way is to visit my Web site or e-mail me. My contact information is on the last page of this chapter. You can also ask for a copy of my *DBR Business Mastery Newsletter,* just put that in the subject line of your e-mail. Contact me to schedule speaking engagements.

WRIGHT

Any parting comments?

BAKER-RECENIELLO

You can be jazzed and electrified. The key to happiness is doing what you deeply value and love. This new criteria can help you make decisions as to what to do with your limited time more successfully. Look at any task in front of you and ask if this will add to your dream or distract. When you are committed to your dream and you have this knowledge, the universe will get behind you to have it in your life. It is miraculous. Eastern philosophy describes this alignment process beautifully. It will bring things to you and support you in ways you could not have imagined. *Our truest life is when we are in our dreams awake.* —Henry David Thoreau (1817–1862)

To your wildest dreams and joyful fulfillment!

WRIGHT

What a great conversation. I appreciate the time you've spent with me today. I've learned so much and you've given me a lot more to think about. I appreciate that.

BAKER-RECENIELLO

Thanks for the opportunity. And, thanks to all of you, the players in my life, who make my life a success.

ABOUT THE AUTHOR

Deborah Baker-Receniello is CEO of DBR Life Strategies & Business Coach. Deborah has advanced degrees in Counseling Psychology and Business Administration and is a Certified Life Strategies and Business Coach. She is a noted speaker, author, and trainer. Deborah partners with you to design and grow yourself personally and your businesses, attracting more clients and making more money. Deborah is the author of: *Why It Works! The Science Behind Manifesting Everything You Desire, Play a Bigger Game! Proven Strategies to Design and grow Your Successful Small Business*, and *101 Great Ways to Live Your Life Volume 2*, co-authored with Brian Tracy and Zig Ziglar, et al.

Deborah lives in Olympia, Washington, with her husband, David, and son, Douglas.

DEBORAH BAKER-RECENIELLO
DBR Life Strategies & Business Coach
360-989-9997
deborah@dbrlifecoach.com
dbrcoaching@comcast.net
www.dbrlifecoach.com

CHAPTER FOURTEEN

The Road to Success

An Interview with...

ANDREA MICHAELS

DAVID WRIGHT (WRIGHT)

Today we're talking with Andrea Michaels. Andrea is a leading pioneer in the meeting and events sector, years ago creating an industry where there was none. For more than thirty-five years she has established the trends, paving the way for others to work nationally and internationally. Recipient of over thirty-three special events Gala Awards, she was the first inductee into the event industry Hall of Fame. A member of the Women in Business Hall of Fame, she has also received two SITE Crystal Awards, and an MPI Global Paragon Award, among other industry recognitions. Prominent events include the opening of the Las Vegas Venetian Hotel and Resort and Vancouver's GM Place. Other high profile events include NASA's Space Shuttle Development Conference, and the Hong Kong Tourist Board's multi-city Road Shows.

Her ability to produce mega events for thousands is legendary. An upcoming memoir, *Reflections of a Successful Wallflower,* will reveal her remarkable career. Andrea is a sought-after speaker for numerous global educational conferences. Her seminars on creativity, profitability, and production have earned her international recognition.

Andrea, welcome to *Stepping Stones to Success.*

ANDREA MICHAELS (MICHAELS)

Thank you.

WRIGHT

So tell our readers, what is your secret to success?

MICHAELS

Whatever success is, I don't think I've reached it yet. But I believe in it—I don't think there is another option. So I always strive to aim at being successful. I don't know how else to put it in a more simplistic form. If I don't have doubts, then ultimately I'll succeed. It's striving for success that motivates me and perhaps makes it seem to others that I've reached "success."

WRIGHT

So belief is the secret. I've never heard that.

MICHAELS

I think you have to believe. Success involves persistence—just keep putting one foot in front of the other and keep moving forward is what it takes.

WRIGHT

So what have been your greatest successes?

MICHAELS

I think creating something out of nothing is my greatest achievement. When I look back at when I entered the industry in the 1970s, a meetings and events industry as we know it now did not exist. In 1973, when I first entered the world of events, a special event consisted of a three-piece band, hotel linen that hung an inch off the table, a bud vase centerpiece, and no special lighting or frills. That was what was called an event. A meeting might have had overhead projectors, a microphone, and a speaker standing in front of an audience with no real audio-visual support. It was functional and bare bones.

Somehow this just seemed like an opportunity for me. I looked at that opportunity as something I'd always wanted to create, such as theater. I wanted to be Cecil B. DeMille. I had so many dreams, and here it was—an open opportunity to create something out of nothing.

In the early seventies, a client approached me and said, "We are having a bicentennial celebration; what can you do?" Then the client asked, "Do you have a band for us?" I thought, "Well, that doesn't reflect two hundred years of a company's history. What about creating a theme for the event?" At the time I didn't even understand what a theme was, because no one did what we now know as "theme parties."

So I worked with the client to deliver something that became a guest experience. When the manager of the hotel we were going to use said, "You're doing *what?*" suddenly I discovered that not only was nobody else doing this type of event, they didn't even understand it.

From that early success we grew into creating theme events, decorative events, and then adding sound, lighting, specialty entertainment, and acts that maybe were previously only seen in theaters and circuses. We were getting the message across that we wanted to create experiences. When people go to a movie, when they go to the theater, when they watch television, it's all about what experiences these activities bring into their lives. Events shouldn't be any different.

So now, when you have terms like "experiential marketing" and "experiential events," you will know that the event I described above was the forerunner of them all.

It was the same with meetings. I always felt that a meeting was more than a talking head on stage standing behind a podium and lecturing an audience. A product launch had to create an emotional response to what the client was trying to sell and that can't be done through a static picture.

So all of these things I consider my greatest achievements—helping found an industry, which in today's world is just huge and didn't exist when I started. So yes, it was fun being a pioneer. It still is.

WRIGHT

I'll bet you really enjoy watching the Super Bowl thinking, I started all of this.

MICHAELS

Well, I didn't start the Super Bowl any more than the Opening Ceremonies for Olympics. I would much rather compare my journey to watching the Olympics in Beijing, and saying, "You know, some of the things they're doing I did first. Some of the things enabling them to do these massive productions that are so tasteful and so beautiful were the end result of years of introducing fresh and new ideas into my industry." I love watching what other people have created because now it's teaching me something new.

WRIGHT

So what challenges have you encountered and overcome on your pathway to success?

MICHAELS

I'm glad you see it as a pathway. So do I. Well let's see—hurricanes, floods, tornadoes, power outages, wars, riots, picket lines, the economy falling apart—those are just some of them.

WRIGHT

Other than that, Mrs. Lincoln, did you enjoy the play?

MICHAELS

When you've been in the industry long enough and you tackle large projects, you're bound to find lots of challenges that come along.

WRIGHT

So would you tell us what your definition of success is?

MICHAELS

Great question. Well, I'll repeat myself and say that I haven't achieved it yet—I still think it's in my future. There is so much left to do. I'm proud of what I have accomplished, and I want to achieve more. I don't know if I'm ever going to reach a place where I can say, "Okay I feel that I'm a success." Once I'm there, am I going to strive for more? I'd rather strive for more.

WRIGHT

So what do you think the tools are that a professional needs to have to be successful, both professionally and personally?

MICHAELS

Perseverance, balance, and the ability to cope are the vital tools necessary. Every kind of wrench is thrown in your way, personally and professionally. Love what you do and have a real passion for it. You have to have a very strong sense of ethics and morality and the ability to give, not just receive. Also needed is the ability to treat everybody kindly and fairly, and to be honest about what you don't know and yet want to learn.

WRIGHT

In these challenging times, how does one maintain success?

MICHAELS

With a wink and a prayer! My industry is totally dependent on our clients. I don't manufacture a car that has to be sold, so, if they don't produce it, there is no product to be launched. Therefore, if the corporate world isn't finding the need to do events at the moment it's very, very hard for me to keep business going. When that happens, I look at it as a time to look for other avenues—a time for strategizing with my clients and not just being a fulfillment company. It's not that they need five hundred envelopes and I can give them that; but rather, I have to ask, "What are your needs at the moment? What are your challenges now? How can we work with you and assist you to raise morale, to sell product, to just be the company that you want to be? What are the cost-effective solutions?" Success in today's world is in becoming a strategic partner with your clients. If you sit and wait for them to literally place an order, it's never going to happen.

WRIGHT

How do you nurture success in others?

MICHAELS

Encouragement, pats on the back, creative brainstorming, and making everybody a part of the team that works together for an end goal is a good way to nurture success. I think education is also vital, so we encourage everybody on our staff to take classes to learn new things, to travel, gain experiences, network as much as possible, be part of every organization that holds meetings, trade shows, or special events, and to have a lot of fun while they're doing it. We try to do fun things in the office together, whether they are potlucks or birthday celebrations.

We started publishing (since the beginning of January) what we call the *Good Newspaper*, and we send it out to everybody we've ever even met. It has nothing but good news in it; there is no promotion—no advertisements—it just features what good things are happening in the world, and it goes out every week.

WRIGHT

So describe a typical day for our readers. I mean, what are the activities and actions that qualify as successful?

MICHAELS

How much time have you got? I generally get up around 5 AM and just get my wits together, check e-mail, and respond to clients in Europe and Asia by e-mail. I don't want to come into the office at 9:30 and find that I've got three hundred e-mails waiting for me, so I try to do that before I even get dressed.

The first thing I do is go to the gym, almost every day. Then I reward myself for doing that by going to Starbucks, and then I come into the office. If I'm in town, generally we'll meet with the staff to find out who's doing what, who needs help on what, what has to be accomplished during that day, and then really spend as much of the day either being a support to the team creatively or in production, reviewing proposals, reviewing budgets, and getting together with everybody as much as I can on an individual one-on-one basis.

At the end of the day, when they all go home (and everybody here does work pretty late), that's when I start on my own projects—the proposals, the creative writing, and reading industry magazines. I generally turn off the computer between 9 and 10 PM. This includes weekends too because I find that when I'm alone I can do twelve hours of work in three hours.

WRIGHT

That is a full day.

MICHAELS

It is a full day, but it is a very stimulating day. Many of my clients are also my friends, and hearing from them and corresponding or talking with them, no matter where in the world we are, is enriching on so many levels.

WRIGHT

If you could teach success, what would the curriculum be?

MICHAELS

First, I think I would do a class in psychology. Psychology teaches people about peaceful communication, and illustrates communications skills. This is where you can realize your goals through win-win situations. I think most people are reactors and as a result they don't really get what they want.

If I could teach one skill to anybody, it would be creative listening. I think really listening to other people is the greatest tool on the way to success. Think of what can be accomplished if you really understand what someone else is saying, clarifying what they want, and then finding a way to deliver it, whether it's personally or professionally. I think communications skills would be number one on my curriculum. I would also include creative writing, another communications skill that can be so expressive.

I'm a technology idiot, so as much as I would like to say that everybody should be wizards in Twitter and Flickr, and all that kind of social Internet communication, I don't understand it myself—I still have yet to learn it. Nevertheless, I'm sure it is very important today and something I should know.

I would also include social behavior or manners because I think that is a skill set that is getting lost. I would teach international protocol, international communications, and how to deal with other cultures. As we expand our world and expand our businesses, we have to realize it's not just our way we have to respect, but we have to be open to other ways of thinking. We have to understand and respect everyone, and I think that's an eye-opener. We all tend to get complacent—that we here in the United States know best, but we don't know everything. There is so much to learn and we need to be open to it.

WRIGHT

So how do you achieve balance in life on the road to success? You mentioned balance and a list of characteristics a few minutes ago—is balance a way you define of success?

MICHAELS

Another interesting question. I achieve balance, I believe, because I've got some primary loves in my life—my family. They will always come first to me. I have two beautiful grandchildren, courtesy of my wonderful son and daughter-in-law. Watching the world through the eyes of a child is rejuvenating and fulfilling. When something comes up in business where I think, "Oh no," and start to feel what could turn into stress, all I have to hear is the sweet voice of my grandson saying, "I love you Nonna," and nothing else really matters.

I don't stress out easily, and I'm sure that's one of the secrets on the way to success. People have asked me why. It's as though you could probably light me on fire, and I would just stoically glaze over and stay calm. But I compare it to my beginnings. I was born in a concentration camp. My mother had to run for her life as a young woman. We escaped across the Adriatic Sea in a rowboat and went into hiding in Italy for years.

There is absolutely nothing about a job that can stress me out because the reality is that, on a scale of one to ten, everything is a momentary two. A wilted centerpiece or a power failure for three minutes is not the end of the world, and because I truly believe that it's not the end of the world, my clients don't make it the end of their world either. It's a glitch—it can be fixed. If you're not going to read about it in the *New York Times* a hundred years from now, it isn't that important. If someone doesn't die or get horribly sick before my eyes in a life-threatening way, and if it doesn't threaten lives, then it's fixable.

WRIGHT

You talked about morality and ethical behavior before. How do ethics play into success?

MICHAELS

I believe that I owe everyone around me total honesty and behaviors that respect them; I think people are worth that. I've certainly been exposed to more than my fair share of people who don't share that philosophy, but I would rather believe in the good in people and treat them with kindness and trust. I'd rather get disappointed along the way than come from a negative place, because I just don't want to fill my life with negativity. So I do believe that we owe ethics to everybody with whom we deal—good ethics, trust, loyalty, honesty, and fairness are ultimate.

WRIGHT

We talked before a little bit about success in changing times and maintaining success, but when confronted with adversity, as you would define adversity, how do you handle it?

MICHAELS

Keep moving, put it behind you. There is adversity every day in every moment if you look for it, and there are challenges to be overcome. I look at adversity almost as opportunity. In other words, here's the economy, and it's a disaster, but in it there is great opportunity for everybody. You just have to think about it creatively.

So, from my perspective—in the meetings industry—what are the opportunities that arise in market shares? What things have we not done when we were just so busy moving along and working just to fulfill the needs of our clients and not thinking strategically about where we could go after that? What's new? What could we add to our repertoire, and our arsenal?

For example, at the same time people are being laid off, meeting and events departments in corporations are disappearing, but this doesn't mean the companies don't still have a need to meet. So we have to take a look at how we can strategize. We go into these markets and to the corporations and say, "We can be your meeting-planners while you have no department to fulfill that function." There is always opportunity.

I met with some friends of mine from India recently, and they're facing similar problems. However, they've identified some of the most growing opportunities in India as liquor, tobacco, and condoms. So, no matter how bad the economy gets, these three markets are being greatly promoted. I don't know if condom sponsorships would be received well, but there are opportunities out there. We just have to identify them.

WRIGHT

So how stressful is the road to success, and how do you handle stress?

MICHAELS

As I mentioned, in all honesty, I just don't stress out that much. I think it's in perspective. My perspective is that this is a business and I run it like one. I love it; it's part of my family in my mind and I'm very protective of it. However, there isn't anything that could happen in business that would stress me out that greatly.

I know our bank account is not as flush as it was a year ago; it will be again because the pendulum swings. In the past thirty-five years that I've been doing this, we've experienced these situations before. This isn't the first time. I just prepare for them and ride them out.

I've always kept money in the bank because that old "rainy day" syndrome does come around every so often. When these downturns occur, we're prepared for them. Obviously, we can't last forever, nobody can, but it probably doesn't hit me as badly as it does other companies that have not prepared for it.

WRIGHT

One last question—I'm wondering what's up next for Andrea Michaels. What plans do you have? You have a book coming out titled *Reflections of a Successful Wallflower*, what's that all about?

MICHAELS

I decided I wanted to write a book about my event experiences because everybody I meet asks me how I got to where I am and wants to hear some of my stories (I've always been a storyteller). So I decided okay, I'm a writer, I love writing, why not write a book?

Most of the book is about my experiences in the last thirty plus years of doing events, but I also tie it in with how it relates to personal experiences. I'm very much a proponent of successful women in business. I have mentored many young women, I've hired many young women, and I've supported many young women. When I entered the business, it was very hard all those years ago for a woman to be taken seriously in a man's world, going to corporate America and trying to sell services and be taken seriously.

So it has involved baby steps. I encourage women to believe that they can have fulfilled lives in both their careers and with their families by being calm and strategic and believing in themselves.

I'd like to teach more classes and finish my book. I'd like to do things I haven't even thought of yet and I don't even know what those things are! One day I wish I could produce a Broadway show. But, in the meantime, I do a lot of mini versions of it for corporate America. They're fun and they're creative. I'd like to explore working in countries to which I've never traveled and find new things that no one has ever even thought of to do and then do them and have a whole lot of fun doing it.

WRIGHT

Well, what an interesting conversation. You are an interesting, interesting lady. I'm sure that our readers are going to get a lot out of this chapter.

MICHAELS

I hope so.

WRIGHT

Today we've been talking with Andrea Michaels, a pioneer in the meeting and events sector. She created an industry where there was none. She established the trends, paving the way for others. She is a sought-after speaker for numerous global educational conferences. Her work and seminars on creativity, profitability, and production have earned her international recognition. I don't know about you, but I think her comments on balance and tenacity are really great ideas.

Andrea, thank you for being with us today on *Stepping Stones for Success*.

WRIGHT

Thank you very much. I am always available to our readers for support.

ABOUT THE AUTHOR

ANDREA MICHAELS is a leading pioneer in the meeting and events sector, years ago creating an industry where there was none. For more than thirty-five years she has established the trends, paving the way for others to work nationally and internationally. Recipient of over thirty-three special events Gala Awards, she was the first inductee into the event industry Hall of Fame. A member of the Women in Business Hall of Fame, she has also received two SITE Crystal Awards, and an MPI Global Paragon Award. Prominent events include the opening of the Las Vegas Venetian Hotel and Resort and Vancouver's GM Place. Other high profile events include NASA's Space Shuttle Development Conference, and the Hong Kong Tourist Board's multi-city Road Shows.

Her ability to produce mega events for thousands is legendary. An upcoming memoir, *Reflections of a Successful Wallflower,* will reveal her remarkable career. Andrea is a sought-after speaker for numerous global educational conferences. Her seminars on creativity, profitability, and production have earned her international recognition.

ANDREA MICHAELS

Extraordinary Events
13425 Ventura Boulevard
Sherman Oaks, CA 91423-3998
818-783-6112
amichaels@extraordinaryevents.net
www.extraordinaryevents.net

CHAPTER FIFTEEN

Use Your "Treasures Within" to Achieve Success

An Interview with...

LOUISE COHEN

DAVID WRIGHT (WRIGHT)

Today we are talking with Louise Cohen. Louise enjoyed an exciting fashion career in New York City, a fulfilling career as a licensed clinical psychotherapist, and inspiration with a worldwide service organization dedicated to spiritual development and world harmony. She also enjoyed creative expression as a jazz vocalist and traveled worldwide living in many cities including London and Paris. This mosaic of life and professional experience has inspired her to develop Positive Attitude Coaching to encourage her clients to have a broader view of success. She heard many people expressing a longing to live their life with different values even though they had achieved material success and fame. Louise is convinced that people can find a harmony between their desire for "material outer success" and the "inner success" that is based on respect for self and others.

Louise Cohen, welcome to *Stepping Stones to Success.*

LOUISE COHEN (COHEN)

Well, thank you so much David; it's really exciting to be a part of this project. I feel it has an important message for everybody

WRIGHT

So tell me, what is your definition of success—what is the meaning of success?

COHEN

David, I'm glad you asked that question. I was interested in this project because I think it's really important to help people explore what success means to them. I think it should be a unique and special answer for each individual. If we look at the popular idea of success it is often focused on material gain or position.

I was curious to see how the dictionary explains success. It says that success is the gaining of fame, wealth, or social status. That didn't surprise me. But I was pleased to see that it also mentioned the accomplishment of an aim or purpose. This is the aspect of success I want to encourage people to explore.

It's sometimes very difficult to have the strength and courage to listen to your own inner voice and try to achieve your own special goals. That is why I try to support clients to look for new answers to questions they might not ask themselves. For instance, what kind of human being do you want to be? What do you want to achieve in your work or in your life or in your relationships? What's your life purpose beyond your material goals? Do you want to try to fit in with the popular mold of success, or do you want to follow your own path?

I think we have all been uniquely created to reach higher and deeper on our journey for self-discovery and fulfillment. I also see, as many of our psychologists have written, that in different stages of our lives we are presented with different challenges and ideas of success.

Let me give you an example from my own life because I think it will show you how we can often change our goals as we are presented with new life challenges. When I was in my early twenties, my idea of success was to leave the Midwest and go out to seek the world of fame and fortune. For me that kind of success meant living in New York City. My biggest challenge of course in my early twenties was to persuade my conservative parents to let me take this adventurous step. When I look back now I have to applaud them for their altruistic love and courage. I know they really wanted to keep me safe and home with them, but they let me go anyway.

My secret dream was to be a jazz vocalist and my practical dream was to work in the fashion industry. Creating a dream and committing to hard work are important first steps to success. Through hard work, and what I would say was an unrealistic confidence that only the young can have, I carved out a wonderful and creative career in fashion marketing and advertising. I loved the success, the glamour, the excitement and I even had an opportunity to live in London and Paris during this career. I never got bored with my work in fashion and yet my ideas of success started changing.

Going through some unexpected life challenges and difficulties, I began to hear a new inner voice telling me that my personal values were changing. Of course I tried to ignore that voice because to follow it would mean that I would have to give up the comfort, success, and satisfaction that I had already achieved. Also, I couldn't imagine returning to college at that time in my life.

Interestingly enough, the title of our book, *Stepping Stones to Success*, holds an important key to making any difficult changes. The key is step-by-step. I was able to accomplish a graduate degree and become a licensed psychotherapist and resign from my executive career one step at a time, one course at a time, and one difficult decision at a time. Through many of these experiences I learned that the concept of step-by-step is really an important aspect of overcoming obstacles to achieve new success.

WRIGHT

So what are the obstacles people face in trying to achieve success?

COHEN

Well, one of the biggest obstacles that I see, David, is people struggling with a general *negative attitude*. I heard this great quote recently. I think this quote says it all; *"A negative attitude is like a flat tire, you can't go anywhere until you change it"*— *Wendy Marshall.*

Some people think that you're ignoring the problem when you use a positive attitude; in fact, it's just the opposite. Obstacles can't move without action; but first you have to clear your mind of your negative point of view and assess the problem objectively from all sides. Once you have gathered all your information you can then make a *choice to use a positive attitude.* This opens up your creativity for new solutions.

Another obstacle to success is getting *attached to unrealistic expectations.* We frequently have difficulty accepting things as they are and we create our own expectations. I often hear clients say, "Well, what's wrong with having expectations?" Of course there is nothing wrong with setting goals and having standards. But what happens if these goals or standards can't be achieved at that time—what do you do then? Often we become discouraged because our expectations aren't being fulfilled in exactly the way we plan and we stop going forward.

When I talk to clients about "letting go," they sometimes confuse it with "giving up." Sometimes you may have to give up the expectation or goal temporarily. The key to success is not to keep struggling if it doesn't seem to be open at the time. Put your energy into something new that can be achieved in the present. This will give you a sense of accomplishment that will give you new energy to return to the challenge later.

In a way, it is truly unrealistic to expect a situation to work out as we planned because there are too many factors that come into play. You know the expression, "Life is happening." We never know what will come next.

Let me give you some simple examples.

You leave for work early but there is an accident on the road. Of course you are late for work. You feel guilty and upset. Instead of getting on with the day, you spend the whole day retelling the incident to everyone.

You plan a special party. You make great effort to arrange every detail. Nothing works out as you planned. You spend the whole evening noticing all the details that aren't working out, instead of enjoying the evening that has been presented to you. These attitudes and actions aren't formulas for success.

This is where using steppingstones to success really works. Most people who are successful don't stop the journey when their expectations haven't been met. Taking one step after another, they reframe the expectations and they create new possibilities.

I also see *hidden negative voices* and *self-judgments* as obstacles to success. It is surprising to find very successful and positive people unaware of their hidden negative voices. These self-judgments and fears become so much a part of us over the years that we don't even realize we are carrying around all this extra baggage. Many clients are surprised when they become aware of these "uninvited guests that never want to leave." It is amazing to see the new energy and clarity that opens up for people when they confront their hidden fears and self-judgments.

David, there are many obstacles we could talk about, but I'll mention just one more—our *ego*. Of course I'm not talking about the ego that gives us strength to move forward and accomplish goals. I'm talking about that ego that refuses to get help when you're going through a challenge or that ego that thinks it's always right. My favorite is the ego that won't let go in an argument, even if you don't believe your own point of view. I can now laugh at myself when I think about my stubborn ego.

With the variety of problems surfacing in the world today and the many new challenges for individuals, it is going to become necessary for people to take in new opinions, new support, and let go of solving problems in their usual ways.

For me, it was really a challenge at a certain point in my life to ask for help. But I was presented with a number of crises that I could not solve in the usual ways. When I finally let go and allowed myself to accept new support and information, I was amazed at the creativity and energy I experienced to find different solutions.

Recently I have been sending out a weekly e-mail titled "Changing Obstacles into New Possibilities." I started it because I was hearing a repeating refrain from clients and colleagues about their fears of "the state of things." By hooking into fears, you lose your ability to solve problems creatively. Most of us are not in a position to make policy changes in the government or world markets. But there is an area where we can effect change. From both professional and personal experience, I have seen the power of making changes in one's own inner attitude

So the good news is that we can transform our obstacles and create new possibilities for success.

WRIGHT

Well, that is good news. So will you share some basic strategies that you use to empower clients to create more possibilities for success?

COHEN

David, there are many similar strategies that have been used by psychologists, therapists, and coaches for years; but I really like to encourage clients to experiment and decide what works for them. I sometimes use the expression "trial and error," but it really isn't error it's more experimenting. You have to *practice, process your experience,* and *eliminate* what doesn't work for you.

For instance here are some basic strategies I encourage clients to explore:

- Try apologizing when you're wrong.
- Try to stop and listen when you're in conflict.
- Try congratulating yourself for even one small success instead of waiting for compliments from others.
- Try complimenting someone else sincerely.
- Try to create a friendlier workplace instead of complaining about the negativity from managers and colleagues.
- Try practicing gratitude for the many gifts and blessings in your life, especially when you're feeling discouraged or bored.
- Try laughing at yourself when you make a mistake.
- Try asking for help.
- Try making a commitment to be kind to yourself and others.
- Try fine-tuning your radar to alert you when you are being overwhelmed and then set boundaries.
- Try cultivating appreciation for the inner gifts of your spirit.
- Try managing your own time and energy instead of blaming others for your frustrations.

Changes don't happen with one effort, but old patterns can be changed with practice and commitment. It's always wonderful to see the surprise and sense of accomplishment when clients experience new power, life balance, and success after practicing some of these strategies.

WRIGHT

So why is life balance so important for achieving success?

COHEN

David, I think that is an important question to think about in striving for success. Over the years, I have worked with many clients. Even in my business career the same issues always came up:

- I never have time for my family,
- I never have time to do something fun just for me.
- I never have time to offer some service to help others.
- I am always too tired to accept social invitations.
- I am always too tired to explore new directions in my life and career.

The list could go on and on. I know we could each add something to the list. What is interesting about these comments is that they were said by many people who had achieved material or career success, but had no sense of success and wellbeing about their total life.

Finding that balance between professional life, family life, social life, and other special activities is an important aspect of achieving health and wellbeing. But I'm talking about a different concept of life balance to give one's life new meaning. As I began to observe my life and study spiritual development, I realized that we have all been uniquely created with a spiritual, mental, emotional, and physical aspect that gives us the potential to live our life with perfect harmony and balance.

You don't have to have any particular faith or belief to experience this, but I see it as an important key to success. When your balance is off, that "perfectly created system" tells you something is wrong. For instance, you may start to experience a succession of physical illnesses or you may start to feel like you need to shut down emotionally. Maybe it is taking you twice as long to accomplish your work and think creatively in your problem-solving.

Some people talk about feeling an emptiness and a disconnect from themselves. It confuses them because they seem to have all the material comforts and worldly success they have dreamed about all their life. Some people talk about feeling like they are on a treadmill going nowhere.

Of course, there may be some mental, emotional, and physical problems manifesting in these conditions. However, I also see them as signals from our spiritual aspect telling us that we are out of balance with the Divine Origin that creates the harmony of all things in the universe. I love this aspect of the work because I see the positive changes that develop when clients first find the courage to admit that their life is out of balance with their spiritual aspect. It is wonderful to see them taking the risk to explore the aspects of themselves that they have been neglecting.

When I look back on my past, and remember the times I was experiencing great stress and disharmony, I now see I was looking for answers in all the wrong places. When I became aware of the importance of understanding my spiritual condition, I saw my life gradually begin to come into balance. When I started this process for myself, while sometimes challenging and painful, it became exciting and life-enhancing as time went on.

WRIGHT

You talked about life balance as an important aspect to achieve success. You also mentioned learning to understand your spiritual aspect. How do these aspects help one achieve success?

COHEN

In working with many people over years, David, I could see that if we are disconnected from that part of ourselves that tells us what we value and how we can love and respect ourselves and others, eventually we may experience disharmony in our lives. This negativity then begins to chip away at our sense of success and wellbeing. As I said before, I had seen it with people no matter how much they had achieved material success and fame.

Isn't it amazing that we think we can set our own balance of life and completely ignore that higher balance given to us by the Creator? In a way we have everything upside down because we are often putting top priority on our material aspect. Yet, the highest part of ourselves that contain all the wisdom we need to create a life of harmony and prosperity, we put last on our list.

I know many clients talk about feeling like they're trying to swim upstream when the current is going in the opposite direction; I certainly have experienced this for myself. I realized that when we are going in the opposite direction of the principles that the Creator has given us to be successful, it takes tremendous energy to try to continue to achieve any progress or lasting success.

Again I have to clarify that tuning in with spirituality is not about following a particular faith or ritual. However it certainly can be a way to start opening up to your deeper inner truths. I understand spirituality as an individual's sense of peace, purpose, and connection to others, as well as one's belief about the meaning of life.

As we develop and start to create a positive spiritual aspect, our health, our relationships, and even our financial stability starts to change for the better. Whether we have a particular faith or no faith at all, we have all been created equally to tune into that divine wisdom.

Through a number of unexpected crises in my life, I began to learn that I had forgotten the gifts of that "perfectly created system." Prior to this I had experienced many wonderful training sessions, practices, and a rich connection to the Jewish faith from my childhood. But these crises awakened me to the realization that I had taken many things for granted and I had forgotten gratitude in my life, including the "gift of my life" itself.

I don't think there are any accidents in the universe. Have you heard the expression, "when you're ready for the teacher, the teacher will appear?" At this time of crisis I found Sukyo Mahikari Centers for Spiritual Development. They have Centers in seventy countries throughout the world and their Web site is www.sukyomahikari.org.

At the Spiritual Development Centers, their efforts are focused on two important trainings. One is a practice of light energy, which uncovers our radiant soul to allow us to achieve our true potential. The other practice is about our attitude. Everything we think and do is influenced by our attitude and it affects everything important to us. Even in science today they are experimenting with the nature of higher energy and talking about the concept that thoughts can form or affect reality.

It was interesting to learn how to find new keys for happiness and success in the three-day spiritual development course. They gave information on how to give light and practice the universal principles along with other interesting experiences and knowledge about spiritual development.

But in the beginning, before I ever decided to take the training, I was so grateful to be able to be in an environment where I could feel vibrations of peace and beauty. I also realized I was in a place that allowed me to experience a childhood dream. Even as a child, I hoped that people of all differences could learn to get along. It was a dream come true for me to find a place where people of different races, religions, languages, etc. were striving to work out their differences as a way to create a better world.

Through this experience I began to find new meaning in my childhood faith, and I learned without a doubt that we have a Divine Creator who wants us to love and be successful.

WRIGHT

So what drives you to be successful?

COHEN

It is interesting that you would ask that, David, because I see my drive for success has changed. In my earlier career in the fashion industry in New York, I think there was a desire to achieve success in the "outer world." This meant relationships with famous people, creative success in my fashion career, good reviews from company heads and colleagues, and a good bottom line. I still understand the excitement of trying to achieve these practical and worldly goals.

But as I began to awaken to new inner goals, my drive for success changed. What drives me now is to help others become successful by finding their own special qualities within. For me it creates a sense of fulfillment and success that is different from the achievements I experienced in the material world. It's so exciting when I see a client go through some new discovery of their inner strengths and values that allows them to create a different kind of success in the material world.

That discovery drives me to encourage clients to keep chipping away at the obstacles that block them from trying new things, and learning to see themselves in new ways. I want to help them uncover the unique gifts and abilities that have been given to them by their Creator, even if they have no spiritual beliefs at all.

WRIGHT

You talked about gratitude before; what does gratitude have to do with success?

COHEN

It is actually quite simple because when we're focusing on *what we don't have*, it's impossible to experience any sense of success, no matter what we have achieved. Practicing gratitude, (now I emphasize *practicing* again), is one of the most powerful tools I have seen for creating life success and satisfaction. It would seem that we would be automatically grateful, especially in the Western world, because of our amazing prosperity of science, technology, freedom to think and believe as we please, and incredible material abundance. So why aren't we happy?

Well, of course, that answer is for each individual to explore themselves. But I think that some of the answers can be found when we look at that tension between "the material outer goals" and "the inner goals" based on the universal principals. As I mentioned earlier, I learned that I had taken for granted many of the wonderful gifts and blessings in my life. However, I only realized it after I had experienced some crises and challenges that were beyond my ability to solve on my own.

In reaching out and looking for new answers I learned about the universal spiritual principles such as gratitude and using positive language to solve problems. I learned that there is a spiritual power in the essence of a word. The words that express gratitude can move everything in a positive cycle and it has the power to create things. Of course, we do need to discuss a problem to come up with a new solution. But if we use words that express complaint and dissatisfaction, they can create a potential for something to collapse.

For me this was a big change because I spent many years trying to solve problems and overcome obstacles with anger and complaint. Can you believe that? I had a good temper. I would justify my actions and anger by saying that the goal was to right some wrong, or help someone who couldn't help themselves.

Well, that was the goal most of the time, but I also had begun to realize that there was a self-righteous ego in there somewhere and I needed to be right all the time. So at first the practice of gratitude was really intellectual and I didn't always feel sincere. But then I thought that gratitude was a universal principle given to us by the Creator. Could my ego be that big that I wasn't even willing to try to practice it? And looking at my past filled with anger and complaint, I had to admit those attitudes certainly weren't bringing me happiness.

Interestingly enough, as I began listening more instead of yelling, offering an apology when I was out of line, and finding situations that I could sincerely express gratitude, I started to experience unexpected success with many unsolvable problems.

WRIGHT

So will you give us a simple example of how you practice gratitude?

COHEN

Many professional therapists and coaches have all created wonderful exercises on gratitude practices, but I'll give you one of the simple practices that I use sometimes:

As I open my eyes and look around my bedroom I see the sun streaming in my window, I express gratitude to the Creator for being allowed to see the sun and how much I had taken my precious eyes for granted.

In the next breath I realized the profound mystery that the sun was shining in my bedroom and in different places all over the world at the same time.

In the next breath I realized I had taken for granted "my next breath," and I felt like repeating over and over to the Creator, thank You very much.

As I stepped into the shower and turned the knob, water came out. Water is becoming a precious gift in many places all over the world, but I have it in abundance without any cost or effort; again I said thank You.

And what a mystery! When I turned the knob a little to the left, the water becomes hot, and look how my fingers bend to turn the knob and look how my feet and legs hold me up to stand in the shower; thank You very much.

Look how my eyes close automatically to protect me from the soap and water; how miraculously we have been created.

What about the soap and washcloth? How many people made the effort to produce the soap and washcloth so that I could take a shower; thank you, everyone.

The practice could go on and on, but when I started the day with a gratitude practice, my whole state of mind was completely different as I went out into the world. Of course it's easy to practice gratitude when you see the beauty all around you, but how do you practice gratitude when there is a crisis? Actually, what I found is that you receive the most rewards when you try to practice gratitude with difficult challenges.

I'll give you an example again from my life. There was a period in my life many years back when I was suddenly out of a job. I was working as a social work consultant in New York City and the grant for the program was cancelled unexpectedly. It was hard to remember gratitude when the many efforts I made to send out resumes were answered with silence. Of course my feeling of fear began to manifest in the beginning, but I decided to try to transform the feelings of fear into a positive attitude and a practice of gratitude. Wonderful changes started happening when I let go of my fear and my ego and I started practicing gratitude. Friends began to help me in so many ways it was hard to imagine so much generosity. In the past I had so much pride I would never let anyone know I was having a problem.

The most amazing experience of gratitude came with close family members. During this time of financial challenge I decided to move back to my city of origin. Interestingly enough I was able to get a wonderful job within a few weeks, but I decided to move in with family for a six-month period to build my finances again. Of course this was a great blow to my ego, but it also brought me an unexpected new experience of love and gratitude.

I had a very special relationship with these relatives and I had a great deal of love for them. My brother and I had a special bond, but when we were children we often fought and I would leave the family table in tears and anger. Even though we were adults, it was easy to fall into old childhood patterns again. But now when I felt my temper flaring, I would think about the love and generosity of my brother and sister-in-law taking me into their home and I would silently say, "thank you." Well, it literally changed the nature of our lifetime relationship. It was wonderful to get to know my brother in a new way. The practice of gratitude gave me a new foundation to stay quiet instead of reacting in anger. I found he had many wonderful qualities that I could never see because I was always losing my temper.

I have to say it was a lot more joyous to experience a new relationship of respect and love instead of winning an argument. I could argue really well, yet it didn't bring me much joy; but what a surprising joy gratitude brought me.

David, I think it is interesting to note that my experience of gratitude wasn't unique. In the field of positive psychology, the current research is showing surprising results in the practice of gratitude from top corporations to individual relationships. There are actual studies that show a common experience of success and wellbeing from a variety of businesses, cultures, and individuals of all generations when they started practicing gratitude.

And in the Sukyo Mahikari Spiritual Development Centers, worldwide, businesspeople, politicians, educators, scientists, medical professionals, and people in the creative arts are all reporting that the practice of gratitude has developed many new opportunities for creative problem-solving, success, and respect in their environments and relationships. It's amazing to see how a simple practice of gratitude is really transforming businesses, relationships and families.

WRIGHT

Louise, I think you have talked about a number of interesting experiences of success for yourself and clients. Are there some special points you want people to hear so they can learn from your success?

COHEN

David, there are so many wonderful lessons I have learned in working with people and just living my life. The good news is that obstacles can be overcome and we can start anew. But let me outline a few ideas that I know can be steppingstones to success:

- Flexibility and Persistence are important strategies for achieving success. Don't give up. If one strategy doesn't work try a different one and keep trying.
- Get your ego out of the way. Getting support and information from others is a great key to success and it opens up new creativity and ideas.
- Success is not always an easy flow up—the waves continue to go up and down. The lessons you can learn as the waves go down give you the most important information and strength for future success.
- Get help in changing your negative attitudes. Sometimes the old negative patterns are hard to break, but your attitude change is absolutely necessary for lasting success.
- Start tuning in with your spiritual aspect so you can tap into the innate gifts, strengths, and wisdom given to all of us by our Parent God.
- Gratitude helps to build your positive attitude and tunes you into positive energy that helps you overcome challenges.
- Learn to honor yourself by accepting both your strengths and liabilities. You can certainly begin to experience a new peace and satisfaction.
- Practice letting go when something isn't working as you planned. Holding on just keeps you stuck and delays your experience of something new in the future.

- Don't waste time wishing you had done something differently. Reflect on the negative event or your negative behavior and use a positive and constructive attitude to create something new.
- Learn how to apologize. It is an action that can create new strength and success in all aspects of your life.
- Learn to laugh at yourself even when you're in crisis. Laughing is one of the most wonderful gifts we can give ourselves, and it is absolutely free. In fact, it's one of the most perfect natural medicines that exist in abundance—if we use it.

WRIGHT

So what makes your perspective unique?

COHEN

David, let me start by first pointing out that this is a wonderful time for many people to grow and create lives of success and wellbeing. There are so many incredible teachers and professionals out in the world dedicated to elevating people's lives and the world around them. The beautiful thing about this effort is that people are working together and sharing their knowledge and experience. So I would have to say that while I'm trying to develop a unique perspective, it grows out of a spiritual and professional knowledge given to me from the generosity of the Creator and many colleagues.

As I mentioned previously, I'm working on what I see as a constant tension between our desire to be successful in "the material world" and "the innate success" that is based on respect for self and others.

Practicing a positive change of attitude, with universal principles such as gratitude and respect, can become powerful tools for success. It is interesting to see that when you combine these principles with practical career and life goals such as career advancement, career change, life balance, relationship quality, and even financial stability, you are able to tackle these goals with new energy and clarity.

While it may seem that practicing attitude change takes a good deal of effort, the good news is the tremendous sense of accomplishment and strength that starts to manifest as these practices become more natural. And, in fact, you can experience a sense of feeling lighter and lighter as you harmonize the tension between your "outer worldly goals" and your "inner values."

For myself, I can say that I used to be a very serious child. Now I often feel like a happy child. There was a wonderful sign I saw recently that said, "It is never too late to have a happy childhood."

It has become clear to me in trying to help others achieve a "true success" and my efforts to strive for it myself, that it will make a difference if you take the journey to search for the "Treasures within." Even if you have no spiritual beliefs, these gifts from the Creator are waiting to be uncovered. I'm convinced that the journey to find the treasures within is an important part of the steppingstones to success.

There is a quote on one of the pages on my Web site that says,

Often what we take for granted is where the treasures lie.
Often the treasures we are seeking, we already own.
They are within ourselves and others.

WRIGHT

Very interesting, it's an interesting perspective on success—one that expands most other definitions that I've heard. I really appreciate all this time you've taken answering these questions for me. I've really learned a lot here today. I've got a lot to consider about success and how to use gratitude to achieve it.

COHEN

Well, I thank you so much for your patience and allowing me to share what I feel have been wonderful experiences from my clients and my own life. I hope these experiences will help others begin their search for their treasures within.

WRIGHT

Today we've been talking to Louise Cohen, a licensed clinical psychotherapist and success coach. Her professional and life experience has inspired her to develop Positive Attitude Coaching. She heard a longing from so many people to find a harmony between what she calls "the material worldly success" and "the innate success"—the often unexpressed desire—to live life with a genuine respect for self and others. I don't know about you, but I think she knows what she's talking about, at least I'm going to listen.

Thank you so much Louise for being with us today on *Stepping Stones to Success.*

COHEN

Thank you David, it has been a real privilege to share some of these ideas and participate in this wonderful project.

ABOUT THE AUTHOR

LOUISE COHEN enjoyed an exciting fashion career in New York City, a fulfilling career as a licensed clinical psychotherapist, and inspiration with a worldwide service organization dedicated to spiritual development and world harmony. She also enjoyed creative expression as a jazz vocalist and traveled worldwide living in many cities including London and Paris. This mosaic of life and professional experience has inspired her to develop Positive Attitude Coaching to encourage her clients to have a broader view of success. She heard many people expressing a longing to live their life with different values even though they had achieved material success and fame. Louise is convinced that people can find a harmony between their desire for "material outer success" and the "inner success" that is based on respect for self and others.

LOUISE ANN COHEN, MSW, LCSW
Positive Attitude Coaching
PO Box 957641
Hoffman Estates IL, 60195-7641
847-271-7220
louise@positiveattitudecoaching.com
www.PositiveAttitudeCoaching.com

CHAPTER SIXTEEN

Succeed in Your Purpose

An Interview with...

LAURI WILLIAMS

DAVID WRIGHT (WRIGHT)

Today we're talking with Lauri Williams, author, speaker, professional career trainer, and consultant. She has been teaching and mentoring people on the principles of success and attaining rewarding and productive careers and pursuing their purpose for success in their lives. Lauri Williams has a master's degree in Human Resources and holds many established professional credentials in her field. She is no doubt an established expert on the topic of "Success." Lauri has taught on success principles for many years. She has since decided to share her teachings to those receptive to manifesting success. Lauri further began formulating her success principles in 2004 as a great demand for it existed. She has completed and is publishing the sought-after principles in her upcoming book,

Success Belongs to You: Find Out Why. It will be in publication by November of this year, 2009.

"Begin your journey today," she says. "On the road to manifesting your success, today is the day you take total and complete control of your life and thoughts in every way." Don't limit yourself another day, you're a successful being, begin to increase the level of success you deserve today. Before you begin, you must know it will require you to change your level of thinking and aim toward increasing your level of success. The sky, however, is the limit—you can do it. Successful thinking requires you to move beyond your comfort zone, but it is obtainable. You can do it because you already possess the talents, skills, and abilities within you to draw the kind of successful lifestyle you desire. Yes you have the success power in you to do it—if you desire it, stay strong, believe you can, and position yourself to take the journey to get you there. All you need is a little help and encouragement in developing and stirring the power within you."

She is here and to do just that—encourage you. Remember, you deserve to increase your success. She says, "Do it today."

Lauri, welcome to *Stepping Stones to Success*.

LAURI WILLIAMS (WILLIAMS)
Thank you, David.

WRIGHT
I know you've heard many, many definitions of success, but how do *you* define success?

WILLIAMS
Well, David, we all equate success to a lot of different things and in many ways, but one true clearness or outline or definite statement is that success is knowing and living your true purpose in life. And that, my dear, is "Success." Our modern dictionary defines success as an attainment of one's aim, wealth, or fame, etcetera, but how can you, unless you know what your true purpose is? You can't progress forward or live a peaceful and content and successful life in confusion and misery. So, I believe knowing your true purpose is the key.

WRIGHT

Aside from personal role models, who are the people who have served as your role models for success?

WILLIAMS

Aside from the personal examples—my parents, my pastor, spiritual leader—I would say Marc Victor Hansen, Jack Canfield, Tyler Perry, Oprah Winfrey, Napoleon Hill, Arnold Schwarzenegger, and Tony Robinson. And the list goes on. They serve as role models, although I have not personally met them; I would love to meet them one day. I felt that I knew or could relate to them and could relate to their past struggles as well as get to know what drives their present success. I could relate to that and it encouraged me and motivated me to pursue my destiny in life.

WRIGHT

What would you say would be the biggest contribution to your professional success?

WILLIAMS

I believe the biggest contribution would be my spiritual relationship with my Creator, and the spiritual leader God placed in my life to teach and help me to learn, to grow, to think on success, to learn and apply wisdom, and to persevere. Indeed, I would say that wisdom and perseverance are central keys to success in life and the life after.

WRIGHT

What do you think are the biggest obstacles that people face in trying to become successful or lead successful lives?

WILLIAMS

The biggest obstacle is fear; however, there are many obstacles. Some factors however, depend on an individual's circumstances and situation, but primarily the common elements would be fear. We know that FEAR an acronym for False Evidence Appearing Real, so perception would be one.

Not believing in one's self would be another or a lack of desire.

Another element is being complacent and/or content with life and where they are or not wanting to grow mentally or spiritually. The important element is to have a desire or a motivation to want to break through the obstacle of being fearful of what might happen or what might not happen.

I would say that the biggest obstacle for many people would be fear.

WRIGHT

How does one know what one needs to be successful?

WILLIAMS

I know what it took to manifest my success. It depends on an individual's situation, circumstance, and the power of belief that he or she has within. But for me essentially manifesting success—the life I have—took perseverance. It took faith, patience, persistence, and above all believing in myself and that I could do it.

WRIGHT

Would you tell our readers about what drives you to be successful?

WILLIAMS

The thing that drives me to succeed is purpose. I believe I am successful and I was created to be successful. Likewise, we all are. We all were given a form of power and what we do with that determines our level as to how far we will pursue our innate success. Until people come into acknowledgement or agreement of what their destiny is for their life, their strengths, and talents, I believe that these are what drive people to be successful. Carl Jung mentioned that he who looks outward dreams, but he who looks within awakens. So, until we can look within ourselves and know who we are and what our gifts and talents are, we may be stagnant and not fulfill the purpose we have.

WRIGHT

Many people today are talking about balance, and so many books are being written about balance—especially life balance. Do you think it's important to balance your success in your life and if so, how do you achieve balance?

WILLIAMS

Yes, I do believe it's important to balance your success in life. If there is no balance in your life, you won't be able to maintain your success. So balance equals consistent success.

I balance success in my life by having clarity for the important things in life. First and foremost is my belief in my Creator and time for seeking wisdom and strength to stay on the course of the journey of life that I was given.

To have "me time," is another element of balance. I believe that you must have "me time," if you don't take time for yourself and find out what things keeping you going, you will wander through life not knowing your success and what you were meant to experience.

A final would be relationships. It's important to have stimulating communication from family, friends, or others. No man (or woman) is an island. So others can sometimes help you in seeing the bigger picture in life.

Prioritizing is another important element in balancing success.

WRIGHT

What is the message you want people to hear so that they can learn from your success?

WILLIAMS

The message I want others to hear is that success is theirs. They have the potential within to achieve whatever it is that they want to achieve in life. It doesn't matter who they are. It does, however, require faith—believing in yourself, focusing, and staying strong during hard times.

If people don't give up and if they continue to be persistent and maintain the success they have, whatever level they choose regardless of the obstacles, they too will live contented and successful lives. As spoken in my upcoming book, *Success Belongs to You,* there are four letters that spell out the acronym FAME—Focus, Affirm, Meditate, and Expect. If you take hold of those four principles and apply them consistently, they can measure the course of success in your life.

WRIGHT

Focus, Affirm, Mediate, and the last was Expect.

WILLIAMS

Right. You have to expect. With expectation comes a strong desire. Desire develops feelings and emotions that leads or guides you to take action. So definitely expect.

WRIGHT

You talked a minute ago about people who influenced your life, such as your parents and your pastor. You also mentioned Mark Victor Hansen, Jack Canfield, Tyler Perry, and Oprah Winfrey. How can people help other people to succeed?

WILLIAMS

We were all put on this Earth for a reason—to serve a purpose. I believe that people can serve twofold in helping others succeed. I call it the M&M factor ("Mentors and Motivators"). You have those who will mentor you. A mentor is someone you trust or an advisor—the tutor who is providing knowledge about how to help you get to your destiny. The motivator would be one who serves as a coach or cheerleader to spark encouragement during low times in life (I believe we need that).

If we can look at the M&M factor and see where we play a part in helping others succeed, then we can truly see that this is also success. When we are successful and as we move to various levels of success, we come to know that success is not just for us, but it's for others around us too.

WRIGHT

So would you then say that you are successful and if you are, how do you measure it?

WILLIAMS

Yes, I would say that I am successful and getting better at it every day. Measuring my success comes in various ways. But to keep it simple, my success is measured spiritually, mentally, financially, and physically through accomplished goals, my prosperous business, and helping others achieve their goals and realize their true purpose for success in their lives. This makes me successful too.

My accomplished goals are manifested success. The goals accomplished with the books I have written have helped encourage others. I have a book out now titled *Six Steps, Six Figures*. It has helped many people from different backgrounds, from military to college students—those who want to make a career change. The book is available in Barnes & Noble. I would say that this book project, *Stepping Stones to Success*, is definitely an accomplished goal, as well as my upcoming book, *Success Belongs to You: Find Out Why*.

WRIGHT

In the beginning, when I was introducing you, I read something you had said—"Successful thinking requires you to move beyond your comfort zone, but it is attainable." What do you mean by "successful thinking means you've got to move beyond your comfort zone"?

WILLIAMS

If we look around us and we look at creation, if we look at even the objects we are sitting on, and objects that we use, we know that at first, they were a thought. A cabinet maker first thought of making cabinets or a dressmaker first had a thought to design a garment before designing a wardrobe. Initially it comes with the level of thinking that we have.

Once we can take hold and discipline our thoughts toward success, then that can help motivate us to another level where we pursue and act upon that and accomplish those things we think about that will bring success into our lives.

WRIGHT

Another question is in the same vein. You have said (and I'm really interested in what you mean), "All you need is a little help and encouragement in developing and stirring the power within you." So success is something that someone else has to help us with?

WILLIAMS

At times have had various points in our lives when we can't focus and we can't seem to see the forest because we're down among the trees. We are here for one another. As we help individuals, we are actually helping ourselves. We were birthed or created from our Creator with powerful success energy within us, and sometimes it takes a little encouragement if we are at a point where we can't really manifest that. Sometimes it takes those around us—whether it's the mentor or the motivator—to help us see what strengths or talents we have that we can be a contribution to society.

WRIGHT

Lastly, Lauri, what principles, if any, do you use for succeeding?

WILLIAMS

The principles that I mentioned previously—the fame factor—is where I focus on disciplining my thoughts toward succeeding and accomplishing goals and helping others stay focused on what their true purpose is for their lives. We were put here on Earth to be a success and a success for others.

Secondly, I continually affirm or speak success and positive words.

Next, I meditate; it helps to meditate. Sometimes I'm bogged down with thoughts, but when I'm meditating upon success it helps to manifest success for my life and I see fast results.

The last principle is expecting. I believe that with expecting you have to have a level of desire to carry out actions to manifest abundant success within each of us. No expectations—no desires—and no actions lead to no results.

Those four principles are definitely the elements I use.

WRIGHT

Well, what a great conversation. I really appreciate all the time you've spent with me here this afternoon to answer these questions about success. I think you've got a new twist on some things about success. You never did mention money, and fame, and all of that as success. Was that on purpose?

WILLIAMS

I was reading a book by Dr. Claude Olney titled *The Buck Starts Here*. He wrote, "Do what you love to do and the money will come." Those were just elements or add-ons. Until you are content and know what your true purpose is for your life, you won't really enjoy the money you acquire to the fullest and you won't have contentment. Contentment comes with knowing your purpose. So again, do what you love to do, find out what your talents, your strengths, and your levels for success in helping others, and that level of financial security will come, along with abundant wealth, knowledge, and experience. This will give you much pleasure in being able to enjoy it and share it with others.

WRIGHT

Today we have been talking with Lauri Williams. Lauri has a colorful background. She owns Optasia Career and Training Services, LLC, a veteran owned company exclusively providing professional services in the area of keynote speeches, training and development, workshops, and much more. Lauri earned a bachelor's degree in Human Services from Wayland Baptist University in Plainview, Texas. She also earned a master's degree in Human Resources Management from Troy State University in Misawa, Japan. Lauri is a minister. She is a certified professional speaker, a certified job search trainer, a certified Train-The-Trainer, a certified Master Career Director, a certified employment interview consultant, and author. For many years she has been teaching and mentoring people on the principles of success and attaining rewarding and productive careers and pursuing their purpose for success in their life.

Lauri, thank you so much for being with us today on *Stepping Stones to Success.*

WILLIAMS

Thank you for having me.

ABOUT THE AUTHOR

LAURI WILLIAMS, author, speaker, professional career trainer, and consultant. She has been teaching and mentoring people on the principles of success and attaining rewarding and productive careers and pursuing their purpose for success in their lives. Lauri Williams has a master's degree in Human Resources and holds many established professional credentials in her field. She is no doubt an established expert on the topic of "Success." Lauri has taught on success principles for many years. She has since decided to share her teachings to those receptive to manifesting success. Lauri further began formulating her success principles in 2004 as a great demand for it existed. She has completed and is publishing the sought-after principles in her upcoming book, *Success Belongs to You: Find Out Why.* It will be in publication by November of this year, 2009.

LAURI WILLIAMS
P.O. Box 94797
North Little Rock, AR 72190
877-771-7513
(501) 240-3491
lauriwilliams@optasiatraining.com
LLLJ123@hotmail.com
www.optasiatraining.com

CHAPTER SEVENTEEN

Developing Leadership & Peak Performance

An Interview with...

DRAKE BEIL

DAVID WRIGHT (WRIGHT)

Today we're talking with Drake Beil who has said that great leaders inspire with an ability to share their vision. They motivate others to levels of peak performance through excellent team-building and coaching skills. Ultimately, successful leadership is about getting other people on the same track of quality and, more specifically, getting the right things done, the right way, and at the right time. Leaders weave strategic and operational elements to influence others with professional communication skills. As needed, leaders demonstrate a wide range of additional abilities in many areas including conflict management, critical and creative thinking, decision-making, financial management, problem-solving, and time and stress management.

Drake welcome to *Stepping Stones for Success.*

DRAKE BEIL (BEIL)

My pleasure to be here.

WRIGHT

So what is your definition of leadership and will you give some specific examples?

BEIL

Simply, leadership is the art of getting the right things done, the right way, at the right time. That's the fundamental path of good leadership, and ultimately to a higher quality of life. It is present in all organizations and in all living organisms. The further you stray from the path, the harder it is to survive. If you don't believe me on this, check with Darwin!

A friend and associate of mine, Dr. Mark Kimmel, and I wrote a monograph called the *Fundamentals of Quality* for the largest training and development organization in the world, ASTD. After searching for excellence, companies were then searching for quality and they asked us for a map.

We came to see that quality, like life, is a series of small improvements. You occasionally but rarely have gigantic improvements happen, but rather a daily and infinite series of small steps headed in the right direction is really what it's about. Living with imperfection is the nature of the leadership path, but with a clear vision, at least you know the destination.

So having a vision of what the right things are, and sharing that vision effectively, creates not only the leadership path but also the management direction. Most strategic planning is designed to find that vision, carve it out, and then translate it operationally so we can create the most effective pathways to get there.

WRIGHT

So what are some of the key dimensions of leadership?

BEIL

Well, along the same lines there are two basic issues: direction and support. We need to know where we're going and we need to know how we're going to get there. Extraordinary leadership is moving people there enthusiastically. Most successful leaders have both the vision that we look for as followers and the ability to communicate that vision to get people motivated and inspired to act.

Essentially, these are strategic and operational issues. Ken Blanchard and Paul Hersey had it right when they wrote *Situational Leadership*. They talked a lot about direction and support and how they interact. They described four stages of developing managers, and I think it goes further because I believe they were really defining the path of peak performance in leadership.

Ironically, that's both good and bad. If you think about key visionary leaders in history—the greatest leaders of all time—who would you think of; who comes to your mind? People like Gandhi, Martin Luther King, John F. Kennedy, Lincoln, Caesar, and Christ? Well, do you know what they all have in common? They were all assassinated! So when I start my leadership course at the University of Hawaii, I often begin by having everybody call out famous leaders. Write them down and you often get an entire list of people who were killed or wanted dead. Then I say, "Welcome to leadership training." It always gets a guarded laugh because that's a real concern. The nail that sticks out does get pounded. Not only is having a vision important and having the ability to communicate that vision critical, but there's also some healthy respect for how much vision people can take at one time, and at what point does that become literally dangerous for the leader?

In Hawaii, there's an old joke about the political leadership here. They say local politicians wait to see which way the crowd is moving and then run to the front. However, as pragmatic as that may be (and as truthful), that's not a useful definition of leadership. Leadership literally is carving out that path with a vision that is both exciting and indeed memorable when it occurs. John F. Kennedy's "put a man on the moon by the end of the decade" is such a clear vision and so motivational. M. L. King's dream is now President of the United States.

So a number of the leaders we cherish, historically, in our minds and in our hearts, have this ability to create a vision. It's a greater vision in fact, because it's not just for themselves, but for all. Often new ideas confront the status quo. That's a threat for many people because status quo is progress. That's why support is so important. I believe it's the fuel that gets the leadership machine moving. The vision alone can't do anything, it's only when it's implemented that you have the potential for progress.

WRIGHT

In the business world, leadership is often about profit. What are the main factors that drive profitability?

BEIL

Leadership and profitability are inextricably intertwined. PIMS, a research group in the Bay Area, did some interesting research. They took a look all the financials and a range of other elements from thousands of businesses and looked at profitability with regression analyses to see if any key factors emerged. There were two. One was the size of the market share that the business currently had and found from low to high that there were some advantages in both directions. The other was the perception of service quality. In other words, people cared quite a bit about being served well, and the most important part of this idea was that they wanted to buy something of quality. They willingly paid more for it, and were generally happy to do it!

If you put them on a graph, you have Market Share as one axis, and Service Quality as the other. That forms an interesting little matrix. There are four basic groups, as you can imagine, and they define companies by business strategy.

For instance, if you have high market share, but a low perception of quality, that's not necessarily a problem. A lot of the big box stores have no service, but you can walk in and buy mass quantities of things at great prices, so they have carved out a profitable niche for themselves. The quadrant of the high quality and low market share can also be very profitable. Think of Mercedes, Prada, Ritz-Carlton, Rolex, and Louis Vuitton. These brands are not ever going to have Coke-like market share, but they can charge a lot more. All of the name brands prove this niche is also valuable because people are spending tens of thousands of dollars more every day, whether it's a handbag, or luggage, or things that obviously could be bought for a lot less.

The real action obviously, is what happens when you combine high market share and a high perception of quality? Now we get into some very rare air because there are only a few companies. Maybe you can think of a couple of others, but Coke maintains massive market share by communicating the perception of quality. Apple also comes to mind and they're actually gaining market share right now. I think AT&T is really smiling a great deal. They were in the right place at the right time with Apple and their numbers are turning now as a result of that and the perception of the quality of the iPhone. Another one, for me, is Nike. People will pay huge money for a Swoosh.

Starbucks is another. I know they're closing a bunch of stores now, but sometimes consolidation is good—it's just like pruning a tree. If you don't garden properly, unchecked growth will be a problem. But Starbucks redefined an industry. They proved you could charge a fairly healthy amount for a basic commodity that you could get in probably twenty other nearby locations. But maybe we pay a little bit more for a decaf skinny vanilla latte, or whatever, because we like it.

So, successful leaders understand that those two elements of market share and service quality determine the ability to create higher and higher levels of profitability. You can either look at ways to increase your market share, especially on your more profitable lines, or you can create or increase the perception of service quality in the minds of your customers.

On the customer service side there is an element of yield improvement (not simply yield management) that is very important to all businesses. Ironically, most businesses do *not* have a plan to increase yield. I'll be more specific about that because it is a secret to higher profitability. Running a restaurant is a tough business because you have lots of competition, challenging labor costs, and often the cost of goods sold is high.

Let's say that you and I go out to dinner and we go into a restaurant. Because we're just average guys, maybe we order hamburgers and Cokes. The ideal question would be, in that restaurant, what's the most any customer has ever spent or actually could ever spend? What if we started with drinks and maybe had some appetizers, then we both had a soup or a salad and a little plate of specially items. Then we had main courses with matching wines. Then we had desserts and after-dinner drinks. Now compare that check with the check of the hamburger guys. One cover. Two people. But look at the difference to the business.

Clearly you can see you have a range of what your typical customer might be able to contribute to the bottom line. But you have to design a process, a sequence, or experiences—a path for customers that allows them to spend more. Then you need trained associates who can offer nice choices to make customers happier, who can act as trusted guides, not annoying gougers ("want fries with that?").

In our hospitality work with luxury hotels, we design the arrival experience to see how many ways we can make you happier as a guest. Let's say that you're going for honeymoon or a getaway weekend at a beautiful resort. Well, you probably reserved a regular room to get the best deal, as most people do. But if we can see that you're on your honeymoon or are a romance couple, and we offer you a suite for only few dollars more, you might like that. If it is going to be empty anyway, even a few dollars more is pure profit. Maybe there is a special romance package that you might like too. The housekeepers are still cleaning one room and all the rest of the services are the same. But again, we actually get greater revenue from the same customer. Whether it's in a restaurant or a hotel or in any enterprise, there are always ways to extend the customer's profitability.

As another example, we did proprietary research with banks and savings and loans that proved the more accounts that they had with any customer, the less likely the customer would close their account(s) and withdraw all of their money. If you only had one account it was easier to close down. The moment that you had several accounts you had traction. Multiple accounts also created higher levels of yield per customer and you can imagine how that influenced operations.

Or, you walk into a retail store. I used to work for a very large conglomerate and one of the departments was a huge paint area. Zillions of cans of paint and this and that and I observed. I'd see customers walk in and say, "Hey, can I have a gallon of paint?" The sales staff/service team members would say, "Yeah here's your paint," ring it up, and boom, the customers were gone. So we said, "Well, wait a minute. That customer will be back in an hour because he (or she) forgot his brushes, and then he needed thinner and never realized it, he doesn't have gloves, and he didn't have the right bucket. Did you really do anything to help this customer by ringing him up quickly? Does he get home and get mad because he forgot all this stuff, and now he's got to go back? Why didn't we create the opportunity to provide better service by offering appropriate choices?"

Here again, service quality affects profit and it gets operationalized through a service team that understands yield improvement and is literally taking advantage of the blessings of every customer.

WRIGHT

Then what is the relationship between leadership and team-building?

BEIL

At a first pass, leadership is the combination of directive and supportive behaviors that develop relationships. The directive aspect being, here's my vision, here's my direction, here's our mission, here's our goals for the day, the week, the month, the decade. Let's *go!*

Then it is balanced by the supportive aspect with how you ensure the people who are getting this done actually have the tools they need and the skills they need in order to do it, and do it well! It's easy to say, "charge," but if they don't have the skills or the tools, if they don't have the equipment, if they don't have the training, then that can be an awful waste of resources.

So the relationship first between leadership and team-building is a) getting everybody moving in the right direction, and b) giving them the kind of support they need so they can be successful when the time comes. There are a lot of supportive roles that can be developed by a leader and nurtured in their associates.

For instance, empathic leadership is really important. Showing that you understand how followers feel and providing some emotional support is important, but balance is the key. Too much empathy and you may be wasting time, and too little empathy may be showing you don't care. You can only do so much team-building.

Another supportive behavior, "empowerment," was a very popular word for a long time in American business. American industry has gone through this series of quasi-improvement strategies really kicked off by Peters and Waterman in *The Search for Excellence;* their book was so profound. But the problem is, despite their brilliance, how many companies do you know now that are searching for excellence? Probably not that many. The same "leaders" who wanted excellence also needed quality. When they finished their quality programs, they needed total quality because regular quality wasn't enough. Then, when they finished total quality, they went to process improvement, and continuous improvement, and then to empowerment, and so on in search of a better buzzword.

This is all basically the same stuff. It's sound organizational development work based on the right vision and direction, providing solid goals, smart objectives, and providing the proper support, whether it's empowerment, encouragement, or simply training your people well.

The tipping point in team-building is not just training them well but responding well when someone (inevitably) makes a mistake. You can learn a lot about a leader, manager, an organization (parent) from the way they respond to a mistake done by one of their team members (children). Too many people are too quick to blame others for problems and mistakes. Maybe we're broken early by a school system that focuses on finding errors, so that when we find one, we can't wait to pounce, as if that will cure decades of painful education. But that's a defining moment with any team member. How does management/leadership respond to a mistake?

We do a lot of training with managers on this, and the key words are, "I'll take responsibility for working this out; here's how I can help you." Not, "You idiot!" or "Sorry, that was David over there, he always screws things up; if we could just fix him we'd be fine."

Successful leaders really need to be able to provide the kind of support that protects their people. If a mistake or a problem has been made, they handle it. Obviously, too much protecting and you've got a lot of cover up issues, and legal and ethical challenges; but too little protecting, and you've got defensiveness, blaming sessions, and finger-pointing practice for everybody. You must provide support but again, similar to direction, too much or too little also will create some lessons that bring you back to balance.

WRIGHT

So how does peak performance develop, and how does effective leadership make that happen?

BEIL

We were talking about support and direction. If you think about those two in a graph as well, with one axis as direction and one as support, the person (whether it's a child learning how to walk or an adult learning how to drive a stick shift car) goes through the same four stages, defined by the amounts of direction and support that are needed.

For instance, if you were starting a new job—let's say this was your first interview—you might want a little bit more direction about what to say, when to say it, how to say it, and how long you say it. You really want a lot of tangible things that are, in a sense, highly directive because you haven't done it before. The more you can identify these things that can help you, the easier it will be for you to take those steps in the right direction.

Did you ever learn how to drive a stick shift car? Remember the first hill you were ever on?

WRIGHT

Oh yeah.

BEIL

You're thinking to yourself, "Okay, one foot on the gas, one foot on the brake, one foot on the clutch. Um, wait a minute—emergency brake." What if somebody sneaks up behind you, now you're thinking, "Go back, go back, back," because you know you're going to roll. You know what to do and have to bear down and really concentrate on your training to be successful.

So in the beginning of any task or new learning, the more direction provided, the better. So think of that as stage one. Whether it's learning how to use the cash register or counting out your money, discovering where the bathroom is in the office, or figuring out what questions to ask in your first interview, you usually need a lot of direction in any job when you start.

Now let's say we've been doing this job for a couple months. I'm not your first interview. I'm your thirtieth interview. You've got a lot of these under your belt. I'm not the first hamburger, I'm your one hundredth hamburger order. You know how to ring it up, you know a bunch of other things too, but you may not be perfect. So from a leadership perspective (and we can also look at this as a path to peak performance), I can't keep telling you what to do at that point and at this stage two of your development.

If I do keep telling you what to do, you begin to wonder what I think of you—if I trust you. I can begin to say, "David, did you ring that up the right way?" and then you do it and then two days later, I ask again, "David, did you ring that up the right way?" You'll think, "Wait a minute, what's going on with this guy? I've already done this!"

So at a certain point the leader has to know when to back off on giving direction. Now, the associate at this stage still doesn't know all that he or she needs to know yet, so you actually have to "cherry pick" the moments when mistakes are made where you can do some coaching and counseling. This is critical training that is necessary to push associates over what I would call a learning curve, where they *now* know 51 percent or more of the job. Actually, it's a demarcation line to stage three.

In a lot of companies we work with, the associates do a hundred things in a day. They do ninety-nine perfectly and make one mistake and they're only going to hear about one thing. That's a very odd way to do performance improvement because at a certain point people will never admit a mistake. If they do, they're going to be pointing fingers and blaming rather than taking the risk of getting their heads chopped off. It's a real cause of dysfunction all through the workforce.

But let's assume we can coach them over the learning curve and get them to a point where they know more about the job than they don't know. Now you begin to have some veteran employees who have different challenges because they need much less direction now, but they need a lot more support. They need support to be able to come in and do that one more day and to just stay as motivated as they can and to do the kinds of things they know they're supposed to do, rather than doing the minimum, minus one, because they know they can get away with it.

That's a real challenge there—some people never get out of stage three. While some employees quit and leave, these people quit and stay. They just noodle around and live "lives of quiet desperation," as Thoreau said. The real key to stage four is when you know what you don't know. You can learn and start to polish the gem—polish your own diamond—at that point because you keep developing. Now here it gets interesting. These are people who don't need instructions. In fact, they already know and they've already done it by the time you ask them. That's how you know. Peak performers self-identify.

I'll give you an example that's even more tangible on how the four stages of development can be cued via language in a mixture of direction and support. Let's say you and I are doing a seminar, and it's the first time that I've ever worked with you. There is noise outside and you might want to say, "Drake, I want you to go outside, quiet those people down, escort them down the hallway, maybe get their names, find out what is going on, and come back and tell me what happened." I'm going to say, "Yes sir." It's great because this gives me the direction I need. I know just what to do and I can do the best I can to be successful.

But let's say we're working together a while, and we've done twenty or thirty programs. There is noise outside, but your cueing to me might be a little bit different because I'm not in stage one—I'm in stage two. You might say, "Drake, there is noise outside. I think you should go out there and quiet them down, what do you think?" The "what do you think" part of the message (I call it "what do you think management") actually engages the other person. What that indicates is I believe you have useful ideas in your head and rather than my just telling you what to do, I'll give you suggestions. You tell me what you think, and now I'm coaching. We're cooperating. We're collaborating. It's a different thing than "go there and do this."

Cuing for people in the third stage—the associate who should know—is different again. Let's say we've done hundreds of these seminars. At that point, if you and I are doing a program and there is noise out there, you might look at me and say, "Drake, there is noise out there, what do you think we should do?" You don't even give me a suggestion. Why? Because you think I should know. The moment you start telling me what to do, indirectly you're now actually saying that you don't think I'm smart enough to know what to do. It never gets stated, it's all unconscious understanding, but associates know how it makes them feel.

Now what if I'm at the highest level? I'm a stage-four seminar rock star! You and I have been doing these for a long time. We are smooth together. There is noise out in the hallway, you look in my direction and guess what? I'm gone. I'm already out in the hallway. There is no need to say anything. That's what I mean when I say "peak performers self-identify."

Now here's the irony, in business, in most cases: What happens when you get people who are at that stage four level—the peak performance level—what do we do to them? We promote them! We promote them back to stage one, so now they're incompetent managers, as opposed to incredibly talented salespeople. I mean, the worst thing in the world is to promote your best salesperson to manager. Might as well shoot yourself now. Totally different profiles, totally different skill sets.

In fact, when I come in and start to work with companies, often they'll ask me to do some leadership and management assessments. The first thing I'll try to find out is who are considered the biggest troublemakers. Why? Because they are often the only ones brave enough to create some possibilities that a change could be made somewhere. Again, it's the idea of the status quo being fine for most, but that's what these guys are bucking against. I'm always interested in finding out who's on the edge—those who are considered the "problem"—and I'll listen and talk with them. Obviously I'll talk with them objectively because who knows what axes they may have to grind; but nevertheless, they will have valuable insights.

Albert Camus, who is one of my favorite writers, wrote that the only true good in the world was the act of rebellion. Rebellion was the only thing you could be sure of because the person who was rebelling was moving from something bad, toward something better—at least in his or her mind.

WRIGHT

In that same vein, what are your favorite types of motivational strategies?

BEIL

Well, I love designing performance-based incentive programs. I call it gain sharing, and that's not profit sharing. Gain sharing offers associates a piece of the pie, but only after management has taken the biggest slice. So let's say you expected 5 percent to 10 percent growth in a year. Well gain sharing starts there and says, all right, let's say we grow 10 percent. My question to you as a manager—as a leader—would be, if you grow more than 10 percent, how much of that "more" are you willing to put on the table for your associates? It's not profit sharing—it's gain sharing. We've already passed the goal—we've clobbered it—so how much of that are you willing to give back to the associates?

We custom-design those programs by industry, whether it's airlines, car rentals, hotels, manufacturing, retailing, wholesaling, you name it. If people say they can't measure it, they're either not trying or they're lying. If you can't measure it (as Ken Blanchard says), you can't manage it. Of course we can measure it, the challenge is can you measure the right stuff? Once you can do that you can definitely implement a gain sharing concept that will motivate everyone involved.

I was working with a telecom client two years ago and the company's numbers were in the basket, I mean they lost money two years in a row. Another year of this and the CEO knew he would be fired. He called me, now willing to try a change.

People often don't like calling consultants; it's somewhat of a dual-edged sword. You don't want to admit you need help, but you need help. What do you do?

Anyway, I was called in and they had missed their goals for two years.

"What do you want to do?" he asked.

I said, "I'm the dumbest guy in the building at this moment, but let me talk to some people and find out for you. To start, what's your goal for this year?"

He drew a line in the sand.

I said, "Great. Let's say you beat that by 5 percent, would you be happy?"

"Absolutely—we'd be delighted."

"How much above that line are you willing to give back to your associates?" I said.

His eyes went up and I could see he was puzzled. "What?" he asked.

I said, "Yes, if you beat that number, are you willing to put 20 percent, 30 percent, 40 percent of the extra on the table and split it with your people?"

He really had to think about that. It took him a couple of days to get back to me. This was money they didn't have and they were fighting about it for days. So he finally came back to me and said, "Okay, 15 percent. We've all agreed we can do that."

"Fine," I replied.

We did a full company meeting. Everybody understood what the goals were, what happened if they reached it, and they laid out a game plan.

At the end of the year, it was amazing. Every single person in that company acted as one. I mean, they didn't waste a paperclip. The average employee got a check of over $1,700, and it was right at the holiday season, too! These are rank and file people. That's huge money; it's life-changing and it was all there anyway. What made the difference was that the people cared more because they owned a piece of the pie.

In some of the designs, we like both individual and team incentives. If the team accomplishes a certain level of performance, everybody gets paid, regardless of how well any one individual did. In some cases people had purely support roles. But without them, the quality of work could not be done. So in a way they're as vital, but in many cases they won't be recognized.

The Chinese are a major power in the world and on their path toward this growth they discovered something. Did you ever hear the story about all the Chinese farmers? They had collectives set up and for the most part the collectives were functioning reasonably well. But at the highest levels, to encourage and experiment with an entrepreneurial spirit, the leaders said to these various collectives, "Farm 90 percent of the land. Once you've finished the collective work, we'll give you the other 10 percent and you can grow crops there for yourselves. Whatever you sell from that 10 percent you can keep." Okay fine. Well, within a couple of years the amount that was being grown on the 10 percent was equal to the amount that was being grown on the 90 percent.

The extra profitability—the excess capacity—is there; it's always there. People have the ability to surprise, to outperform, and to do fantastic work. It's there in every organization I have ever seen. The challenge is how do you capture that peak performance? How do you develop the right people? How do you provide the support they need to follow through? Then, how do you manage the results to recognize them and give them a piece of the action? The most successful companies are certainly doing that, whether it's in stock options or bonus plans.

I'm really not crazy about generic bonuses; I really like tying things to performance whenever possible. It's so much cleaner, it's very straightforward, and gets everybody onboard heading in the right direction, and working together toward a common goal.

WRIGHT

Does leadership change cross-culturally or do the same basic principles hold?

BEIL

We consult in over twenty countries and I've found that while language and nuance change, the basic non-verbal messages are consistent. That creates a platform for building rapport and developing partnerships.

We do a lot of work in China and I often say to the people I'm working with there, and very humbly, "Your English is lot better than my Mandarin. I'm studying, but thank you for your patience, just bear with me." A little humility goes a long way sometimes, especially cross-culturally. A lot of what we take for granted in this country is new territory for other countries. A healthy level of respect is important for leadership success worldwide.

America has a tremendous position in the world and one of the greatest opportunities in history to do something that really hasn't been done before—to create a level of prosperity globally. But look at the American students today—how many of them know a second language or a third language? Whereas if you look at a European or an Asian student, that's not even a question, it's a given—they are bi- or tri-lingual. It gets even more dramatic, especially if you're looking at a larger scale or the bigger picture cross-culturally. I may be a little bit off on this, but some of the data I have seen suggests that the top 25 percent of the high school students graduating in China are more than all of the students graduating in the United States combined.

Now multiply that by the next ten or fifteen years. It's a very interesting picture. We have some challenges in front of us and the United States is a heck of a machine. If we can adapt cross-culturally, and use some of these basic principles that have helped us grow, the future is bright. In another context, our real job is to help grow others. The moment we can create the level of prosperity in other places that we already have here, we will win the war we are really fighting. By no means do we have it all solved in the United States. We have tremendous poverty, education, and economic issues to work out, and these are important leadership goals for the future.

WRIGHT

So how do critical and creative thinking play important roles for leaders?

BEIL

This is one of my favorite topics because most people don't actually know how to think. This may be surprising to you but did you ever take a class called thinking—"Thinking 101" or "Thinking 201"? Probably not, and that's exactly the problem. No one ever taught us how to think. You would have to admit that thinking skills would be a useful subject, don't you think? If I had a chance to redesign the educational system, I'd probably start that curriculum pretty early, and keep cycling through it at higher and higher levels.

Part of my doctorate research was on the nature of comprehension itself and how people come to learn. Bloom, Guilford, and Torrance each did excellent research on the nature of thinking, and their models are surprisingly complex.

In our approach, there are four stages of critical thinking that lead to problem-solving. Stage one begins with collecting information about the world around you, and this is the importance of sensory perception. Stage two brings those unique perceptions together into meaningful patterns. Those patterns can vary because it's an aspect of creativity called convergent thinking. Then the third stage is applying those patterns and ideas, not only to the situation you're in, but also to new situations in the future. The fourth stage and highest level of critical thinking is evaluation—figuring out if what you did worked, and deciding whether you would do it again.

So as an example of how problem-solving evolved, let's say we go back to the beginnings of civilized, organized life as humans. Here's the beauty of this—thinking hasn't changed for 50,000 years. We're still the same species and the process is the same, only the content changes. If you and I are walking down the dirt road as cavemen and we kick a few pebbles, we'd notice that they roll. We might see the shape of the pebbles and notice they roll, but we're not really thinking yet. This is stage one. We're just collecting data.

We walk a little further and we feel the ground shake in a tremor and it quakes again and a couple of boulders get dislodged on a nearby hillside and roll down the hill. We look at the boulders, we watch them roll. Again we notice the round shape, but we're still not thinking yet.

Well, maybe we come into a clearing and we see a couple of our fellow cave members from cave forty-two. They're trying to pick up a log to bring it up to the cave for firewood. The log is heavy and they're having a hard time lifting it, but when we look at the log from the side, we see the same round shape. We remember images of pebbles and boulders, and boom: *round shapes roll!* That's the moment of the birth of a thought. So we'll walk over to the log, I don't know what we might have said 50,000 years ago, but we might have just grunted and pushed the log. When the log rolled, an idea was born.

Now, once we saw the log roll, guess what we did in cave forty-two? We became "round rolls" specialists! We started making wheels didn't we? We went crazy for wheels. We put a couple of wheels together and a couple more together and put a piece of wood flat on it, and we could haul heavy stuff around. Maybe later on we trained one of the animals in the yard and hooked him up to the thing and had him haul it around. Then we put a couple of those wheels on a plank and went up to the top of the hill and gave it a little shove, creating the first go cart. Right after that we invented brakes. Steering became useful too. Pretty soon we had a Mercedes.

It's always the same process and it starts by collecting information. If all your senses work properly, you're blessed. The beauty is that we work with whatever we can get, tending to trust information from our favorite senses most. The problem is, once you have it collected, how do you actually form it and structure it to be useful?

For instance, I could say to you, "What do these have in common: cougars, mustangs and pintos?" What would you say? Would you answer, "Animals"? That's absolutely correct. Somebody else might say they're cars, and that person would be right also. I've even had people say "horses." And I said, "Yeah, except for the cougar, you're right." Sometimes the mind deletes things that make it harder to be right so it just forgets those things and focuses on what it likes. (It's the principle of hearing what you want to hear!)

The idea is that convergent thinking often will have two or three right ideas. The school system has a hard time reconciling that because we've got a red pencil mentality in most cases. Management is like that too when training employees. We shouldn't be involved with trying to catch them doing things wrong and correcting errors, we should be involved with trying to catch them doing things right and identifying where they actually come up with brilliant and creative ideas.

WRIGHT

With all of your experience down through the years and all of your success, it sounds to me that your inclination is toward consulting and coaching. How does coaching play a role in development of the leadership toolkit?

BEIL

Well, in a similar way, if you think about those four stages on the path of peak performance, they're similar to the critical thinking process. The first stage is where we're teaching them what to do, when to do it, and so on. That's not really coaching, it's a data dump and only after they have a little bit of information can we work with them.

How do we form patterns for them out of all the information? That's when we coach them. Can you explain or demonstrate or deliver some informative or useful support? If you can, people will apply those ideas in similar and new situations, evaluating what worked best. It is especially important to coach people through those early mistakes without making them feel terrible. In a sense, make them feel supported and encourage them to learn—that's the real key. If a good leader can be a good coach—someone who can develop people—it's considered exceptional because great coaches are rare.

For example, I love Pat Summit, the Lady Vols coach in Tennessee. She is amazing and literally talks about how she uses direction and support in her approach with her players.

Another amazing coach is Chris McLachlin. President Obama named him the most influential sports person in his life. Chris is an old friend here in Hawaii and a tremendous coach. He not only won ten state volleyball championships here in Hawaii at Punahou School, his teams went undefeated for ten years. Now, if you've got new kids every year, it's hard enough to win a title, much less go undefeated for a decade. So there was something going on there.

Coaching is more than just providing good feedback, it's helping people set objectives that are doable. Stretching objectives, it's tracking performance and then recognizing even small steps in the right direction.

I remember when Chris gave me a tennis lesson one day as a favor. He hit me a forehand and I launched it toward South America. He said, "Good racket preparation." Then he hit me a backhand and I hit a shot that hasn't come down yet. He said, "Good foot speed to the ball." I hit another one way out of bounds and he said something else positive. He consistently found the one thing I did right every single time I hit the ball. By the end of the hour my head was a collection of all the right stuff. I imagine that if he did this with you or with your team, with your associates, with your employees, or if parents did that with their children, over time they would shape them in the right direction.

Let's say you have a company with twenty people and every single one of them catches one person doing something right daily. All are trained to recognize excellence immediately, specifically, and with all sincerity. By the end of the week you've got a hundred positive moments where you're moving people in the right direction. By the end of the month, you've got four or five hundred of these. Well, at a certain point you've got critical mass and everybody is now moving down the right path together. That's why coaching plays a huge role in the whole developmental tool kit.

However, not everybody can coach. Too much of the coaching is throw the chair and scream and make them afraid. That may have worked in the past but if we're going to compete on a global scale cross-culturally, that just doesn't work anymore. Maybe it does in some places, but I think we're smarter than that and there are better ways to build commitment and develop competence.

WRIGHT

Well, what a great conversation. I have taken notes here copiously. This is great information. I really appreciate all the time you've spent with me this afternoon to answer these important questions. I really have gotten a lot out of this and I know our readers will.

BEIL

I appreciate that very much. I think it's a real honor to be able to talk with you and if it's helped anybody in even one simple way, then it's been a good day for both of us.

WRIGHT

Today we've been talking with Drake Beil. He is an international management consultant based in Honolulu who teaches companies how to achieve peak performance through leadership development, team-building processes, and performance-based gain sharing programs.

Drake, thank you so much for being with us today on *Stepping Stones to Success*.

ABOUT THE AUTHOR

Drake Beil is an international management consultant. He is a leadership and organizational development specialist who is focused on the worldwide hospitality industry. Starting his private practice in 1980, Drake currently has clients in over twenty countries that he serves from his home base in Hawaii. Drake's doctorate centered on learning theory. He is adjunct professor teaching the Executive MBA course on Leadership at the Shidler College of Business, University of Hawaii, and for the Hanoi School of Business. He is author of *Business Solutions for the 21st Century* (Pfeiffer & Co., 1994) and co-author of *Fundamentals of Quality* (ASTD, 1992) with Dr. Mark Kimmel. He is a keynote speaker and practices Bikram Yoga.

DRAKE BEIL, EdD

Drake Beil & Associates
A Division of Solutions, Inc.
55 South Judd Street, PH-2
Honolulu, HI 96817
Office Phone/Fax: 808.587.5832
Direct Line: 808.223.3223
drake@drakebeil.com
www.drakebeil.com

CHAPTER EIGHTEEN

How Does Your Garden Grow?

An Interview with…

JAMES MURRAY

DAVID WRIGHT (WRIGHT)

Today we're talking to James R. Murray; James is a seminar speaker, after, before, and during dinner speaker, he is a keynote speaker, and a "no count" speaker. That accounts for his being an ordained minister, professional clown, quality control engineer, bartender, and therapist. Throughout his diverse career Jim always finds himself involved with the steppingstones of self-discovery. This approach is contagious; those who participate with Jim find it an enjoyable experience. He has entertained audiences of one to five thousand (not counting parades). Instinctively realizing that there are vast differences in personalities and learning styles, Jim adjusts each presentation to enrich all concerned.

James Murray, welcome to *Stepping Stones to Success.*

JAMES MURRAY (MURRAY)

Thank you very much, David.

WRIGHT

So you have an interesting and diverse background. Is there a common thread?

MURRAY

I think there is. The diverse background has been steppingstones, and each one of them was lead by curiosity and a need to know.

In the electronics field it was very straightforward—if you put something in here, you got something out there. If there was a problem and if you looked long enough, you found a solution.

The next step was dealing with people. As a supervisor I discovered that I wasn't communicating very well. After attending a communication class I really became curious about people. I went back to school to understand why people act the way they do and I became a counselor. During this time I discovered people were a lot like electronics—if you put something in, you got something out. If there was a problem and if you looked long enough, you would find an answer.

WRIGHT

So how does clowning fit into the picture?

MURRAY

Well, interestingly enough that started off as wanting to do humor therapy. I found that when people were laughing they weren't thinking about their pain and their bodies seemed to heal quicker.

When I went through Clown School, I discovered that when you put on makeup you could take on any personality. You could be happy, sad, mad, or glad, and nobody knew the "real you," because you were hidden by the makeup.

Personality is a derivative of the word "persona," which is defined as "the social façade an individual assumes" or in other words, the masks (personality) we wear.

If you look hard enough you will see the real person and not the mask.

WRIGHT

So how do you balance life and relationships on the steppingstones to success?

MURRAY

It is a balancing act with four variables:

10 percent	Nutrition	What one consumes
10 percent	Activity	What one does
10 percent	Environment	What is going on around one
70 percent	Mental Attitude	How one views the world

Nutrition: the sum of the process by which an individual takes in and utilizes nutrients and food substances.

Activity: the process and quality of life that an individual carries on or participates in.

Environment: the aggregate of social and cultural conditions that influence the life on an individual.

Mental Attitude: relating to the total emotional and intellectual response to perception.

There are those who specialize in each area. Health food stores for example, specialize in nutrition. Gyms specialize in physical activity.

Plenty of folks make a good living on saving the environment. Of course, each has a mental attitude that supports their belief system.

The biggest balancing factor seems to be mental attitude; it affects the other three. A person can be raised in a rich area and not be successful, or somebody can be raised in a poor area and be incredibly successful. It's all about Mental Attitude.

WRIGHT

With our *Stepping Stones to Success* book, we're trying to encourage people to be better and live better. Who has been there for you?

MURRAY

Mom and Dad for their strength in character and willingness to probe the unknown; and my brother, Don, who refused to give up.

Don was born with cerebral palsy. The doctors told our parents that he would not learn to walk or talk and his age expectancy was about twelve years. They should place him in an institution and let nature take its course.

Mom and Dad said, "No, he is our son and he is going home with us. He will walk and he will talk and live like everyone else."

At that time I did not have words for what I was learning from Mom and Dad. But they were unwavering in their dedication to my brother. "He will walk and he will talk." I accepted that decree and that became the focus.

Dad had lived through the hard times and the hunger of the Depression, therefore food was very important to him. So every year a garden was planted.

One day as Dad was working in the garden I asked him, "Why doesn't my brother walk like everyone else?" My father did not say anything but just kept working on that very straight row of the garden.

This time I asked my question louder, "Why doesn't my brother walk?" Without looking at me, and while continuing to work, he said, "You have been helping me with the garden haven't you?"

"Yes Dad, every year."

"You have learned about the garden haven't you," he asked. It was more of a statement than a question.

"Yes sir," I proudly replied. I continued, "I have learned to make the rows straight and learned which ones are the weeds and which ones are the vegetables."

"Have you noticed the radishes, son?" he asked.

"Yes, they are really growing and I can see some of the red as they get bigger. But the carrots are just barely poking through the ground," I replied.

"What about the corn?"

"Nothing yet."

He paused for a moment and said, "I remember that you really like olives don't you?"

"Yes, I sure do—especially when we chop them up in the cream cheese and stuff it all into the celery."

"Did you know that an olive tree must grow for a hundred years before it can begin to grow olives and a pecan tree must grow for eight years before it can grown nuts?" He asked.

"I never thought about that before," I said.

He continued, "Every seed that is planted is on its own timetable; each must grow at its own rate. Your brother is like a seed—he is on his own special timetable. Everything must grow at its own rate and he will walk and grow just like every one else."

Mom would say "What you think about comes about. Everything is done twice—once in your head, when you plant the seed, and then it is created once again when it becomes something that everyone can see."

Begin with the end in mind. When things are not working out, refocus, get your mind off the problem and back on your goal. That was the foundation my folks gave me.

By the way, my brother does walk and talk. He has been married and divorced has a child and he has outlived his doctors.

Today I stand on the shoulders of my parents—their teaching and compassion—and I am still inspired by my brother.

Now I choose to associate and surround myself with thinkers and authors like Deepak Chopra, Dennis Waitley, and Jack Canfield, to name a few.

WRIGHT

There is much talk about positive and negative energy. What's your view?

MURRAY

It is very interesting how the human mind works. We have a need to justify everything—to explain and label everything. If we hear something we do not understand, we label it as bad or negative. If we hear something we like or agree with, we claim it as positive or good. Very rarely do we look to see what is really taking place. We make the assumption that everyone sees and feels life the same way.

When my wife and I first got married I knew we would never fight because we were so much in love. Merging our two households was something we were both looking forward to. I had just finished setting up the upstairs bath and was going downstairs to do the downstairs bathroom. When I arrived, I found she had already completed the task. Here was the first problem in our relationship. You see, the toilet paper was on backward.

So I told her. "The paper is on backward," I said in a strong voice.

"Is not," was the equally strong reply.

"Is too!" And the argument was on.

There were to be many lessons to follow like squeezing the toothpaste correctly and how to eat at the dinner table.

By the way, we have had guests visit the house from time to time and one said to me, in confidence, "I fixed the toilet paper for you, it was on backward."

Positive and negative energy is somewhat of an interpretation—what's good for me, may be bad for you.

One day I asked a gentleman, "Where is a good place to eat?"

His reply was, "That restaurant across the street is a good place to eat, to me."

I asked, "Why did you say *to me?*"

"That's because *to me* it is a good place to eat. I don't know if you have the same taste as I do. I like steaks, but you may be a vegetarian. So it wouldn't be a good place for you."

With that, I discovered that if I included *to me* in a statement, it would assist me in remembering that positive and/or negative is an interpretation and didn't need to be defended. This also served to remind me that *people only do what they feel is right, proper, and/or justified at the time of doing or they could not do it.*

WRIGHT

So I hear through the grapevine that you are called the "Come-Back Kid." What's that all about?

MURRAY

David, I assure you I didn't plan it that way.

I wasn't feeling well and I went to the doctor for a checkup. I received a diagnosis of cancer. Several doctors and several tests later, it was given a name, Non-Hodgkin lymphoma (NHL), stage four. I had a lump the size of a large ball.

The oncologist began immediate treatment. I asked about vitamins and alternative therapy. He said, "I will support anything that gets you well."

In the book *Heal Your Body*, by Louise L. Hay, I read that cancer was defined as:

- deep hurt,
- a longstanding resentment,
- carrying hatreds, and
- grief that eats away the self.

This information struck a chord deep within me. I failed at a business and had gone bankrupt. You bet I was still grieving and angry, and the resentment was growing. To me, it was about life or death.

I went back to what my folks had taught me. I got my mind off the problem and back on my goal and I said, "Looks like we've got a problem. I don't need that, I want to be healthy."

Now I focused on health and happiness and in about forty-five days they could not find any lumps, bumps, or pictures but they continued the therapy for another six months to make sure it was gone. "Remission" is a wonderful word.

The next was a heart attack. I was standing in line at the airport. Suddenly I began to perspire profusely and could not stop coughing. In between coughs I called my wife and said, "Come back and pick me up we need to go to the hospital."

"Why?" she asked.

"Something isn't right," I coughed.

We drove like racecar drivers to the emergency room. When they asked me to sit down I said, "I think I am having a heart attack." In less than a blink of an eye I was in surgery.

There have been many advances in the medical field. Rather than open heart surgery, the doctor went up through my groin and installed a couple of stints.

Once again I had something to contemplate. What thoughts and emotions had I been harboring? The cancer issue had been solved but what was this? Working, of course. It was necessary, but then in a flash there it was—I had been squeezing all the joy out of my heart in favor of money and position and I was angry about it. This was no longer acceptable. Once again I had the choice—"Change Your Thinking, Change Your Life."

Will I be the "Come-Back Kid" or the "Slow-Learning Kid"? For me, for some reason, every adversity gives me new insight. Those mind-altering and physically challenging events allow me to see differently. There is so much to experience in life. I have come to realize that a new thought produces a new condition.

WRIGHT

So then do you think that thoughts affect the body and relationships?

MURRAY

Yes, I do. Health is a constant adaptation. This is a unique relationship with the outer environment (outside the body) and the inner feeling (inside the body).

Cycle of Adaption

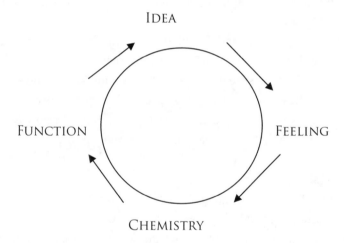

Idea: The cycle of Adaption begins with an Idea or Thought.
Feeling: An interpretation of the thought produces a Feeling.
Chemistry: The glandular system produces chemistry to support the Feeling (neuromuscular reaction).
Function: The body is now ready to carry out the Idea.

If there is a pleasant experience, or thought, the body becomes happy. What is equally true is if a scary thought is present, the body acts accordingly to the chemistry supplied.

What was just described is the Adaptive Cycle. But what happens if the process is altered? What happens if we hold thoughts and emotions and don't express them? This unexpressed chemistry is called "mobilized unreleased energy." This energy has no place to go so it is stored inside the body. If this energy is stored long enough, it becomes toxic to the body. You might say the body has become intoxicated.

The body must do something with this excess. The chemistry continues to build up. Now it becomes time to adapt. There are two choices of unusual behavior to burn off the chemistry. The second choice is to store the unused chemistry in the cells of the body, which is called "unusual cellular activity."

- Unusual Behavior: Anything in excess (e.g., smoking, drinking, exercise, talking—all to burn off the chemistry).
- Unusual Cellular Activity: The chemistry is stored in the cells and joints replacing the normal fluids. This causes dis-ease.

Imagine that we went to work in the backyard building a fence but forgot to bring gloves. Soon our hands would become sore and stiff. If we continued, a blister would begin to form. Then inside the blister would be fluid. The fluid would attempt to put out the fire in our burning hands. This is unusual behavior and the body is adapting to it.

Let us continue to build fences for the neighbors. As we continue the behavior, the body begins to adapt but now the dead skin of the blister is forming a callus to protect the hand. The body has again adapted.

The neighborhood now all has fences and we no longer use our hands. One day in the shower you notice, as you scrub your hands, that the callus falls off. Why? Because it is no longer needed for protection—we are no longer doing that activity. The body again has adapted.

The difference between what was described (a callus) and a tumor is that one is under the skin and the callus is on top of the skin. The body is trying to protect itself in both cases. When we stopped our work in the yard; the callus fell off. A tumor is just like the callus—when we stop the unusual activity (which caused the tumor) the tumor disappears.

WRIGHT

Tell me, why do you call your company Timeless Solutions?

MURRAY

It is called Timeless Solutions Institute because the name most accurately describes what we are all about:

- Timeless: not affected by time.
- Solutions: implies that there is an answer.
- Institute: indicates structure for learning.

On a more private note: When this material was revealed to me by my teachers, I was informed that it was not their material nor was it mine. It has been passed down generation to generation through the ages and no one person can claim to be originator of the work.

The material is available to those who ask the right questions.

WRIGHT

Deepak Chopra speaks of reversing the aging process. Is it possible to reverse the stressing process?

MURRAY

Absolutely. "Stress" is a term we have all heard. Originally stress was called the *general adaptation syndrome* or GAS (a theory of stress). The name "stress" caught on and became associated with a negative interpretation. There are three kinds of stress:

- Distress: Negative event or interpretation; the body triggers the survival mechanism to fight or run (e.g., crying).
- Stress: A neutral event subject to interpretation, sometimes called a stressor.
- Eustress: Positive event or interpretation producing a positive pressure inducing happiness (e.g., laughter).

An event is neutral until an individual places a value on it. The way we view an event modifies or changes the actual experience because the *Cycle of Adaptation* is now in affect.

Public Speaking is a good example to illustrate the three values of stress. Public speaking is in itself just an event. Some people, however, find this extremely threatening. Just the thought of getting up in front of people can be distressful for them. Others look forward to being in front of the room and experience Eustress and enjoy the experience.

A more common experience of the adaptation of stress is when you enjoy an experience. You feel that time collapses, but when you are doing something you do not enjoy, time elongates.

To reverse the stress process all we need do is recognize and/or re-evaluate our responses and consciously choose another. This is a huge steppingstone to success—to be in charge of my own inner state. If not, then everything and everybody else is.

WRIGHT

So what makes your perspective unique?

MURRAY

I have always been interested the mind—how it works and evolves. Apparently in the time of P. D. Ouspensky there were two types of psychology:

The Study of Man as He is: This is where the norm is to expect the conditions that have existed at one time must or will always be the same, therefore the individual is predictable.

The Study of Man as He Can Be: This is related to the varying circumstances of life that can never become fixed and habitual. This indicates that people are able to adjust themselves to completely different external conditions and yet maintain a sense of balance.

To answer your question directly, The Timeless Solutions Institute is about the possible evolution of consciousness.

WRIGHT

So what is the message that you want the readers of *Stepping Stones to Success* to hear?

MURRAY

A pretty simple but powerful statement—a new thought produces a new condition.

It has been said that true insanity is continuing to do what we have always done and expecting a different outcome. Each of us can choose to think differently, and you can experience life as a gift. To sum in all up: change your thinking, change your life.

WRIGHT

What an interesting conversation. I could ask you questions here for the rest of the day because I'm learning a lot. I really do appreciate the time you've taken with me to answer all these questions.

MURRAY

Thank you, David.

WRIGHT

Today we've been talking with James R. Murray who is a seminar speaker as well as a keynote speaker. He is also an ordained minister, a professional clown, a quality control engineer, a bartender, and therapist. I think we have found out today he knows a lot about what he's talking about, at least I think he does.

James, thank you so much for being with us today on *Stepping Stones to Success*.

MURRAY

Thank you very much David.

ABOUT THE AUTHOR

JAMES R. MURRAY is a polished teacher, facilitator, key-note speaker, Master of Ceremonies and storyteller. Jim has a unique gift of being able to communicate with audiences and classrooms with an easy to understand and relaxing manner.

Meditation, Relaxation, Communication, Relationship Strategies (marriage & business) and Stress Management are a few of his favorite topics. His material has been read and heard around the world.

James "Amazin" Murray is the curator of the *Timeless Solutions Institute*. The mission statement is: Understanding the world you live in." Classes lead the individual to a different type of mental activity, to a different way of seeing self and to a new state of awareness. The purpose is to reveal and describe those ideas, ideals, beliefs and decisions one has accepted which are obstacles to peace of mind.

JAMES "AMAZIN'" MURRAY

Timeless Solutions Institute
PO Box 440250
Houston, TX 77244
832.722.8407
tsinstitue@aol.com
www.timelesssolutions.org

CHAPTER NINETEEN

Yikes! What Do I Do Now?

An Interview with...

KAREN STAIB DUFFY

DAVID WRIGHT (WRIGHT)

Today we are talking with Karen Staib Duffy, an executive coach, and President and Founder of Quantum Development Coaching. Her specialties are Strategic Coaching, which is a practical and performance-based form of coaching, and Ontological Coaching, which concentrates on developing Emotional Intelligence skills, new behaviors, and the use of language in leadership. While she typically works with high-level executive teams, she also does life coaching and career coaching for individuals.

Karen, your topic is *"Yikes!* What do I do now?" Under what situations do people tend to ask that question?

KAREN STAIB DUFFY (STAIB DUFFY)

These are moments when we find ourselves tested to the limits of our abilities in very challenging situations. These are typically times when we get some news (professionally or personally) that creates a challenge so daunting we don't even know where to begin. I call these *Yikes!* moments. Our next question is typically, "What do I do now?"

WRIGHT

Tell me more about these *Yikes!* moments.

STAIB DUFFY

A *Yikes!* moment is when we are entering uncharted territory. Major success or major failure looms before us, depending on what we do or don't do, and what we choose in that moment.

A *Yikes!* moment can occur when you face a challenge—maybe even a breakdown—in your life. When I say "breakdown," I mean this in the sense of a time when things are not working the way you had wanted or hoped for. These breakdowns can lead to breakthroughs, depending on how you handle them.

A *Yikes!* moment does not just occur with "bad" news or situations, such as getting fired or getting divorced. It can also be "great" things such as getting promoted to a much larger job, getting married, or becoming a parent.

These are all defining moments for us as people and for our careers. It is through these defining moments that we carve out our destiny and bring our dreams into reality.

There are a million ways people can find themselves in a *Yikes!* moment.

WRIGHT

How do these moments relate to success?

STAIB DUFFY

Success does not just come in a steady string of lucky breaks and brilliant opportunities. Success is created through flexibility, learning, and resilience. Everyone goes through periods of great duress and difficulty. We all have *Yikes!* moments. We all have them on a regular basis. There are always challenges. Success and mastery in life come from rising to meet the new and the overwhelming. One can meet it head on or sideways, up or down, over or around, but mastery comes from and through responding instead of merely reacting.

WRIGHT

Will you tell me what you mean by responding versus reacting?

STAIB DUFFY

When we just do what we typically do, we are reacting from habit. We are making choices in a knee-jerk way without further thought. Of course, a habit can be a useful thing. It allows us to move through life with less energy than if we needed to continually pause and reconsider everything before we made a move. But when something is not going well or when we suddenly face the overwhelming, we need to pause and make a change. Simply reacting will just produce more of the same, which we no longer want. When we react out of habit, we have no control. We have no choice. We are not in charge any more.

WRIGHT

What should we do instead?

STAIB DUFFY

I am suggesting that instead of just reacting, we respond. Responding requires that we hit the pause button and reassess before we take an action. It requires that we manage our thoughts, our emotions, and our actions. It makes us engage our creativity and adapt at a deeper level. Responding is a form of mastery and it comes from learning in a transformational way. This kind of transformational learning changes you, expanding who you are and what you are capable of.

WRIGHT

How does one learn in a transformational way?

STAIB DUFFY

One of the things that we do best as human beings relates to our capacity to learn, to change, and to adapt in life. Darwin spoke of survival of the fittest. I prefer the phrase "thrival (as in 'to thrive') of the most adaptable."

We all have expectations. Most of the time we do not realize how deeply ingrained our expectations are until they are not met. Sometimes our expectations themselves preclude us from seeing new possibilities for change and success.

When we let go of expectations, we pause and start observing with fresh eyes. These observations lead us to new insights and a totally different viewpoint on what is taking place. This expands what we might do about it. Letting go is different than giving up. Letting go is about releasing your expectations.

WRIGHT

What causes us to lose our ability to adapt and learn?

STAIB DUFFY

As we go through life, we acquire a set of beliefs or assumptions that work for us most of the time. They lie in the background of our thoughts. They create a filter. What we "see" in life is only what gets through that filter. We tend to reject thoughts and learning that do not flow easily and comfortably through the filter. Without knowing it, we become rigid.

When life throws us a curve ball or a situation in which our beliefs or assumptions no longer work, we are forced to change or remain stuck and dissatisfied. When we begin to change "who we are" at the level of our thoughts and emotions, we can start to create and recognize a new set of defining assumptions and move to a fundamentally different approach.

Failure occurs when we give up and we declare ourselves to be a failure. Then the game is over. We are not a failure just because we have a difficult situation to deal with. Even though the challenge is daunting and we have no clue where to start, we can still move into success.

WRIGHT

What would you offer as a way to proceed?

STAIB DUFFY

There is always a way to do something differently than the way we are doing it now. There is always some new learning that can take place. When we are in a *Yikes!* moment, we have moved into a growth edge. A growth edge is a spot of confusion, turmoil, lack of clarity, uncertainty, and maybe even a bit of pain. A growth edge is where we are challenged to expand in life beyond the boundaries of who we are or more precisely, who we think we are. A growth edge is a good place to be, since without it, we are stagnant. Yet in that moment, it may not feel particularly good. How we handle the *Yikes!* moments helps us to set the path for growth in a new direction.

Success in life is measured by how we handle these truly difficult times, when the task in daunting and complex, the pressure is crushing, and we don't know what to do. If you are in that kind of spot now, you have arrived at a growth edge.

Let's look at some possible *Yikes!* moments. They can come when your career is in jeopardy. Maybe there has been a merger or acquisition and you do not know if you will make the cut. Maybe you find out that you will be getting a new boss and it is a person with whom you have never worked well in the past. Or perhaps you know nothing much about him or her. You do know, however, that many new managers like to bring in their own people.

A *Yikes!* moment also can come from a shrinking economy that causes us to lose a job or face a demotion, even though our performance has been fine. Now that the system is broken, we have to get creative and start learning again in order to thrive anew.

A personal *Yikes!* moment can come with the loss of a spouse or partner, through illness, death, or divorce. It can come from a misunderstanding or betrayal by a friend or colleague. It can arrive when you become a parent and find yourself stretched to the limit of endurance.

There are as many *Yikes!* moments as there are people and events. It is also important to note that what might be a growth edge for you could seem like just so much common sense for someone else. A growth edge will be unique to you. What is important is that, for you, this is a space that requires expansion and flexibility.

As we each approach our unique challenge, what drives our actions in the moment is our mindset, our worldview, and our filter. Embedded in our worldview are hidden assumptions or beliefs that drive our actions.

WRIGHT

Are you saying that we need to take a long hard look at our beliefs and assumptions to achieve success?

STAIB DUFFY

Yes. Often we do not even know that these assumptions are there, but they are. In addition, even if we do know we have this or that belief, we do not see our assumptions as something we can change. We treat them as truth, big and immutable.

We can find our beliefs or assumptions most easily in the stories we tell ourselves. Once we have uncovered these assumptions and put them up for reconsideration, very interesting things start to happen. Their power to bind us starts to slip. Hidden outside of your assumptions are other choices and actions you can live instead. Once you begin changing your assumptions, you can come up with a new way to handle a situation that might otherwise leave you stuck. You free yourself to be different again, to learn something new, to adapt and thrive once more.

Do not accept your assumptions at face value. Question them. Feel free to change them.

WRIGHT

How do we go about changing our assumptions?

STAIB DUFFY

There are several ways to start changing your assumptions. For starters, ask yourself: Could the opposite also be true? If so, when and how? If your assumption is, *"Jack is just a jerk; he doesn't care about other people's feelings,"* you will be quite annoyed with Jack. If you revise this thought to, *"Maybe Jack was up all night with a sick child or working late on that project that is due this afternoon, so he is just exhausted right now."* This latter thought leaves you open to recall some other times when Jack might have been very thoughtful or considerate. If you are working with the second set of assumptions, you may find yourself feeling compassion for Jack, rather than annoyance.

Another technique is to be on the lookout for dead-end thoughts. A dead-end thought does not let you go anywhere or do anything with it. An example would be a statement such as, *"That's just the way I am."* There is nothing you can change here, no circumstances under which you could be different. Another way of phrasing this thought could be, *"This is how I choose to be"* or *"I have been this way before, so I prefer to continue to be this way."*

But you can change this thought stream. For example, compare these previous thoughts to, *"I have been this way before, but I am choosing to be different this time."* A more concrete example of this kind of thought would be, *"I am shy"* versus *"I am usually shy, but today I will go to the party with Ann and she will help me to meet new people."* Now there is something you can do to initiate a change in your actions and, from there, a change in results.

If you have tried two or three things that you thought might work in a particular situation without success, and you are about to try them again because you cannot think of anything else, it is especially important to start questioning your assumptions. If this is where you are, you are stuck in a thought loop. A thought loop is a story you tell yourself that does not lead you anywhere but keeps you going around and around with no new choices. This thought loop will have key assumptions embedded in it.

An example could be: *"If I am demoted, I am a failure."* There is nothing you can do with this. Nothing is in your control. Change your story to get out of that thought loop. *"If I am demoted, I am a failure"* can become, *"The economy is rough right now, but this is still a good job. I will do my best, and soon another good opportunity will come along."*

Another example could be taking a thought such as, *"There is no meaning in my life. It is just a constant struggle"* and turning it into, *"There is meaning in every breath I take. There is meaning in the influence I have on all those whose lives I touch. There are challenges but there are also many moments of easy bliss. I choose to allow those moments of easy bliss."*

Yet another example might be changing the belief that *"Success means that I am on top of everything and nothing is difficult for me"* to become, *"Success means that I handle difficult situations with grace, grit, and dignity."*

Can you see how each story has different assumptions embedded in it? Can you see that by questioning your assumptions you can find a way of breaking out of being stuck?

WRIGHT

Is there anything else we can do in these moments?

STAIB DUFFY

Yes, indeed. Look at the emotions you are feeling as you go through your day. The assumptions you hold will bring you to a specific emotional state, such as fear, frustration, happiness, or peacefulness. Did you know that you can choose your emotions? You do not have to just accept whatever emotion is served up to you! There are methods for shifting your emotions out of a feeling that you don't want and moving into a feeling you would prefer.

We can create a distinction between emotions and moods. Emotions happen in reaction to external events and are sharp and intense. Moods are internally generated and less intense. The reaction to a specific event will trigger an emotion in you and that reaction will be unique to you. Someone else may have a completely different emotional reaction to the same situation you are dealing with.

Begin by paying close attention to what you are feeling. Can you find a word to describe how you are feeling? Is it fear, anger, resentment, resignation, frustration, confusion? Is this the emotion that you want?

Often what we are feeling is not just one emotion, but a blend of emotions. This can make it tricky to assess, as each emotion is closely followed by the experience of a different emotion. The first emotion will peak and recede, to be followed by the next emotion. Knowing this can help when you are trying to identify what you are actually feeling. Once you have noticed the emotions you are currently feeling, you can consider which emotions you would prefer. Perhaps you would prefer peace, joy, abundance, love, clarity. As you change your assumptions, the emotions that are generated shift as well.

WRIGHT

How do your thoughts and assumptions affect your emotions and your reaction to the world?

STAIB DUFFY

As an Ontological Coach, I work with two basic models of how we interact with the world. Ontology is the study of how we are the way we are as humans.

In the traditional model, which is what most of us use, we start as an observer who takes an action, which leads to a result. If we like the result, we move on without any further consideration. If we do not like the result, we try a different action. If this works, great; we are done. If not, we try something else. If this still does not work, we are usually stymied and stuck, going around and around.

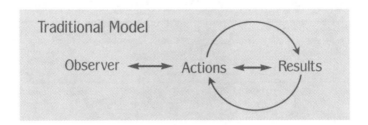

At this point we have reached a growth edge and we need to pause and change how we are observing. This is when we move to Ontological Model 1 to get us out of the loop:

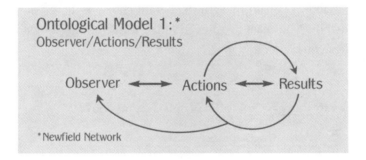

Once we start observing how we are observing, Ontological Model 2 gives us a way to learn differently. We contemplate how the thoughts we think (language), the emotions we feel (emotions), and the way we hold energy in our body (body) all come together to create our worldview (filter). Our possibilities for action flow through our filter. Because our language, emotions, and body must be coherent with each other, we can start with any one of them and use it to rebalance and regroup. When we have hit a growth edge, we need to go back to assess how we are observing and begin the process of learning at a deeper level.

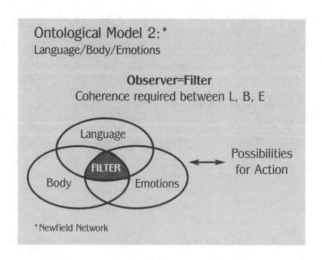

This type of learning is very intense in that it expands who you are. This is called ontological learning, transformational learning, or double-loop learning. This process allows you to make a deliberate choice in how you respond to an event versus how you react to an event. Like a tree adding rings of growth each year, it makes you bigger and more resilient.

WRIGHT

How does this process affect the people around you?

STAIB DUFFY

Our moods and emotions are contagious and affect those with whom we are interacting. One aspect of engaging in a *Yikes!* moment is about managing turbulent emotions during trying times for a better outcome. Senior-level executives are very aware that their decisions have a significant effect on their organization and the people around them. But all of us have an influence on ourselves and others all the time through our emotions as well as our decisions and actions.

So, if for whatever reason, you are in a *Yikes!* moment, do not despair. Do not give up! Instead, pause and regroup. Question and observe. Observe and question. Pay attention to your emotions. Listen to your inner narrative. Consider the actual words you have selected and the assumptions driving the story. When dealing with a big mess, sometimes of our own making, we need to regroup and reevaluate before we move to the next step.

Another key strategy is to breathe! Breathe deeply. If you are somewhere quiet, listen to your breath. If you are somewhere noisy, just do the breathing anyway. Whenever you think of it and wherever you think of it, breathe. Breathe deeper and deeper. Do this four or five or ten times a day. It will calm you down, even in the midst of an incredible crisis. Breathe deeply. You will make a better decision.

WRIGHT

What can we expect as we try what you have suggested here?

STAIB DUFFY

When you move to take on a great challenge, it typically unfolds in a series of small steps. Start taking it one day at a time, one thing at a time. At each point, you will have the opportunity to choose. The shortest distance in a spiritual sense is not usually a straight line. The path curves a lot, and sometimes even doubles back! Life has many twists and turns. At times, the path might be foggy and there will be little clarity about what to do next. But as you make your choices, the next aspect will be presented to you. Great good can come from a bad situation. Wonderful learning can unfold when things are not easy. We can make such situations easier or harder for us by what we say to ourselves as we turn to face our most difficult moments.

Let's look at some specific examples. When the economy goes south and we lose a job or a home, we can slump over in defeat or we can start again and try some new approaches. When all is going well for us, we can become arrogant. When we struggle, we can become more compassionate and empathetic to the plight of another. When we face the loss of a loved one, the fragile beauty of living and loving can become evident to us. We can choose to shrivel up in the face of loss or we can keep our hearts open by realizing that every day we have together is a day that can never be taken away. A potential loss can make us very aware of the beauty and song of life that we miss when we just rush.

Some times in our lives are more challenging than others but there is always a different way, a happier way, a new possibility waiting for us to see it. We can approach this learning from a scientific point of view, including recent research that shows how our thoughts actually create physical changes in our brains, or we

321

can approach it from a religious or spiritual point of view. Either way, what we think, what we feel, and what we intend are important.

WRIGHT

Will you give me an example of a new approach?

STAIB DUFFY

Look at whatever you consider to be your major strength. A major strength can be a major drawback. It is so easy to overdo a strength. Something we are good at will garner us much praise. Since we are good at it, it will have historically led us to successful outcomes. Because we have experienced so many good outcomes, we do it more and more and get even better at it. It becomes part of our fabric—part of who we are.

That all works fine until one day it does not work as well. We get less than satisfactory results. So what do we do? We do more of it! Because, of course, that is what we are good at, and it usually works so well. We continue to use it, even though it is no longer the best choice or even a good choice. And then, even if it is still not working, we will usually redouble our efforts because we believe that it eventually will work again. Furthermore, we usually think we cannot do the opposite, so that solution is unavailable to us. These are all signs that we are overdoing a strength.

Very often, a daunting challenge will require us to do the very opposite of what we think we are good at. For example, if you are well known as a diplomat and as a person with whom everyone gets along, it is highly likely that resolving your predicament will require you to be direct and handle a confrontation. It will be something that you cannot delegate or ask anyone else to do. You will need to do it yourself.

There is a saying that "When the only tool you have is a hammer, it is tempting to treat everything as if it were a nail." Well, if there is no nail and you are using a hammer, all you end up with is a hole in the wall. This applies to using your strength in a situation where the opposite is more appropriate. Using too much diplomacy when a more blunt conversation is needed (or the reverse, of course) will not lead you to the successful outcome you are seeking.

Many times when you are in a *Yikes!* moment, you have entered a space where your hammer is no longer useful and is in fact likely to be counterproductive.

When you are in a situation that has you going around and around, consider what you would typically do, then hit the brakes and do the opposite. If you are assertive, back off and listen. If you are great at confronting challenges head-on, you may need to be diplomatic and perhaps indirect.

WRIGHT

Isn't this difficult to do?

STAIB DUFFY

Well, when you first try this, you will be lousy at it because it is not a skill you have been perfecting for years. It is a skill you have mostly ignored. But it is important to start trying.

This is called behavioral learning, as opposed to conceptual learning. This type of learning requires time and practice. You will get a little bit better, a little bit better, and then better again. The goal is not that this will become your new defining strength. No, the goal is to be able to perform the needed skill just a little bit better so that you have more flexibility and a larger assortment of potential responses when you really need them. When your responses are more nuanced, you are likely to achieve the desired outcome.

WRIGHT

Is success the ultimate goal of all this?

STAIB DUFFY

Yes, but one of the big questions is how do we define success? Is it making a lot of money? Attaining a certain position or level in a company? Starting and running a company of your own? Must it be big or is small and profitable okay? Could it be raising your children to be happy and healthy? Being happy and contented with yourself? Finding a new job? Making a connection with the divine? Finding meaning and purpose in your life? Handling a very difficult situation with grace and dignity? Having more flexibility or leisure in your life? Success could be any of these things or some combination of these things. How you define success for yourself will be a key part of the next step. If you fast-forward your life and imagine yourself successful in five or ten years, what would it look like, feel like? Then look at the decisions you will need to make to achieve this.

Life will always throw you curve balls—situations that seem beyond your ability to cope with—and will require further learning and expansion. We can never stop learning. The trick is to learn from a space of enjoyment and perhaps even fun. Let go of the assumption that learning has to be hard and painful. Maybe the situation is difficult, but maybe it won't be, once the learning starts to kick in.

WRIGHT

What is your definition of success?

STAIB DUFFY

I would like to suggest that success is about how you feel! It is an emotional state, rather than a particular job, a certain amount of dollars in your savings account, a particular house, or a certain partner. Success in life can be found in feeling good about what you are doing and how you are doing it.

Most of us look to buy things to make us feel better or to feel happy or sexy or accepted. We buy an item to capture a particular feeling, even if only temporarily. We look at someone else's big house and we think, "Oh, they must be so happy." A bigger house, the better job, a marriage, a divorce, having children, a new car, trendy clothes—most of the things that we chase after in life are actually a diversion from what we are really seeking. What we are actually seeking is the emotion we think might come with the bigger house or the new clothes. Feeling happiness or contentment with what we have and, more importantly, with who we are is success for me. Most of us want to feel a sense of joy and abundance as opposed to scarcity and fear. What if this feeling of joy and abundance is the ultimate success?

And here's the key: We create our emotional state. We get to choose how we feel. We can choose to generate the feelings we want by engaging in the process we have been talking about. We can feel successful or happy or confident, in part by the questions we ask, the assumptions we make, and the stories we tell ourselves. We create the emotions by how we hold our bodies—how we stand and sit, our facial expressions, and our posture.

If you are completely lost as to how to start, I would invite you to begin with gratitude. What are you grateful for? Once you have generated a different emotion, you will find that new alternatives will present themselves that are more in keeping with this new emotion.

Here are two questions to consider: Can we seek to learn and to succeed from a place of joy and contentment? Who says learning has to be hard? Learning with joy feels like play, but we are still growing and expanding.

Many of us are perfectionists. We are told always to seek excellence. Excellence and striving for improvement are important values, but these can also be overdone. Perfectionism can leave you constantly dissatisfied. Excellence is not attainable in every situation, is not always really necessary, and is ephemeral at best. What if sometimes good is good enough? When does it not have to be perfect? It can be useful in these situations to rephrase from "I *should* do—" to "I *could* do—" This emphasizes your choice in the matter. If we sometimes declare that good enough is enough, we are free to enjoy these moments as well. We can choose where and how we strive, and where and how to relax.

Furthermore, when we do attain perfection, it is good to remember that perfection in this physical world is only for a moment—a fleeting space of beauty, like a flower. There will be many times when you will get that moment of perfection. You might wonder, if it is fleeting, why bother? Because there are billions of flowers and trillions of moments of beauty and perfection. We won't experience them, however, unless we pause and savor them. This all goes back to our mindset, to our thoughts and our assumptions, and to the stories we tell ourselves as we go through our days and rise to meet the challenges in our lives.

Ask yourself: When and where in my life do I declare that what I have is enough? When and where in my life do I declare joy and abundance? When and where in my life do I declare success?

WRIGHT

How would you summarize your message?

STAIB DUFFY

We are each powerful in the moment! This is a good time to hit the pause button and make a deliberate choice in how we are responding. The intention and energy we choose to bring into the world in these moments are important. We affect each other as we make our way through these situations. Our choices make a difference.

First, make time for reflection. It does not have to be a big block of time. It can be ten minutes here and there. Or an hour. Or a day. Work with whatever time you can carve out. Start to observe. Breathe. Breathe deeply.

Second, question your observations. Differentiate between facts and assumptions (or beliefs). Question your assumptions. What are you assuming is "true"? What if the opposite of your belief were "true"? Watch out for dead-end thoughts that leave you with no option for choice or change, then restructure these thoughts.

Next, look closely at the stories you are telling yourself. What are the actual words you are selecting? What happens to your story if you change the assumptions? Your story is *key* because it guides your thoughts, and your thoughts guide your actions. Change the story. What new assumptions can you incorporate into what you tell yourself? What do you think is your greatest strength? What do you think you cannot do? Try doing what you think you cannot.

Lastly, ask what emotions you are feeling. What would you prefer to be feeling? By shifting your thoughts and moving your body, you can choose your emotions. Start living the emotions you want to feel!

Remember, what you are not changing, you are choosing. Choose your success.

ABOUT THE AUTHOR

Karen Staib Duffy's background includes over twenty-five years in large corporate America and considerable experience in management, risk management, sales and business/product development, primarily in the investment banking and financial services field. She is an Ontological Coach, certified through Newfield Network's Coaching for Professional and Personal Mastery (CPPM) and a Professional Certified Coach (PCC) with the International Coach Federation. She has held a variety of roles in coaching and executive development, including three years as Regional Managing Director with Korn/Ferry International. Before establishing her own firm, Karen was Managing Director at one of Chicago's leading financial institutions, Banc One Capital Markets (now part of JPMorgan Chase). She has an undergraduate degree from Northwestern University and a master's degree in Business Administration from the University of Chicago.

KAREN STAIB DUFFY

Quantum Development Coaching
kesduffy@hotmail.com
www.qdcoaching.com

Secrets to Success Uncovered
The 10 Stepping Stones
By Dr. Steve Cady

There's no secret about success.
Did you ever know a successful person who didn't tell you about it?
—Kin Hubbard

Secrets—what do they mean to you? They might mean something hidden or something untold or possibly something to be uncovered—principles that can help you in a new way. The 10 Stepping Stones for Success are based on powerful stories and approaches for improving our lives.

The men and women interviewed in this book are some of our most accomplished thinkers, coaches, speakers, physicians, educators, professionals, counselors, and leaders on personal growth and development. They have committed their lives to a calling that has taken them out into the world to make a difference bigger than themselves. They have taken risks to live what they believe. They have worked with people from all walks in life. They have walked in all corners of the planet. They have seen some of the best and worst in humanity. Yet, they still believe in us. They believe we can be whole human beings—doing great work in the world. I am honored to have been included among them and excited to have a chance to look more deeply into their interviews to unlock their collective secrets to success.

If they were to sit in a room, share their approaches, and come to agreement on common principles, what might they conclude? I have reviewed their comments and merged their advice into common themes in the form of 10 Stepping Stones to

Success. While the steps to success are basic, they can both challenge us on one hand and encourage us on the other.

As you read through the interviews, you undoubtedly picked up on themes. I'm curious if you uncovered the same themes found in the research conducted here. This is the essence of qualitative analysis. This technique was used to examine the interviews—breaking their comments into key thoughts, cataloguing them, categorizing them, and then providing you with a re-integration of what was found.

Qualitative analysis is not an exact science, and I offer the following as my summary of their wisdom and expertise. I have connected their words into a collective story of success. While the guidance in this chapter is not my own, it is my interpretation based on categorizing their wisdom. This chapter may seem a bit "clunky" as I am doing my best to stay true to the original words, phrases, and concepts found in the interviews. As a result, you will find the interviews woven together into a tapestry of advice called The 10 Stepping Stones to Success. My desire is to spark your curiosity to dig deeper into the interviews, make your own connections, and uncover the collective wisdom found in this book.

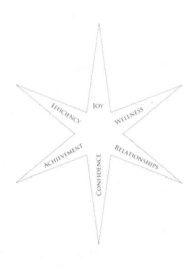

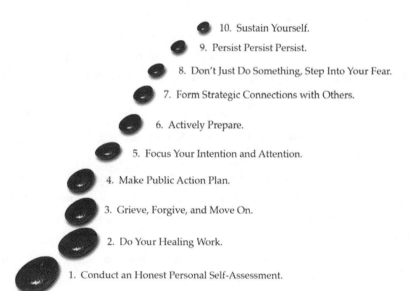

10. Sustain Yourself.

9. Persist Persist Persist.

8. Don't Just Do Something, Step Into Your Fear.

7. Form Strategic Connections with Others.

6. Actively Prepare.

5. Focus Your Intention and Attention.

4. Make Public Action Plan.

3. Grieve, Forgive, and Move On.

2. Do Your Healing Work.

1. Conduct an Honest Personal Self-Assessment.

3 H's for Success

The symbolism of stepping from stone to stone represents a core action for you to take as you maneuver along the river of life. The advice here can help you to break through old habits and limiting beliefs—to develop new habits that bring you more joy, confidence, wellness, love, efficiency, and achievement—to move into a higher state of being your best self. The 10 Stepping Stones can be gathered into three symbolic cairns called The 3 H's for Success—Healing, Harnessing, and Helping. Cairns are piles of stones used by people in nature to serve as markers on our journey. Hence, the stepping stones have been gathered into three broad areas for personal growth and development.

Healing is looking inward –
taking care of self in order to better serve others

Healing connects the mind, body, and spirit. The experience of personal healing is often described as going deep to connect with the hidden wounds created by the trauma of the human experience; releasing them through embracing the pain, coming out of isolation, sharing the experience, and being thankful for the lessons. Regardless of how charmed life seems, the human experience embodies trauma of some kind. Being wounded is natural. Facing a wound seems unnatural, yet is healthy and necessary. As Harri Holkeri said, "you cannot make easy decisions unless you commit yourself to hard solutions."

Stepping Stone 1. Conduct an Honest Personal Self-Assessment.

The first step in healing is to understand yourself in order to build on your strengths in a manner that diminishes weaknesses. Golletz talks about building our uber strengths. He goes on to propose as an entry point for discussion, "you must accept that you are not equally and infinitely capable of all things." Therefore, it is important to "understand your strengths and weaknesses in a precise and granular way. Knowing them starts with feedback." Focus on assessments that define specific actions. There are three ways to conduct a self-assessment: self-reflection, standardized tools or inventories, and feedback from others.

As you conduct your self-assessment, listen differently. In order to get a new result, it is necessary to conduct your assessment in a new way. Michaels encourages us to be honest about what we don't know and want to learn. This includes being honest with yourself and others. Cohen states that "It's sometimes very difficult to have the strength and courage to listen to your own inner voice and try to achieve your own special goals." She goes on to emphasize that the key to self-assessment is in the questions we might not ask ourselves. And, as Duffy suggests, this can include looking at our beliefs and assumptions to achieve success. These assumptions can be found in the stories we tell ourselves. Don't accept them at face value, question them. She suggests asking the question, "could the opposite be true?" Challenge your dead end thoughts, such as, "that is just the way I am." Differentiate between facts and assumptions. DeStefano and Faust both provide very practical questions you can ask yourself regarding your career, job hunt, and interviewing.

The self-reflection process includes looking at our bright side and our dark side. Are you willing to own your addictions? Rohrer describes how addictions come in many forms. She suggests that you look at the deeper reasons of how and why you are using the addiction to "dampen your feelings and why you are doing that." In the process of doing your self-assessment, be ready and willing to allow an emotional release as a key component of your personal growth. DiLallo describes how he, "sobbed and felt a deep remorse and responsibility for how I had treated others in my past." He goes on to share that it is important to take care of our intrapersonal life and listen to our hearts—become "inner activists."

The greatest movement comes as you move toward your light—your strengths. The experts strongly emphasize the important of identifying your talents, gifts, and core capabilities. Too often, people stay in the weakness finding, and this can be dangerous as it can lead to developing weaknesses.

Finally, consider conducting as assessment by gathering feedback from others. There are a variety of questions that ring true among the interviews. Beil takes a critical thinking approach that make the self-assessment process quite practical. First, collect information about the world around you. Second, organize the information into meaningful patterns. Third, apply the pattern to situations today and in the future. Fourth, figure out if what you did worked. Beil goes on to describe a story of how important it is that we focus on positive patterns, finding those things that we do right is the key to our success. If you catch yourself and others doing things right daily, you are going to start moving down the right path.

Stepping Stone 2. Do Your Healing Work.

A thoughtful self-assessment can begin to dislodge blocks, particularly blind spots that can keep you from knowing where to begin your healing work. Where do you start? One thing is clear among the interviewees. Begin with healing yourself. Faust jumps right in. She speaks of transition as the key to doing healing work, "you must care for yourself first, then the rest of your world." The interviews tend to focus on healing in a few key areas: physical healing, emotional healing, relationship healing, spiritual healing, mental healing, and habit healing.

A consistent message for the healing journey is to identify the "baggage" we carry and the trauma or events that help to create the baggage. In an inspiring story, Murray describes when he had to face sequence of cancer and a heart attack. His key to healing was recognizing the cause could be related to deep hurt, longstanding resentment, hatreds, and grief that were eating away at him. In response, he focused on health and happiness and in about forty-five days the cancer was gone. As for his heart attack, he recognized that he had been squeezing all the joy out of his heart in favor of money and position. What he came to learn is that new thoughts create new conditions. In both of his health crises, he used a mental and spiritual approach combined with modern medicine. Both were important to his healing.

This leads to the next point. Often the various types of healing are so interconnected that they are addressed with certain interventions. For example, Chopra describes how you can reset your biostate up to fifteen years younger than your chronological age. The key is to break out of the prison of prior conditioning. If you think you should feel old, then you are locked into that prison of pre-conditioned beliefs. Healing begins with changing three perceptions in regard to the following: aging, the physical body, and dying. And, one key to healing is deep rest that includes sleep and meditation. DiLallo suggests taking time to relax, reflect, unwind, and do nothing. In his Peace2U approach, he has found people respond well to guided experiences that help them to meditate and de-stress. In general, the experts recommend that we understand and ensure we have healthy levels of stress in our lives, called eustress.

Another area commonly mentioned is how important nutrition is to healing and reversing the aging process. Interestingly, exercise is often mentioned along with diet. The experts encourage us all to have our own forms of exercise that involve good old-fashioned sweating.

The bottom line message is stop ignoring and start working on yourself. Use robust approaches that have a history of success in helping people heal. For example, Rohrer provides "Six Simple Steps to Emotional Freedom." She demonstrates how the wounds we experience often lead to our addictions. She recommends that you consciously use your wounds as a personal "pattern-busting" strategy. She goes on to suggest that you don't run away when you get your "buttons-pushed." Notice and run toward them. Quit looking outside yourself for a quick fix. Go inside to discover if the hurt can be traced back to their origination, make the connection, and release the energy. This is why Stepping Stone 1 is so important to Stepping Stone 2. Look inside, identify, embrace, and then do your work intentionally to heal. Use both non-traditional and traditional approaches together to design a personal healing approach that works for you.

Stepping Stone 3. Grieve, Forgive, and Move On.

Healing means change for good. Yes, it means to become more whole and yes it means to become healthier. It also means to leave behind parts of ourselves that no longer work for us. With this leaving behind comes loss and emotions. These emotions, if ignored, can cause us to revert back to old patterns and, in essence un-heal or re-injure ourselves. For example, consider events from early in life that have not been addressed. The experts say that wounds from early relationships can serve us and inform us, yet we need to recognize them for what they are. In the interviews, there are personal stories of tough childhoods, from parents who were alcoholics to no parents at all. Others describe great families, yet describe other kinds of challenges such as Michaels being born in a concentration camp, escaping with her mother in a rowboat, and hiding in Italy for years. A consistent theme is that they shifted control of their life from outside to inside. They didn't let self-pity get them down. Rather, they noticed and took responsibility for their lives. They allowed themselves to be forgiven by others and they forgave themselves. The consistent advice is to forgive and move on to living the life you yearn to have. The five steps in the grieving process are:

- Denial—"All is fine, I'm doing just great."
- Bargaining—"There has to be a quick way to fix this."
- Anger—"This is wrong. I'm mad at…"
- Sadness—"I'm sorry, I feel so guilty and ashamed."
- Acceptance—"I forgive you, I forgive me, I'm ready to move on."

Sometimes people get stuck and don't move out of healing into harnessing their power. They get hooked on the grief associated with healing. The physiological experience of sadness and shame associated with healing can become all a person knows and, when acceptance and joy are finally experience, it is foreign and uncomfortable. The person's reaction can then be to self-sabotage in order to go back to the feelings of sadness and shame. That is because we are more accustomed to the chemicals our bodies produce that are associated with these emotions, like an addiction.

By allowing yourself to go through the grieving process, you can let go of old parts of the self that no longer serve you and open a space for adopting more healthy and affirming ways of living. DiLallo provides a quote from Carl Jung, "The healthy man does not torture others—generally it is the tortured who turn into torturers." He describes himself as a recovering bully who learned much of his behaviors from his father. It was forgiveness and getting to a place of peace and love with his father that has allowed him to translate those early experiences into living his personal mission. He noticed the pattern, did his personal work, forgave, broke the cycle of bullying in his family, and moved on to harnessing his power to do great things in the world.

Healing experiences set you up to move to the next stepping stone. The experts suggest that it is in these moments that you and only you can make the choice to break free of the cycle that has held you back. DeStefano describes a concept called inflection points. These are moments when you are surrounded by a clear need to change. It is a moment when you will descend or jettison into another ascending arc. It is analogous to taking your life to the next level as mentioned in several interviews. These inflection moments are opportunities to reinvent you. Moving to the next level can include discarding complexity and embracing simplicity. When you do this, life is clearer and more concise—you'll find it's easier to live with fewer distractions. Taking these steps will help you move on to the next set of stepping stones.

Harnessing is the process of clarifying your gifts and talents, defining and refining them

Harnessing creates an ennobling and inspiring vision for the future. Creating such a vision requires tapping into your soul's deepest passion - having an authentic conversation in which you claim what fires you up. Then, it involves translating that inspiring vision into a public action plan for manifesting your dreams. This is no time to be shy about living your calling in the world.

Stepping Stone 4. Make a Public Action Plan.

The experts recommend a basic checklist for crafting your action plan. Clarify your purpose. Choose and prioritize your goals. Develop clear and concrete deliverables that can be measured. Create a flexible roadmap and timeline for implementation. Then, allow your plan to unfold and adapt your plan based on what you learn at each step on your journey.

It is through your goals that you manifest your purpose in life. These two points serve as the fodder for an action plan. Sometimes you can create your goals and use them to help you uncover your purpose. For example, ask yourself, "if I achieve all these goals, what will be different in the world." Your answer is your purpose in life, often referred to as a personal mission statement. The other way is to craft your purpose or mission statement and ask yourself, "what do I need to achieve in order to fully live my purpose." For example, Chopra suggests that you take time each day to focus on: who am I (purpose) and what do I want (goals for success)?

When crafting your purpose statement, Waitley emphasizes its power when he says that, "what you want in life turns you on much more than what you need in life." And, if you listen you will hear your own wisdom guiding you. A key theme in all the interviews is that you are unique and have something special to offer. Williams represents the general message from the experts when stating that, "we are all put on this earth for a reason."

Next are goals. Goals are broad areas of focus that are integral to your purpose in life. Prioritize your goals, which means put the big stuff in first. For each goal, make sure your include those things that nurture you. In almost all the interviews, family and close friends were mentioned as important to balance in the process of achieving goals. Williams goes on to describe the benefits of providing detail for each goal—develop measures for success spiritually, mentally, financially, and physically. That is, commit to deliverables for each of your goals. Deliverables are specific tasks to accomplish in the next few months to year. Then, use these details to develop an implementation plan or roadmap—a timeline for getting things done. Infuse a focus on quality into your plan, as Beil recommends. That is, remove waste and increase your timeliness.

Once you have developed your action plan, share it with others. Make public pronouncements that you own and don't be embarrassed by the audaciousness of your purpose, goals, and action plan. One of Canfield's mentors says, "success is not a four letter word." Confidently explain why you care about the plan and give specifics on how you are going to get there. A subtle, but important, message that emerged from the interviews is the need to craft a concise and easy to understand action plan that you and others can use. Consider, for example, The Lesson of the Buss as told by Weldon. In a big city, people get on the wrong bus because the instructions are confusing and cumbersome. The advice is to be clear about how your plan directly connects to your purpose—your passion. Share it concisely; yet not so fast or cryptic that it is hard for others to join you—to support you—to collaborate with you.

In one compelling story shared by Waitley, a 10-year-old boy participating in a workshop with adults on life planning came to him a bit discouraged by what he was witnessing in the adults. The boy told him that most of the adults were talking about playing golf and socializing. The boy wanted to know what he could do. Waitley gave the boy an assignment as a game called Write the Future. Forty-five minutes later the young boy returned and astonished the adults with a plan for his life—clear and concise. Sure enough, years later, Waitely turned on the television to see this little goal setter floating around in space on a tether as an astronaut just like he publically stated in that workshop.

In addition to sharing your plan publically, find ways to join forces with others and create collaborative ventures. Design your own performance-based incentive program called gain sharing. Get others involved in your action plan and give them some ownership, as they contribute to your success. Successful people have a knack for getting others on board with their passion. They connect passion among people so that individual and collective dreams are realized. By doing this, it enables you to connect with others, enlist their support, and mutually support them in doing good work in the world. Bottom line, share your success with those who have been instrumental in making it happen. Turn your action plan into a team plan for success.

One practical way to make this happen is to shift your passion to a "we" focus by removing the "I" and putting more "you" into the description of your plan. How will your plan serve and tap into the talents of those around you? Make a case that invites others to join forces with you. Weldon suggests that you write a five to ten page letter to someone you serve. Don't use the word "I" one time and notice what you learn. And, finally, be able to describe your passion, your purpose in one sentence. In the end, you will be able to answer the questions: Who are you?, Where are you going?, and How are you going to get there?

Stepping Stone 5. Focus Your Intention and Attention.

Does your intention keep your attention? Intention is about choice and attention is about focus. Intention is described in step four above—choose your purpose, goals, and action plan. Then, develop the habit of focusing your attention on that intention. Another way of asking this is—are you paying attention to your intention? A common agreement among the experts is that our brain can run us or we can run it. They strongly emphasize that we are in charge of our thoughts. They don't claim to be perfect at this, but what they do claim is that they work hard at training themselves to habitually focus their attention on what matters. In Michaels' interview, she states, "I believe in it—I don't think there is another option. So, I always strive to aim at being successful." Williams concurs by suggesting that our focus is the key. Overall, you can train your brain and whole self to bring your personal mission, vision, goals, and action plan to the forefront.

The power of bringing your intention to the forefront can be demonstrated with the latest research findings; quantum physics is mentioned among several interviews. For example, Baker-Receniello describes how our subconscious influences our success. Because our thoughts create matter, we "reap what we sow." She goes on to describe how the atomic world is nothing like the physical world. It's not really solid. She further elaborates on brain research and how our brains can change in moments due to its plasticity. She provides a list of tips such as "commit to focus on the present moment and make whatever your current task is the most important."

A simple way to begin is to pay attention to the positive, small successes, key supporters, and expectations for living your passion. Use this approach to remove roadblocks and uncover new pathways to success. Cohen describes, "obstacles can't move without action; but first you have to clear your mind of your negative point of view..." She goes on to describe how we can allow small challenges, failures, and problems to become the focus of our thinking long after the event is over. Reframe your expectations toward possibilities as the practice of gratitude. Start with waking up and noticing what you are grateful for, the small things, all around you. The more you do this, the more you will attract things to be grateful for into your world.

Stepping Stone 6. Actively Prepare.

This stepping stone is straightforward. Go and attend classes, workshops, read, ask questions, and more. Listening is a common thread in all the interviews and this directly relates to education. Really listen and integrate what you are learning, and read, read, read. Take notes and document your learning. There are so many resources provided in person and on-line. Take the time each day, week, and month to be learning something about your passion. Canfield's main focus has been on the stories of people who have overcome insurmountable obstacles. He says that we can learn from the stories of others in ways that can shift us and save us a lot of time. He reads one book per week and in ten years has read 520 books, putting him in the top one percent of people knowing important information. DiLallo describes how education became his "healing potion" and he is a lifelong learner with a "beginner's mind." Consider enlisting the services of experts like those interviewed in this book as Faust suggests. Hire them to take you through their simple step-by-step processes. Make sure that you adopt a method that has a track record of success.

Next, move from reading to practice. You know you have learned something helpful when your behaviors change and the results are better than before. The experts describe a variety of ways such as discipline, trial and error, and experimentation. For example, Faust suggests, as you get ready for the next steps, such as a job search, get a friend to listen and help you prepare for the interview. If necessary tape record yourself. Find creative ways to practice before going "live."

A final piece of advice is to ask for what you need, which is directly connected to the previous stepping stones. By completing the previous steps you will have a better understanding of what you need to be successful. In the asking, separate what you want from what you need so that you can be clear about what is important to getting started. Frank elaborates on the ask as negotiation, the art and a skill in which we communicate with others to seek a common ground to reach a mutually satisfying, sustainable agreement. She goes on to describe the "solutioneering" procedure that reframes non-agreements as opportunities. Be careful to ask in a way that ensures a win-win situation. It is win-lose that creates wars. Frank goes on to provide an acronym that is based on the word LISTEN that can help you to develop conscious skills and tools for ensuring you get what you need in order to take action. This leads to the next stepping stone.

Stepping Stone 7. Form Strategic Connections with Others.

This is a fancy way of saying, be thoughtful about whom you partner with, whom you hang out with, and whom you ask for help. There are a lot of ways to describe this and it boils down to the people you include in your personal circle of influence will rub off on you. Canfield suggests that you surround yourself with people who have qualities and habits you aspire to have more of in your life. This seems to be very important point made by the experts. They recommend that you gather together a set of mentors to provide guidance. Think of it as a Personal Advisory Board where each mentor provides a unique perspective. Make sure that they are willing to act as a mentor and have the necessary time. Also, pick mentors that are modeling what you want in your life. Frank encourages us to craft an agreement that is satisfying to both people. Consider using her model to help you develop a formal or informal mentoring contract.

In addition to mentoring, consider whom to partner with on projects and other initiatives. Join forces with people who model healthy habits and attitudes for success. It's also clear that you shouldn't waste your time on people that are not ready to be healthy and productive with you. If you are in a chronically sick relationship, it is imperative that you change it or leave it immediately. Move on. Move toward the more healthy and vibrant people who will encourage you to rise to your best self. The experts describe the people they partner and collaborate with as friends. It seems that their significant accomplishments are with people they care about.

Another related theme is the notion of manners and consideration of others. Each of the experts talked in different ways of being thoughtful, using good manners, being respectful of people from all stations in life, and being kind to one another. Notice their interaction with the interviewer, David Wright, and how they exemplified such consideration. Golletz tells of Andrea Agassi's impeccable manners and how he insists that people who work for him conduct themselves in a similar manner.

And, finally, consider making your approach easily available to others so that they can be mentored, informed, and encouraged by you. Become a teacher and mentor to others. Michaels makes her work available for others to adopt and use. She takes an "open source" approach to her work. She has forged new ideas in the marketplace and is glad to see people using her innovations. This also relates to her notion of strategic partnerships. The more you share, the more you are able to join forces with others doing good work in the world. Build a community of practice around your work. Initiate small events that bring people together for meals, celebrations, conversations, and more. Do these things both in-person and on-line. DiLallo proposes that you internalize the philosophy of "my success is your success and your success is my success."

Helping is the action that moves you from a self-focus to another focus

Helping is making a difference in other people's lives. This shift from self to others is profound. Successful people move from healing and harnessing to that of creating. The light of creation overcomes the wounds of darkness - inspiration abounds. Play and joy are experienced. Life's challenges are seen differently. Learning is wonderful and peak experiences are plentiful.

Stepping Stone 8. Don't Just Do Something, Step Into Your Fear.

Personal growth brings change and change brings fear. The most common message from all the interviewees is this - doing something that matters to you will require stepping into your fear. Are you willing to move beyond fear to be your own cheerleader? Frank emphasizes that your enthusiasm and passion are infectious. People want to trust that you are on the right path. If you are doubtful, how can you expect others to believe? It is similar to the notion that dogs can smell fear. Recent research suggests that even mosquitoes can smell fear and stress. In short, your enthusiasm begins with the verbal and behavioral action of belief. Smile, stand, and hold yourself like you believe in your plan. There is the notion of fake it till you make it. You have to act like a winner in order to feel like a winner. In the process, your enthusiasm becomes contagious.

Interestingly, the experts describe a paradox. You must embrace your fear in order to move through it and bring forth that deep confidence that has always been there. Williams provides an acronym for FEAR - False Evidence Appearing Real. She emphasizes, "Successful thinking requires you to move beyond your comfort zone." Fear is your visceral connection to what matters to you. Fear is therefore a sign that you are moving in the right directly. The key, as Faust prescribes, is to, "take a chill pill and calm down." This requires stepping into your fear and staying in it long enough to know you will be OK. View it as an offering to open a window of opportunity to grow and have wonderful new things in your life. DeStefano refers to this as a transition, the leaving of something familiar behind without knowing in advance what to do.

Cohen encourages us to move through fear to confidence step-by-step. Take one step at a time away from one thing in order to overcome obstacles and achieve new success. Put your energy into what can be achieved in the present. For example, one of Golletz's rules is, "knowing what to do and actually doing it are not the same thing." There is no time like now to get started, and it doesn't have to be BIG. Often, the first steps are small. Waitley describes how self-confidence comes from reinforcing those small successes, and Michaels describes how she relishes creating something out of nothing. This is stepping into the unknown.

At some point, you will be called to speak in front of a group to share, sell, invite, and get others involved with your passion. Weldon asks, "What will your comfort level be? Will you be confident, relaxed, and self-assured? Or will you be self-conscious, anxious, and uneasy? Will you have the ability to positively influence them, to persuade or inform them, or to direct their behavior in some way?" The ability to share your passion with others is a vital stepping stone to success. He goes on to emphasize that the only way to develop the skill is to just get started.

Duffy describes Yikes! moments that occur when we enter uncharted territory that can take the form of major success or failure. These become defining moments to help us find ourselves and carve out our destiny, and often provide the impetus to go back and do more healing and harnessing work. Faust gives a provocative way of thinking about this using a technique for reframing such a moment, "Congratulations! If this is the time you have been terminated or laid off, then realize that things do happen for good reasons and this is the beginning of the new you." Be happy and realize that this is not the job for you any longer. DeStefano found in her work with laid off workers that approximately one-third were relieved when they learned of their fate. The key take away from all the interviews is this—successful people really believe a "no," rejection, or failure is an opportunity—a learning moment—and a necessary nudge or push toward something better.

Stepping Stone 9. Persist Persist Persist.

This is the essence of successful habits that Waitley describes in his interview. It is the disciplined structure and action that separates the extraordinary from ordinary. He shares that he is a positive attitude person, but he has come to appreciate that success is more than attitude. The real difference to being successful is found in the work necessary to be a champion in any endeavor.

Persistence doesn't mean doing the same thing over and over again, expecting different results. That is actually the definition of crazy. Golletz describes how some leaders are stressed, self-indulgent, over-baked, and neglectful of themselves and their families. They are hard-headed instead of tough-minded. Being tough-minded is the goal. It is, "the ability, inclination, and discipline to face any situation with strength, determination, and equanimity."

The advice of the experts is that you continuously improve—making adjustments as needed. Admit when you are wrong and that you are making modifications. This is the essence of double loop learning in the present. Duffy refers to creating success through flexibility, learning, and resilience. Cohen describes this as "trial and error." The various experts all emphasize the importance of learning from experience. In order to avoid the notion of "crazy," periodically conduct after action reviews based on the following questions:

What did I plan to do?

What happened as compared to my plan?

What did I learn?

What will I do differently next time?

Baker-Receniello encourages us to use such self-review and learning to grow or reinvent ourselves. Use this awareness to add to your dream and remove distractions. As Beil describes in his leadership approach, the aim is to get to the stage in development where you anticipate and act efficiently—often with no words or explanation required. He describes this as the "peak level."

Finally, the core concept of persistence is never ever give up. Murray tells a story of his brother who was born with cerebral palsy. As a young man, he one day asked his father, "Why doesn't my brother walk?" His dad shared with him that it takes an olive tree one hundred years to produce olives and a pecan tree must grow for eight years before it grows nuts. The message from his father was that we all grow at our own pace. The key is to keep on keeping on. If you do this, you will get it in your own time.

Stepping Stone 10. Sustain Yourself

A sustainable personal practice is about making sure you have support and other things in your life to help you stay the course over the long haul. What will help you re-energize, re-cover, and re-focus when necessary? Something mentioned in all the interviews is service. Pick one or more charities or ways of serving that taps into your talents. Bring your talent in direct connection with the needs of people, animals, nature, etc. Connect your calling to something that matters in the world and to you. Notice the good work you are doing.

Canfield talks about the most influential people in his life and how each person had a vision that involved change. In some way, all inspiration is about a transformation. It is in our hope for the future that we find inspiration. "Do what you love" is a consistent message. It will sustain you through the tough times. If you are not doing what you are passionate about, the person next to you who is passionate will outlast you because they are acting consistent with their core purpose and values. So, don't short change yourself. Do things to connect you to your purpose in life.

Also, be sure to pace yourself, manage your energy, and rely on those you love. Chopra consistently reminds us to take care of our physical being so that we can energetically live our calling. As Michaels advises, save for a rainy day. Savings can come in the form of money to support from those that love you. Sustainable personal practices involve nurturing our relationships because it is this support that is so critical to being healthy. When Michaels feels stressed, all she needs to do is remember the sweet voice of her grandson saying, "I love you Nona," and nothing else matters. Maureen & Laura Osis are a mother daughter team who emphasize how important it is to ensure healthy relationships through conversation. Conversations encourage us and this is particularly important when addressing difficult subjects. DiLallo concurs with a Clear Talk model. Osis suggest a SMART model to guide a difficult conversation. Set a goal, Manage your emotions, Accept differences, Recognize responsibilities, Take time and take turns. One key to their mother daughter relationship is conscientious listening and mutual respect.

Another important aspect to sustaining yourself is to keep positive and stop the "put downs." Allow yourself to be inspired by those around you who tell you that they believe in you. Don't give your power to negative people. Spend more time listening to positive healthy people and stop giving a majority of your attention to the naysayers. While naysayers are resistance and that can be useful information, only give the naysayers the limited time necessary to be informed and then move on.

Last but not least, a common theme that emerges from the interviews is one of humor, fun, play, and not taking ourselves to seriously. Murray's is professional clown, among other things. He went to Clown School and found that when people are laughing they aren't thinking about their pain and their bodies seemed to heal quicker. Maureen Osis describes her daughter's remarkable sense of humor and quotes Victor Borge who said "the shortest distance between two people is laughter."

Bringing the 3 H's to Life

Do all three of these H's happen separately? What happens if one of the H's is not addressed? How do you know when to move from one H to the next H? To answer these questions, consider using the checklist in three ways.

First, and foremost, give time to healing, harnessing, and helping. Notice in which of the H domains you tend to operate most of the time. If you are consistently operating in one of the H domains, then you are likely stuck. Move through the 3-H's fluidly and dynamically. Life breathes through our healing, harnessing, and helping; so give attention to all three domains in your life. Second, if you are stuck in one H, acknowledge it and act concretely in one of the other H's. For example, say you are stuck in *healing*. Start actively doing things to harness your power: dream, envision a future, and set goals. If, however, you find yourself stuck in *harnessing*, take a few small steps to move into helping. Pick one act of service directly related to your passion that you know you can easily do in a three-week period. And, just do it. If you are stuck in *helping*, yet not making progress in living your mission, then move back to healing and do some self-reflection and self-assessment. Finally, allow your passion to draw you forth by writing it down. Write about it in terms of a unique gift you have to give the world. Write as if you are fully living your passion today in this moment. By writing it so, you bring that ideal into the present. By claiming it, you unlock the power of your passion in the here and now.

Benjamin Franklin is one of history's most accomplished entrepreneurs, inventors, writers, sociologists, and leaders—a true Renaissance man. He lived a full life traveling the world in a way that would rival anyone's experience today. He was one of the first ambassadors for positive change in the world. In short, he got more done in his lifetime than a dozen people typically accomplish in their lifetime.

Stepping Stone Checklist

- ☐ 1. Conduct an Honest Personal Self-Assessment.
- ☐ 2. Do Your Healing Work.
- ☐ 3. Grieve, Forgive, and Move On.
- ☐ 4. Make Public Action Plan.
- ☐ 5. Focus Your Intention and Attention.
- ☐ 6. Actively Prepare.
- ☐ 7. Form Strategic Connections with Others.
- ☐ 8. Don't Just Do Something, Step Into Your Fear.
- ☐ 9. Persist, Persist, Persist.
- ☐ 10. Sustain Yourself.

Franklin identified a dozen virtues and then developed a simple approach to make these new habits in his life. He knew it would be difficult to focus on all twelve at once. So, he focused on living one virtue for one week. He called this approach his project of arriving at moral perfection. He knew that perfection was not attainable, yet it was in the striving that he became a better person.

The latest research on how people integrate habits into their lives—the unlearning and learning of new behaviors—suggests that forming new habits can take anywhere from 18 to 254 days pending the habit, with an average of 66 days (see Lally, et al, 2009 in the European Journal of Social Psychology). In short, adopting new healthy habits can vary in how long it takes, pending the habit and the healing work required.

You can be truly successful. The fact that you are reading this book puts you in good company with others who are choosing to live a truly successful life. Here is the most important piece of advice - pick one stepping stone—live it for a week. Pick another stone—live it for a week. If you fail, let it be a part of the process, forgive yourself. Get back up and learn from the fall. Start again. The key is to never ever give up. It is in the learning to fall and get up that makes for real winners in life. I wish you the best; the world needs you now more than ever.

"Dost thou love life? Then do not squander time,
for that's the stuff life is made of."
—Benjamin Franklin

NOTES

NOTES

NOTES

NOTES

NOTES